July 2006.

HERE ENDETH
THE EPILOGUE

A blown husk that is finished
but the light sings eternal
a pale flare over marshes
where the salt hay whispers to tide's change.
- Ezra Pound
Drafts and Fragments of Cantos CX-CXVII

"Sick Cat, Light on the Humber"
- Would-be parodist of the Epilogues
on the Archer's message board, 2004.

It cannot dye so. Heavens King
Keeps register of every thing:
And nothing may we use in vain.
Ev'n Beasts must be with justice slain;
Else Men are made their Deodands
- Andrew Marvell
The Nymph Complaining on the death of her Faun

HERE ENDETH THE EPILOGUE

by Steve Rudd

writing as

"Slightly Foxed"

The King's England Press

2006

ISBN 1 872438 97 0

HERE ENDETH THE EPILOGUE
is typeset and published by
The King's England Press
Cambertown House
Commercial Road
Goldthorpe
ROTHERHAM

© Steve Rudd 2005

All Rights Reserved. No part of this publication may be reproduced, copied, stored in a retrieval system, or circulated in any manner whatsoever without the express prior written consent of the publisher.

This book is sold subject to the condition that it shall not, by way of trade or otherwise, be lent, re-sold, hired out, or otherwise circulated without the publisher's prior consent in any form of binding or cover other than that in which it was originally published and without a similar condition including this condition being imposed on the subsequent purchaser.

The author asserts his moral right to be recognised as such under the terms of the Berne Convention and of the Copyright Designs and Patents Act 1988, as amended.

Printed and Bound by
www.lulu.com
Digital print-on-demand.

Dedication

To Debbie, who will never read any of it, and never understand why I wrote it anyway; to those who *will* read it all and *still* not understand why I wrote it; to those very few, maybe, who will understand why I wrote it without ever *having* to read it, but may or may not do so, as their fancy dictates; to Amy, who will never have to read it again because she proof-read it (the mistakes are all mine, though) and finally to those who just stood on the sidelines and heckled. We are all part of the same cat-smell.

How this book came to be...

In Spring 2004 I started posting a regular message every Sunday night on the BBC message board dedicated to *The Archers*, known by those who use it as "Mustardland" because of the striking yellow background colour of the pages. Although part of the BBC web site which is concerned with the comings, goings and doings of the various characters of this long-running radio "soap" it also contains a message board called "The Bull" which is intended for discussion of anything outside of *The Archers*.

This regular message grew into a weekly bulletin (or "Epilogue") of how things had been going for me in the preceding seven days, mixed with reflections on any spiritual lessons I felt I had learned during the week. Soon I began receiving emails from people about it and the message board "threads" which each message started frequently exhibited a wide range of responses ranging from pro- to anti- to couldn't care less, especially on some of the more controversial postings to do with animal welfare.

Some of the people who had been posting on the message board for a long time and had amassed many thousands of posts between them, took exception to what they saw as my use of BBC facilities for "blogging", and various arguments developed, resulting in my at first withdrawing from posting the Epilogue in The Bull altogether, and then, following further discussions, posting them on another message board on the same site, "The Village Hall".

By a strange combination of circumstances, I had, in the meantime, become involved with the start of I-church, the Church of England's online presence, and as part of my contribution, I asked if they would be amenable to having the Epilogues posted on their message board as well, which they agreed to. For a while, therefore, they were appearing on both *The Archers* and I-church every Sunday.

In the autumn of 2004, Keri Davies, who is *The Archers* message board host, decided that, although the Epilogues didn't actually break any rules for posting on a BBC message board, he would much rather I didn't continue to post it, because it "wasn't in the spirit of the Archers message board" (whatever that means) and the postings were switched to H2G2, a different message board, still run by the BBC, but obviously not so precious about its content!

This book contains more or less a year's worth of message board postings (March 2004 to April 2005) which have been tidied up and (I hope) proof-read with varying degrees of accuracy. Because of the nature of the way these pieces were written (usually composed from scratch on a Sunday afternoon) there are inevitably going to be places where it would benefit from a re-write, but I've decided not to go in for heavy editing, out of respect to "the spirit of the boards"!

STEVE RUDD,
The Holme Valley, July 2006

§

March 7ᵗʰ 2004

It's been a long and busy week, this week, and just when we thought Spring might be going to make an appearance (with the first crocuses showing in the garden) the cold and showery weather has returned to the Valley to make me wish I'd ordered a few more bags of coal for the stove back in October to see us through. It's been such a busy week, that I have hardly had time to reflect much on the greater issues of life, though I have been reading Thomas Traherne again for the first time in a lot of years. In odd moments.

I have been feeling pretty pleased with myself as well. After we weathered the bank meeting, the way ahead has been clearer. Sure, there is lots of work ahead, but that's just work. We have been doing that since 1989. Nothing new there.

But pride always comes before a fall, which is how I ended up this week queueing at the supermarket checkout, in my business suit and tie, only to hear the little girl perched in the trolley in front voice her opinions of me to her mother, in a loud voice that brooked no arguments - "Mummy - that man is UGLY". One has to smile graciously (but thinly) in those circumstances.

Life's full of little hiccups, that usually happen when you are feeling at your most self-satisfied and overweening. It occurred to me that I had been getting a bit like the man in The Little Prince:

"... a certain red-faced gentleman. He has never smelled a flower. He has never looked at a star... He has never done anything in his life but add up figures. And all day he says over and over ... 'I am busy with matters of consequence!' And that makes him swell up with pride. But he is not a man — he is a mushroom!"

I thought back to a time in 1997, when we had just moved into our house. The kitchen floor was a complete mess and had no top floorboards, just joists, with the bottom floorboards underneath. It was very difficult to cook a proper meal, and there was no sink. I was clomping around, eating a cheese and onion pasty, like you do. Tig was eyeing it enviously, from the safety of the doorway, wagging her tail hopefully, but I wasn't in a mood for sharing. My needs came first. Of course, I tripped over a joist, and lost my balance. Because of my bad knee and leg, when I go, I really go, and I fell on my back with a resounding crash, banging my head on one of the beams that would eventually support the proper floor. I lay there slightly stunned, seeing stars, thankful that I hadn't gone right through to the cellar, and trying to feel a) whether I had broken anything, and b) what I could still wiggle, and as I lay there groaning, I was vaguely aware of Tig gingerly crossing the floor towards me, picking her way delicately through joists and wires and tools. Ah, I thought, with a warm glow, bless the mutt, she's coming to try and rescue me. Then, with a swift dart of her jaws, she stole the uneaten remains of the pasty from my outstretched hand, and skittered back with it to safer ground, where she devoured it in one gulp, keeping a wary eye on me as I eventually struggled back upright.

You are responsible for what you tame, like the Little Prince said. But it doesn't mean they feel responsible to you, in return. And if you concentrate too much on material things, whether it's a pasty or a purchase ledger, you are likely to come a cropper. It is only with the heart that one can see clearly, what is essential is invisible to the eye. The only wisdom we can hope to acquire, is the wisdom of humility. So said Antoine de Saint Exuperey and TS Eliot, but not at the same time.

Or, as Traherne puts it: "The WORLD is not this little Cottage of Heaven and Earth. Though this be fair, it is too small a Gift."

Next week, I must try and concentrate on what really matters. Meanwhile, as the turn of another day approaches, and bed beckons, to everyone I am fighting this battle called life for, be you furry or non-furry, RL or ML, if I have forgotten to tell you all how important you are to me, allow me to rectify that now.

March 14th 2004

It's been another busy week in the Holme Valley, but spring still resolutely refuses to come, though the odd bedraggled crocuses have forced their way up through the grass verges, only to be blasted by wind and rain in ever increasing quantities. I have had to give in and ring up the coal merchants in Huddersfield to get some more fuel for the stove, something I had totally forgotten doing, until yesterday morning when they started unloading it in the driveway, and Freddie began hurling himself at the window in the sort of display of coalman-hatred that only a little wiry terrier can muster. As someone wryly remarked in another context, Freddie is the only one in the whole world who doesn't realise he is a little mutt who is nine inches high. In Freddie's mind, he's still a timber-wolf, and a pack-leading hero at that.

Today we decided it had all got too much, all this work, without adding another Sunday to the list of grey days spent hammering stuff into a computer. I felt a bit guilty because the pressure is on to get the hedgehogs web site up and running before SNH start culling them, but in the end we did set off for Ambleside, despite this, and despite the weather. A journey of 105 miles, from our house to the car park, and we rolled in on the stroke of two o'clock, after chasing rainbows up the M6 in a dazzling kaleidoscope of non-stop weather of the sort you only ever get in an English spring.

At Ambleside we watched the river - swollen with much snow, I would imagine - crashing blackly over the rocks by the National Trust car park where hundreds of people swarm every summer, and where Tiggy once watched her new purple frisbee bob along on the tide as it headed towards lake Windermere, making no attempt to retrieve it even though it had cost £2.99. No swim for Tig today, though, too dangerous by far, probably even for humans, had any been mad enough to venture in.

So I spent two hours doing a passable rendition of "mountains in the rain" in water colours, from a vantage point near to the churchyard where Wordsworth lies. Another sort of hero of course, to the many thousands who seek him out every summer.

I have been thinking about heroes and heroism quite a lot this week. Heroism is everywhere, if you look for it. Not only the dedication of the paramedic who rushes towards a bomb blast to help, regardless of the fact that there may be other explosions: but the heroism of the long term carers, those who devote themselves day after day to tending to those with long term illnesses. The postman who turns out in all weathers. The people who re-home lost animals, the people who re-home lost people, if it comes to that. There is even heroism in those who face impossible positions - at work or in their lives - yet still get up and go out there each day and do it and do it all over again the next day.

Mythical heroes carried their power externally, of course. Today's heroes and heroines probably carry it within. Or is potential for heroism something within us all? When the time comes, we are touched by something, some connection with the eternal, that gives us patience and strength?

I don't think I am quite fanciful enough to believe in guardian angels, though of course Blake saw Angels everywhere he looked. He was, of course, as mad as a box of badgers, which may have had a bearing on the situation. Donne says

> So in a voice, so in a shapeless flame
> Angels affect us oft, and worshipp'd be.

When he was writing this he was making an erotic analogy, but maybe in the shapeless flame of the bomb blast, when "the dove descending breaks the air with flame of incandescent terror" the bitter flower of suffering that blooms and is gone leaves behind it the seed of the good which we need to tap into to overcome its perpetrators. Who was it who said you are never given the problem without also being given the means to solve it?

In the flash of the coward's bomb maybe the angels also bestow on the survivors the blind strength we need to pull the girder off the victim. The indomitable nature of the human spirit. I have had lots of discussions on the board - and elsewhere - about the problem of evil, and I have still not reconciled myself to its presence in a God-driven world, but maybe there is a way in which, if the presence of evil stirs in us the capacity to do more good, then, although evil is still loathsome, its presence no longer automatically becomes a cause for automatic despair, because, no matter what horrors befall, we will find in ourselves the ability to become heroes, and whatever we have lost, be it a home, a love, a friend, "like the Mary Ellen Carter, rise again!" "There lives the dearest freshness, deep down things," said Gerard Manley Hopkins,

> And morning at the brown brink eastward springs
> Because the Holy Ghost over the bent
> World broods with warm breast and, ah! bright wings.

Or, as some one equally flamboyant put it, rather more simply, in a thought that went round and round in my head as the tyres ate up the homeward miles past Kendal and Skipton:

> We can be heroes, just for one day.

Sleep well Mustardland. Heroic things are expected of us this week.

March 21st 2004

March comes in like a lion and goes out like a lamb. That's one of the many things that my grandma taught me (along with "always pay your tax on the stake when you bet on a horse, then you won't have to pay it on the winnings") Sadly for us this year, March seems to be going out like a lion as well, at least in the Holme Valley. Not that gran cares: I suppose they have double glazing in heaven.

Meanwhile, down here, for the last couple of days we have been watching with concern as the wind lashes the trees on the hillside down behind our house, in case any of them fall. The poor rooks trying to build nests in the treetops are being flung about like shreds of discarded bin bags in the air, or clinging on desperately, when perched. The owls have been voicing their nightly protests, too.

The dogs have been moody, wet, and miserable, Tig flatly refusing to go out on Saturday morning. She just sat there with her head on one side, eyeing me pityingly for having entertained the fanciful notion that she would go and wee in the garden during a hurricane. As Elias Canetti once wrote

> Whenever you observe an animal closely, you feel as if a human being sitting inside were making fun of you.

The cats are being more stoical. Each one seems to have separately chosen a specific radiator to curl up against, riding out the storm like furry ships at anchor, tuning in their purrs to the radiators' own humming and gurgling, like Tibetan monks tuning in to the universal "Om".

Such a change from earlier in the week, when I really thought we were going into that pleasant stage described by the writer of the Harley Lyric "Alysoun"

> Bythuene Mersh and Averil
> Whan Spray Beginneth to Springe

(They don't write lyrics like that any more. Just as well, since most aficionados of popular music these days barely understand modern English, let alone middle English. Harrumph!) <Dons pipe and slippers >

I have been looking forward to Spring for so long now that I hope it doesn't turn out to be a disappointment when it finally arrives. There is something about Spring that always stirs the Englishness in me. Don't get me wrong, I am not running down Britain, as a concept, but the Scots, the Welsh and the Irish seem already to have clearly defined identities that keep them spiritually nurtured all year round. It may seem weird, but I always feel at my most English for the fleeting two weeks either side of Easter.

Don't worry, I am not going to start straying into the territory occupied by people such as the British National Party. I am very well aware that all wars start with the waving of flags, and this weekend especially serves as another reminder, if we needed one.

No, my English patriotism is reserved for things like dry stone walls, warm beer, thatched pubs, antiquarian bookshops with bells that tinkle when you open the door, cathedrals, brass bands, village cricket, and John Major's perennial favourite, spinsters cycling to matins.

Nor am I claiming these are any better, or any more culturally valid than, say, aloo sag, or a game of boules in a dusty French square. It is just that, for me, something in them stirs the spirits at this time of year. As C Day Lewis wrote:

> You that love England, and have an ear for her music
> The clear arias of light thrilling over the uplands

Of course, there's a long tradition of spirituality being nourished by Englishness, and the English countryside, ever since the first iteration of the legend that Jesus himself visited the west country when young, and is supposed to have walked on the green at Priddy. This is the legend Blake refers to in Jerusalem when he wrote:

> And did those feet, in ancient time
> Walk upon England's mountains green

Not to mention Joseph of Arimathea, sticking his staff into the ground and finding that it had turned into the Glastonbury Thorn. Last time I was at Priddy, I sat on that self same village green, ate my sandwiches, drank my bottle of brown ale and watched the farm hands stacking up sheep hurdles. That's another thing I like about England, you get the feeling that history is always within touching distance. Like if you happen to be in Ripon's market square at sunset, on any day, and a bloke drives up in a Ford Fiesta, gets out, puts on a frock coat and a tricorn hat, goes to the boot and takes out a medieval horn, and blows the curfew blasts, just as the many watchmen of Ripon have done, every night for the last eight hundred years. Of course, they also say that in England, you are never more than ten feet from a rat. Yes, there is a lot wrong with England, but I can't help feeling there's a lot right as well.

Blake (bless him) wanted to turn England into Jerusalem. His idea of Jerusalem was very different from the WI's interpretation, as it included amongst other things, lots of divinely inspired sex and free love. (Although after Calendar Girls, perhaps Blake and the WI are more apt bedfellows than I first thought). There are also forces in the world, as we have seen all too clearly of late, who think our idea of "Jerusalem" hasn't evolved since the days of the Knights Templar, and that we are all "crusaders". They are the fanatics currently trying to enact George Orwell's prophecy for England on his return from the Spanish Civil War:

> Down here it was still the England I had known in my childhood: the railway cuttings smothered in wild flowers . . . the red buses, the blue policemen — all sleeping the deep, deep sleep of England, from which I sometimes fear that we shall never wake till we are jerked out of it by the roar of bombs.

And equally, there seem to be those who think that our freedoms, our route to our own Jerusalem, can only be safeguarded by over-reaction, by abandoning the very things we're trying to protect. A sort of baby/plughole interface. I take Orwell's point when he says that

> We sleep safe in our beds because rough men stand ready in the night to visit violence on those who would do us harm.

But you also need the spiritual perspective, to remind you: like the psalmist says, in the words engraved over the door of the Wakeman's House in Ripon,

> Except the lord build the house, they labour in vain that build it; except the Lord keep the city, the watchman waketh but in vain.

I have been thinking a lot this week about what sort of world we are building, because yesterday, in the course of a gathering of the extended family clan in the run up to mothers' day, my sister in law announced that she was expecting a baby, and I could not help but wonder what sort of a world it will grow up in. A world of unparalleled wonders, undoubtedly, probably unimaginable to us now: a world of freedoms, but also a world of dangers. He or she might yet see us build the new Jerusalem, and banish sickness and poverty, but equally we need to be careful that we're not slipping back once more into the situation described by Arthur Mee in his 1918 classic, *Who Giveth Us The Victory:*

> Do thousands of children come into the world to grasp for life in a slum; to go to school hungry for a year or two; to pick up a little food, a little slang, and a little arithmetic; to grovel in the earth for forty years or to stand in the steaming factories; to wear their bodies out like cattle on the land; to live in little rows of dirty houses, in little blocks of stuffy rooms, and then to die?

Well, Mustardlanders, there seem to be challenges ahead. For Becky and Adrian's unborn child, and for all the unborn children everywhere, we must try our best. We must work and pray, we must not cease from mental fight, We must strive, in short, to make sure we only get rid of the bathwater, and let the babies inherit the earth.

March 28th 2004

Well, once more it's Sunday evening and I am sitting here in my old chair in front of my old desk hammering words into my old computer.

The last week seems to have flown by: the clocks have gone to summer time, but it's still not really Spring. One day last week (Thursday afternoon to be precise) we all watched open-mouthed as hailstones the size of frozen peas pelting down out of the lead grey skies rattled the windows and turned the scene outside to winter in a matter of five minutes.

Dusty and Kitty have been making tentative forays further and further through the cat flap this week, but Russell with the wisdom of an old cat who has seen it all before, remains resolutely possessive of the chair nearest the stove. Nigel has found himself a new Nigel-hole, wedging himself down between the portable oil heater in the office and the desk cupboard next to it, and then slowly cooking himself in his curled up position overnight. This is all very well, but if the last person in the office forgets to check and shuts him in, it means a chilly trip out of bed at 3am to open the door and let him out when he starts scratting and meowing.

It's been the busiest week of the year so far: a massive mailing (for us) going out to the National Trust and other heritage sites as they begin to wake up from their winter hibernation, press release about the Flying Scotsman, hedgehogs, hedgehogs and more hedgehogs, and of course it's the end of the month, which can only mean one thing ... accounts.

I live my life in a sort of battle with accounts. Usually it's guerilla warfare. I ambush a few receipts here, surprise a bank statement and reconcile it before the gremlins have time to retaliate by infesting the calculator, or pick off a few invoices. But at the end of every month, a big set piece battle takes place between me and the chaos of accounts, aided only by my trusty calculator and spreadsheets.

Of all the jobs I have to do in running this business, accounts has to be the worst. I suppose every career has a job that you really don't look forward to, something which hangs over you like a dark cloud. The trick is to keep disciplined, keep at it and get through to the other side as quickly as possible. Like being lost in a wood with night coming on.

Whenever I feel afraid
I whistle a happy tune

But sometimes, especially when it's a bright day like it has been today and I am stuck here at this computer adding up rows of figures, I tend to get a bit like Joni Mitchell describes in "A Free Man in Paris"

You can't please 'em all
There's always somebody calling you down
I do my best
And I do good business
I deal in dreamers
And telephone screamers
Lately I wonder what I do it for

You can't help but regret losing a time when you weren't possessed of such overwhelming responsibilities, not only to yourself, but to others who have placed their trust in you that they'll still have a job tomorrow and that their house is safe.

> I was a free man in Paris
> I felt unfettered and alive
> There was nobody calling me up for favours
> And no one's future to decide
> You know I'd go back there tomorrow
> But for the work I've taken on
> Stoking the star maker machinery
> Behind the popular song

Life is so like a pilgrimage at times like these. The medieval pilgrims set off on their journeys never knowing whether, or if, they were going to get there. There were times when only their own confidence and faith in themselves, and in a God who could make everything come right for them, carried them through. Like Bunyan's character, they had to have belief in themselves

> Who So Beset him round,
> With Dismal Stories
> Do but themselves confound
> His strength the more is…

There are always going to be times when the rain is beating on the window and you don't want to get out of bed. When your car won't start, when the computer crashes, when you walk in the office on Monday morning at 9am and the phone is already ringing and there are large piles of undone things spilling out of your in tray. Times when you have to tell somebody something difficult to say. We have to remember that, as George Herbert said

> A servant with this clause
> Makes drudgery divine
> Who sweeps a room as to thy lawes
> Makes that and th'action fine

So, this week, with a big sigh and a last look over my shoulder at the sunlight out of the window, I am going to shoulder my burden, pick up my staff and my scallop shell of quiet, and get going down the accounts pilgrimage road. I don't suppose the Pope hands out indulgences for completing the VAT return, mortifying though the experience is, but we each have our own Jerusalems, our own versions of Santiago de Compostella, that are just as meaningful to us, our own accomplishments

But don't lose sight of the important things: what we should never do is to use the excuses of responsibility to prevent us from doing or saying the important things. Every time I hear "To Be A Pilgrim" now it reminds me of my father's funeral, and all the things I wished I had said to him while he was still alive. Life isn't a dress rehearsal. I think I need to be careful that I don't let the pilgrimage become a goal in itself. Like it says in the song:

> So if there's someone you care for
> Don't wait until they have shut that door
> Tell them right now and tell them some more
> Tell them how much you love them ...

Have a good week Mustardlanders, Let's hope that, in life as in accounts, we can get the balance right.

§

4ᵗʰ April 2004

We have been waiting patiently for Spring here in the Holme Valley, as chronicled in previous epilogues, and this week it may, just, finally, have arrived. The fuzzy little catkins on the tracery of branches outside my office window have finally broken out, and every time the wind stirs them, they nod frantically sending green shadows flitting about the place.

> Annihilating all that's made
> To a green thought in a green shade

As Andrew Marvell put it in "The Garden". Mind you, with the sun comes the rain.

> Whan that Aprille with his schoores soote,
> the droght of Mershe hath perced to the roote.

And what showers. We have had so much rain this week, it reminded me of the time I was in Ireland four years ago. We stayed there for a week and it only rained twice, once for three days and once for four.

This week, the doggies have been coming in from walkies that have started in bright sunshine, encompassed a downpour of biblical proportions, and ended up once again in bright sunshine. Even Russell has been tempted away briefly from his chair near the stove to have a roll in a patch of sunlight on the driveway where it has warmed the tarmac. Then in a moment it changes and you can watch the rain pushing through the threshing trees in a Mexican wave all the way up the hill.

I have been looking at the garden to see what has survived with renewed interest because, following a meeting with our financial bod this week, it's become pretty apparent to me that we won't be doing our self-build this year, barring a miracle of lottery-winning proportions. So we will be living here for a while yet, and had better get back to gardening. On the plus side, if I work very hard, I can retire in 17 years' time! (But I might have to live off cat food on toast).

Anyway, even though the garden looks like it has been under the sea for the last six months, it does appear that, we have, in some way, come through the winter. Or some of us have, at any rate. Thinking of the ones who are no longer around, as I sit here on my own typing, late at night, I do feel a bit like Henry Vaughan when he wrote

>They are all gone into the world of light
>And I alone sit lingering here

But, we have made it to Palm Sunday, and no doubt if I still went to church, they would have been singing one of my all time favourite hymns today, "My Song is Love Unknown" and the depiction of the mob turning on Jesus after they had welcomed him by strewing palm leaves in his way

>Then 'crucify!'
>Is all their cry

The way the verse turns on that word "crucify" is a dramatic illustration of the power of the mob, which can turn nasty in a second. Something which we have seen this week, of course, in the way in which terrible events unfolded in Fallujah. It's the same power of the mob which the BNP hopes to harness, fed by the comments of people like Dr Carey, which, though no doubt sincerely meant, and uttered with the best intentions, will only be siezed on by the tabloids and others who want to drive further wedges in our society: the same collective madness of the mob that the right wing press is always trying to inflame over asylum seekers, the same collective madness that led to the government killing so many animals needlessly during the foot and mouth crisis. Twenty years ago, we saw it round here, on both sides, during the miners' strike. The same collective madness that allowed the people of Jerusalem to change from praising Jesus to wanting to kill him.

Jesus has been following me around this week. Not literally of course, but it seems that every time I have turned on a TV or the radio I have seen programmes about the Turin Shroud or Mel Gibson's film {I haven't seen the film itself though}. I suppose it is only natural in the run-up to Easter, a time when we're all thinking about regeneration rebirth, resurrection and renewal, and things coming out of hibernation.

Unfortunately, one species this year will be coming out of hibernation, only to be met with certain death. The hedgehogs on the islands of North and South Uist and Benbecula have been sentenced to death by Scottish Natural Heritage, which has refused to put money into relocating them to the mainland, only to spend a greater amount of taxpayers' money on killing them instead. Despite their being an endangered species on the mainland. I can only describe this as organised evil. A display of mob brutality and collective government madness that brings back very bad memories of the worst excesses of FMD, by an organisation that should be safeguarding the lives of flora and fauna, but which is, instead, preparing to kill them in an egotistical orgy of "we know best", simply because they are not prepared to admit they are wrong.

So, this week, we have launched the Hedgeblogs "boycott Scotland" web site. Even though I pray daily for SNH to be struck by lightning, (not fatally, but just enough to teach them a lesson) I have seen enough cruelty and disappointment in this world not to put my faith in prayer alone sorting it out. When it comes to this, I am very much with Cromwell, who said "Trust in God, but keep your powder dry". Especially since the Church has been very silent in its condemnation of this government's dismal animal welfare record. Well, where are you, George Carey? And where are you, Rowan Williams? I know Bishops can only move diagonally, but that shouldn't stop you. Get yourselves up there to the Hebrides and get on with it.

Last year Scottish Natural Heritage's reaction to my boycott campaign was to try and paint me as some kind of animal activist, a beardie-wierdie beagle-stealer with a bomb under my arm. I rebutted this then, of course, but it won't stop them trying again. I have to say that, faced with such obduracy, I can see how people are driven to such means, although I condemn them. It looks like a bitter struggle ahead on all sides, but at least when I get fed up I have got a business to run, for light relief. For the next 17 years anyway. As Ghandi said

> There are times when you have to obey a call which is the highest of all, ie the voice of conscience, even though such obedience may cost many a bitter tear, and even more, separation from friends, from family, from the state, to which you may belong, from all that you have held as dear as life itself"

I would like to close this by saying that SNH is an organisation which is doing its best to fulfil a difficult role and that it has the welfare of Scotland's ecosystem and animals as a whole at its heart. I would *like* to, but every time I *try*, it comes out as "the people responsible for the hedgehog cull should be set to work breaking stones in a quarry until they see the error of their ways, repent, and stop killing hedgehogs needlessly".

11th April 2004

It has been another busy week in the Holme Valley, finding me simultaneously editing, doing the accounts (neglected, in order to complete the Hedgehog web site - I am sure the VAT office will understand…) and getting some marketing for new books out into the world at large. And of course, the perennial planning.

It is, actually, unbelievably, getting warmer. This is an undisputed fact, evidenced by our sudden dramatic fall in consumption of coal for the stove (which means those nine extra bags will now probably sit there all summer) and stirrings of not only our own animals, but also the frogs in the pond, and the many birds now busily building in the trees in the woods down in the valley. Everybody is being busy and industrious. Especially me, even when the sun is shining outside.

That's not to say we haven't had the odd cold night. Kitty and Dusty were to be found, one morning last week, in what can only be described as a sort of "cat lasagne" on the bed in the guest room. Kitty on top of one duvet but under another one, Dusty on top of that one and - *ipso facto* - on top of Kitty, but under the top blanket, so in cross-section it went - perpendicularly - blanket cat duvet cat duvet, reading from top to bottom.

Today we took the dogs out and went playing frisbee on the playing fields at Honley then we drove back with them panting and slobbering out of the window, over Castle Hill with all of Huddersfield laid out beneath us in the Spring sunshine, with the shadows of the chasing clouds making a chequerboard of the Pennines, pausing for a while to drink in the view - the cleaned-up mills, looking like lego from that distance - and wondering which way of the many ways we could go on from that point.

Many of us are at a crossroads this week of course. It is not only a major religious festival, it's also a time to take stock, with a quarter of the new year already gone. There are going to be choices - tough choices, probably - ahead for us all.

A cross can either be the symbol of redemption, like the Christian message of Easter - and/or of change (a cross in a ballot paper that gets rid of an unpopular and unworthy leader), or it can be the cross hairs of a gun sight, a cross of destruction and of death as grim as any found in Golgotha.

As you may know, I am not a Catholic. I am not an anything, in fact, which is one reason why these weekly struggles with spirituality are so rambling and un-focused. I did, however, as part of my hobby of church-crawling and finding mistakes in Pevsner, visit Holy Cross Abbey in Ireland four years ago, and felt myself privileged to see their famous relic, a part of the "True Cross". Now I know what people think about relics, if you reassembled St Anthony he would have more jawbones than you could shake a stick at, etc etc, but there is no denying the power invested in that object there in that rather gloomy, rather plain church in the Irish countryside.

Standing there, looking at the tiny splinter of wood, in its elaborate gold frame, I instinctively felt, as T. S. Eliot put it

> You are here to kneel, where prayer has been valid

The potency of the cross is all around us. If you go to the tiny church at Ruthwell, in Dumfries and Galloway, you can see the earliest known text of the Anglo Saxon poem "The Dream of the Rood", carved on the 7th century stone cross there. The story of the crucifixion, as told by the cross itself.

> I must stand fast.
> As a Cross I was raised - to lift high the Mighty King,
> Heaven's Lord: - I dared not bow low.
> They pierced me with dark nails; -
> the wounds are here to be seen,
> gaping gashes from cruel blows, -
> yet I dared hurt none of them.
> They mocked us both together.

Sometimes, like today, it is easier to feel the presence of the cross as a redemption than a penance. At other times we all have our crosses to bear, and possibly our

bears to cross as well. We have to choose our options by putting a cross in the box, or even by voting with our feet. X marks the spot. Let's pray for the wisdom to make the right choices for the happiness and wellbeing of ourselves and for all those we care for.

18th April 2004

It's been a busy week here in the Holme Valley, and I haven't had time to sniff the flowers. I have spent it largely doing the accounts and then, occasionally, indulging in the comparatively light relief of editing "Hampshire at War". Last Monday, we stole a few hours and hightailed it to the Lake District, and yes, we did see a host of golden daffodils. I spent the afternoon doing a fairly mediocre water colour of St Kentigern's Church at Crosthwaite, Tig had a dip in the river at Keswick, and many camping shops were visited. Summer is I-cumen in. The lambs were skipping, or basking in the Easter sunshine.

Now I am sitting here typing this to the strains of Kathleen Ferrier, and contemplating the even busier week ahead.
Next Tuesday I go to Oxford, for a meeting that only happens once a year. Next week it is fourteen years since my father died. Even though he's still around me in my thoughts all the time, and scarcely a day goes by without me filtering one of my experiences through the net of what he would have thought or done. Time is marching, relentlessly, on. There is a sense of

> In my end is my beginning.

This is the last time that I will post an Epilogue in The Bull, and probably the last time I will post anything there. It's been a very good intellectual discipline for me, over the last six weeks or so, to pause on a Sunday, reflect back on the week, and try and put down a few thoughts about spirituality on paper, and to try and link them to what I have been doing. Especially as normally, the most creative thing I get to write is a press release (not counting the VAT return of course). It's certainly been a help to me, and if anyone else has enjoyed reading what I have written, then I am glad. Conversely, if anyone's been challenged by what I have put, then you probably deserved it.

It's become plain to me that this board isn't really for confession or controversy, however good the confession has been for me. I have been, in vulgar parlance, tossing one off, and there are a lot of people here who have been here a lot longer than me, and I don't intend to spoil the board for them. I am aware, for instance, that a lot of people feel especially challenged and bored (a dangerous mixture) by issues of animal welfare, and of politics. Since I spend most of my time when not sleeping, eating or working, thinking about these issues, especially with potentially two seal culls to fight, the hedgehog cull still ongoing, state murder taking place in Israel, and the local elections and an EU referendum coming up, I foresee the board turning into a battleground over the coming weeks if I carry on posting what I think.

I am determined to ensure that I inflict as much damage as possible on Labour in the local elections, and to campaign as hard as I can for a "no" vote in the referendum. I could, of course, just pretend that everything in the garden is lovely, and not write about anything controversial at all, but I won't do that, because I would not be being true to myself. I'd rather not post, or post elsewhere. It's not as if Blair ever reads this anyway: "calm down dear, it's only a message board".

I wouldn't want anyone to think I am flouncing, or that I have been faced down, or driven off the board. I am quite capable of sticking up for myself, ready, and able, to defend what I believe in, but not at the expense of ruining Mustardland for the rest of you. If anybody particularly wants to keep in touch, my email addy is still in the lockin and I will leave it there for a couple of weeks before I take leave of there, too.

I have a personal reason for leaving as well. I have watched Russell, our oldest cat, get dramatically thinner over the last few weeks, and though he still seems as interested in everything as he ever did, still eats all his food, and still occupies his well-worn chair by the stove, he is coming up to 13 years old, and nothing lasts for ever. I have to face the fact that we might have a parting of the ways. Maybe sooner rather than later. Maybe I am wrong, I hope I am. After all, when a mere kitten he survived eating a rubber band (even then, he wasn't a vegetarian, the immoral little tyke!) which the vet had to dig out of him at a cost of £127.58 inc VAT. Then a couple of years later, he broke his leg, and celebrated coming home with a plaster cast on it, by climbing on top of the wardrobe and having to be winched off by a stack of dedicated humans. So maybe he'll be with us a while yet. Depends what the vet says I suppose.

Personally, it doesn't really matter too much to me about not posting here any more. It would have been nice to get to 1000, but I do also have a couple of jobs to hold down, and two new children's books to launch, and, as Michelle Shocked once so memorably said "The secret to a long life is knowing when it's time to go." Or perhaps more poetically, to every thing there is a season {turn turn turn} and a time for every purpose under heaven.

Good luck, and I hope you all thrive and do well, live long and prosper. And so I take my leave of Mustardland, with the immortal last words of Lord Nelson ringing in my ears:

How the hell am I going to climb that column with only one arm

The Missing Epilogue [25th April 2004] - never posted anywhere.

Well, it's been a busy week here in the Holme Valley, with summer arriving as early as spring was late. 23 degrees today, and it felt like thunder! And it's only April.

Russell has been giving cause for concern, what with his being thinner than ever, and refusing food that other cats would scratch you arm off for, eg scrambled egg, but on the other hand, he's as vocal as ever, and disappeared tonight out of the conservatory door because he could hear the birds in the trees down in the valley. Tig has been bored today, waiting to go out until late in the afternoon, while the epic struggle with the in tray continued.

Hampshire at War is coming along. I am up to page 165 of 345, so only 180 pages to go!

Finally let the stove go out today, so summer is officially here and there are still four bags of coal left which will now gather cobwebs until the autumn. I wonder what we'll all be doing when the stove is lit again. It'll be about October, and some of us will have been off on holiday, fruit picking perhaps. To make a success of this year, I need to have published four or five new books before that stove is lit again. And, of course, bearing in mind Russbags, we may not all see it lit again.

Gyres run on, or so W B Yeats said. Everything eventually becomes its opposite. But the good thing about that is that, all the bad things turn to good. And the good means that we are better equipped with all the good things turning to bad, because we know they'll come good again.

I could make a better construction of this Epilogue, with more time, but the essential things behind it would remain the same, and even if it was twice as long, Dusty the cat would still interrupt it at this point by scrabbling the carpet under the door.

47cv =]]]]]]]]]]]]]]]]]]]]]]]].;/

and then walking over the keyboard when I let her in. Goodnight dear reader, as we all sail on in this strangely shaped ship called Britain. Tomorrow when we wake up it will be a whole new ball game. I'm sorry this epilogue isn't more intelligible. Like all of them it's saying when you find love, love in return. If you don't find love, don't worry, love is seeking you out, whether you want it or not. Gyres run on.

§

2nd May 2004

There was no Epilogue for 2nd May.

9th May 2004

It has been a busy week in the Holme Valley. I am sitting here in my office, at the top of the house, listening to Handel, one of those rare composers who had a broadband connection to God.

I bet you thought you would never see those words again. On Friday, when I fell down the stairs, I would probably have joined you in that thought. Anyway, I survived, but I have been jolted in more ways than one by the experience. But more of that later.

It has, indeed, been a busy week. The arrival of a skip in the driveway last weekend heralded the start of the great bathroom project, which is now at its height. The skip has gone, bearing the remains of the old bathroom and any other rubbish that happened to have accumulated in the garden over the winter. Between them, Jonathan and Deb managed to fill it, which means that we must in fact have had 9 tonnes of rubbish in the garden, plus or minus the odd bathroom suite. It would almost be cheaper to become a Womble.

The animals have been adapting well to the chaos, on the whole. Nigel looks at the exposed floorboards and joists in the shell of the old bathroom, and sees great possibilities for new Nigel-holes. Dusty and Kitty see more of me, now the lack of a bathroom forces me to use the spare shower, which is in their part of the house. Their joy is only matched by their incredulity, at the sight of me on my new exercise bike (no helmet, bell or stabilisers) which also lives in "their" room (aka the spare bedroom) Tig doesn't care if there's a bathroom or not, as long as there's some nice smelly mud she can roll in while she's going walkies, and with our weather, this week, there has been plenty of mud.

This has been the coldest, wettest May I can remember for some time. Four years ago this weekend, I was in a tent in a field at Cressing Temple, launching a book on the Templars, and it was hot enough to have thunderstorms. And it did. Inside the tent. But not this year.

Russell carries on being Russell, one minute we think there's something seriously wrong with him, the next he is devouring rice pud or cheese slices like there's no tomorrow. Which is perhaps the way to do it. Because maybe there isn't. He's got his favourite chair back by the stove, because it was so cold and unseasonal that we had to give in and re-light the fire (cue for a song), something I can never remember before in all the years we've been here. So my five extra bags of coal weren't over-ordered at all, we're on the very last bag now, and next week it's going to be hot and sunny - isn't it?

I can't help but wonder what will have happened by the time I light the stove again, next October. To make a success of this year, for a start, I need to have brought out five new books between now and then, and the new printers work at the speed of a slug in a wet anorak. Time to brandish the magic chequebook? Anyway, let's hope we are all around to find out.

Which brings me back to the staircase. On Friday I got back, cooked a paella, opened a bottle of Mouton Cadet (known in our house as "Apprentice Sheep" as a literal translation) in honour of Sainsbury's Huddersfield (the one with the famous sloping car park where you have to always keep one hand on your trolley) selling it at £3.99 not £6.99 and watched Midsomer Murders - as you do. On retiring to bed, I got to the top of the stairs - minus stair carpet owing to the current home demolishment situation - tripped, and re-visited stairs 1-14 in reverse order this time, ending up in a heap in the lobby.

Fortunately, I ended up just with two large contusions to the head, a wrenched shoulder, a badly bruised arm, and a large gouge out of the left leg where the gripper rod got me on the way down. But while I was laid up yesterday, licking my wounds (actually, splathering them with liquid Ibuprofen) I was thinking long and hard about the random nature of life. In a parallel universe, I might be dead now. In a parallel universe, Greg might still be alive and happy with Helen. In a parallel universe, Anoni's Jerry cat (RIP, very sorry to hear) is still purring happily in the sun. It could be as near as the next room, as Canon Henry Scott Holland wrote in 1910. All is well. In the rose garden, down the path we didn't take.

When I wrote, in my last epilogue, that there were difficult times ahead and I could foresee the whole board turning into one huge spat if I continued to post what I thought, and that this would ruin it for everybody, there were those who agreed and those who disagreed. There were those who couldn't give a stuff either way. I chose at the time to go with what I perceived as the majority. But I have had a number of emails asking me to reconsider, including ones from people who actually have their pictures on this very web site, no less, that I had already thought, well, a bit hasty, maybe in a year or so it might be amusing to come back here.

But if I make a habit of falling down stairs, I may not be able to do this next year. As it is, I probably only survived Friday because of the elasticity imparted to my body by the Apprentice Sheep, and as soon as I work out the French translation of "arse over tit" I must write to Baron Philippe and thank him. Life is a random business. And it's not a dress rehearsal. How many of us wish we'd told our parents how much we loved them while we still could? What happened in the Archers between Helen and Greg happened in part because they didn't tell each other often enough and early enough how much each meant to the other. And also because lots of people could have helped Greg but chose to think he wasn't their problem. If only they had read Donne:

> No man is an Island, intire of itself. Every man is a piece of the continent, a part of the main. If a clod or a pebble is washed away by the sea, Europe is the less, even as much as if a promontory were, or thyself or a manor of thy friends were ... therefore seek not to send for whom the bell tolls, it tolls for thee.

I have to admit, when I lay at the bottom of the stairs on Friday night, I felt, as Eliot put it "the eternal footman hold my coat, and snicker". *Et in Arcadia Ego.*

So, I am back. I can't guarantee not to be a tosser (but then who can?) I can't guarantee not to cause a spat. I can't guarantee not to annoy those of you who think all this is just a massive ego trip and fishing for compliments - though I have to observe that if I was fishing, I would probably use better bait and choose a more fruitful location than opening up to the forensic glare of Mustardland.

Above all I am back because I missed you all, and you mean something to me. And while I can, I wanted to tell you this. And while you can, I suggest you tell it to everybody you know who means a lot to you. And to that guy or woman who everybody seems to shun, the one who might just be on a downward spiral of Greg-style loneliness and depression. I have been there myself, twelve years ago, and it's not a nice place.

> Been down one time, been down two times,
> never going back again

I may not have worked out what you all mean to me yet, but I will have another go after I broach the second and final bottle of Apprentice Sheep. (Don't worry, I am already upstairs!) Which is, in itself, a form of prayer. Ever since Caana anyway. Cheers!

16th May 2004

If anyone reading this has recently lost a pet, you might want to skip this Epilogue in case it brings back bad memories for you.

It has been a busy week in the Holme Valley, and at last the weather seems to have turned in our favour, though until this weekend, the dull days still outnumbered the sunny ones. The garden has suddenly developed a mind of its own, a sort of collective vegetable consciousness that says to itself: "I have got to be four feet higher by this time tomorrow, fed by a diet of rain followed by hot sun followed by more rain."

The animals have been venturing out at first light and returning only in the dusk, to sleep in a pile of cats on the spare bed, while Tig has been seeking out the shadiest spots on the decking, lying there flicking her ears at the buzz of curious flies.

The great bathroom saga rumbles on, in that the new bathroom now has a door, so there is no longer any necessity to signal my occupancy by singing Handel at the top of my voice in case someone should venture along the corridor. There is something of the communal, something of an element of the cat-litter tray about a bathroom with no door.

This week, we've been counting our blessings and considering how lucky we are, something which I do find useful to do from time to time. As some of you might know, we've been very concerned about the well-being of Russell, our oldest cat, and this week it became clear that the crisis was coming to a conclusion. He was having trouble doing simple things like climbing stairs, and ignored his food, spending long periods just sitting, in obvious distress and discomfort. By Wednesday, we'd decided he had to go to the vet, and, given his age, we were steeling ourselves for the worst. Wednesday night didn't exist for me, it was a series of fitful snoozes broken up with waking to the overwhelming knowledge that the parting of the ways may have come.

Thursday was worse, putting the cat carrier into the back of the car and driving off, hoping against hope that it wouldn't be the last time he ever saw the garden.

But, of course, Russell had other ideas. He's always been a survivor, having originally been abandoned in a cardboard box in a hedge, found by the CPL and re-homed to us, eating a rubber band while still a kitten, breaking a leg, and losing several teeth in his 12 eventful years. It turned out that his condition is something to do with his thyroid, it can be treated, even though it's complicated by a kidney infection. After 24 hours at the vet, some of which he spent on a drip and some of which he spent sitting on the lap of a nubile young veterinary nurse being hand-fed chicken breast (he gets all the best gigs) he came back on Friday and he's now snoozing on the sofa in the conservatory. Thanks, at least in part, to the prayers, positive vibes, and general good wishes of several people on these boards, who sent me individual messages of good wishes and encouragement to my email addy. He even had a prayer from the newly appointed pastor of the Anglican I-Church. I also sneaked in a quick prayer myself, to St Padre Pio, for no other reason than having a supernatural entity with the power of bilocation on your side was probably a smart move.

It was only after we'd got him back and were talking about it that we realised that both Deb and I had, separately, each without telling the other, settled on the spot where we would bury him in the garden, a sunny little enclave near the garden seat by the pond where he likes to sit, frog-watching.

So, we may not be out of the woods yet: we might not have won the war, but at least the first battle seems to have gone our way. And it makes you count your blessings: I may have a dicky leg, I am going bald, I'm overweight for my height, I am still bruised all over from bouncing down the stairs last week, but I can still sit in the sunshine on the decking with my favourite cat. I can tootle off like I did this afternoon, and do a painting for a couple of hours, and trundle back with Sir John Betjeman on the radio. I can go to the fridge, or the cupboard, and there's food there. When I run out, I can buy more. I turn on the tap, and clean water comes out {Yorkshire Water permitting} OK, sometimes I can't get to the office on time because Kirklees have a plan to dig up all the roads round here simultaneously. Big deal! I should get a life! Compared to the people in sub-Saharan Africa, or Ethiopia, or Iraq for that matter, I live like a King.

We spend a lot of time in this century of ours striving. On bank holiday Monday I sat in the car by the side of the road doing a watercolour of Saddleworth Moor, and I was amazed by the speed of the passing traffic, and the sheer volume of it. Where were all these people going to, or coming from? What did they hope to achieve?

I was struck by the similarity with Chris White's poem, "Donkeys" where the two donkeys in the field at the side of the motorway are looking at all the people stuck in the traffic jams and are moved to wonder whether the "real" donkeys are those stuck in the cars. Or, perhaps more grandly, as T S Eliot says:

> Teach us to care and not to care: teach us to sit still.

I'm not advocating giving up our comfortable lives, tipping the Apprentice Sheep down the sink un-drunk, and anointing ourselves with sackcloth and ashes, wearing hair shirts. It's not a substitution exercise, it's more like chalk and cheese. If the white cliffs of Dover, where my father and his anti-aircraft unit perched during the dark days of 1940, were washed away by the sea, England would be the less, the same as if a lump of Wensleydale was. We couldn't do without either. We need to try and get to the stage where everybody has the chance to feel as fortunate and fulfilled as I do now. In the meantime, we accept the peace of Sunday and look forward to another busy week stretching ahead. Thanks again, everybody, and thanks to St Padre Pio, if you are reading this as well as being somewhere else.

23rd May 2004

It has been a busy week in the Holme Valley, but not necessarily a sunny one! Summer still insists on being late, cold, and green. Last weekend we had a veggie barbecue to celebrate Deb's birthday, although at the time the celebrations were slightly muted because we had only just got Russ the Puss back from the vet and we were still unsure which way he would go. Apart from that, it's showing every sign of developing into a typically cold, dull, English summer. Ah well, September might be nice. The rain showers in the week have battered down the Great Mullein in the garden so much that Deb had no option but to cut it right back, almost to the ground. Don't know if it'll come up again this year, but the aquilegia from Cressing Temple is bobbing its purple granny-bonnets in the wind.

Tiggy has still to come to terms with the fact that her "puppy" - as she sees him - Russell, is allowed chicken breast while she only gets the leavings, if any. The word "convalescent" does not figure large in her vocabulary. Dusty and Kitty have now taken to venturing out at first light to spend their days at their "summer residence", otherwise known as the top of Mrs Rocky's shed, down the road. Well, if the Pope can have a summer residence, why not the cats. (Although I have yet to see the Pontiff crouched on top of Mrs Rocky's shed, I think he prefers Castel James Gandolfini). Nigel remains his usual stolid self, though he did stage an overnight absence this week, coming back looking strangely tousled, but with a cheshire-cat grin. If I didn't know that the requisite appendages have been safely ensconced in a glass jar at the Greenside veterinary surgery for the last 10 years (another mint imperial, Vicar?) I would say that he'd enjoyed a night of passion. Perhaps it was platonic.

Russell continues his remarkable recovery, following me round and endlessly yowling for food. He is starting to get his shape back, but we all realise the next ladnmark is when he has to go back to the vet on 15 June to see if there has been any permanent kidney function damage. It's amazing the way major changes can realign the way you look at things. Russell has had a really annoying habit of jumping up on the work surface in the kitchen, which of course necessitated turfing him off then blasting it with anti-bacterial spray. While he was really ill, he clearly wasn't jumping anywhere, and this week I came into the kitchen to find he's jumped back up there. "Deb! He's back on the work surface!" my joyful cry filled the house, and we both stood there grinning like idiots at him, while he tried to work out why the script had changed.

Change has been on my mind this week, of all sorts, because I have been immersing myself in reading the works of S. P. B. Mais, of whom we have theoretically committed to a biography, currently being written for publication 2005/2006. Almost forgotten now, in his time he was a doyen of the BBC and during the war was probably as well known as Priestley or Orwell. Mais is a much less sentimental chronicler of the England of the 1930s than dear old Arthur Mee, though he doesn't go as far into the territory of brutal realism as Orwell or Priestley did. In fairness to Arthur, he wasn't setting himself up to be a social commentator, believing as he did that "progress" would solve all mankind's ills: as he said in *Arthur Mee's Golden Year* (1936)

> Faster than imagination this world is moving on. I believe in the possibility of almost everything. The thought of all the wonders time contains does not surprise me. I believe that the poor will be rich and that life will be beautiful for all. I believe disease will disappear. I believe that we shall see and speak to people everywhere. I believe that the glory awaiting us all is greater than the poet says.

Mais, however, is perfectly placed in the middle ground. He spent a lot of time, like I do now, travelling around England and noting what had changed. He knows that you are never far away from history - as he describes a bus journey up the A1, he remarks on the surviving wall of the park at Hatfield, where Elizabeth I learnt that she would be Queen. I have been wondering what he would think if he was around today. He died in 1975, so he did live to see some of the wonders Arthur Mee was talking about - mass communications, television, maybe the first computers.

All these thoughts were running through my mind on Thursday when I had to go to Leeds for a meeting. I was amazed to find how far the M1 has been extended now, into the gap east of Leeds, almost as far out as Selby, and in amongst these open fields now are huge industrial estates, full of plate glass buildings with atriums and smoked windows, only a few miles from Temple Newsam, another site where the Templars once held sway. All these buildings were temples of the exact type of progress which Arthur so admired. But are we any better off?

The English landscape has probably changed as much in the days since we started reprinting 1930s guidebooks, as it did between the war and 1989 when our first reprint appeared. Should we be concerned about this? Of course, the English landscape is a scrawled palimpsest, boundaries have been drawn, features obliterated, and place names re-lettered from Saxon to French.

> Sally is gone that was so kindly,
> Sally is gone from Ha'naker Mill...

Wrote Hilaire Belloc, lamenting, even then, that "Ha'naker's down, and England's done".

> Ha'nacker Hill is in Desolation:
> Ruin a-top and a field unploughed.
> And Spirits that call on a fallen nation,
> Spirits that loved her calling aloud,
> Spirits abroad in a windy cloud.
> Spirits that call and no one answers —
> Ha'nacker's down and England's done.
> Wind and Thistle for pipe and dancers,
> And never a ploughman under the Sun:
> Never a ploughman. Never a one.

There are lots of people around these days who claim to speak for England, and quick to insist that England *isn't* done: some of them, though, are part of the problem, not the solution. They want to hang on to all the bad things about the past, as well as the good. Given half a chance, they'd have the cotton mills running 20 hours a day, and stick the kids back up chimneys. Just because something is a tradition, doesn't mean it is automatically hallowed: in the words of Skunk Anansie, "just because it feels good, doesn't make it right"

In one sense, the vision of "the merrying of England" cricket on the green, warm beer, church bells and spinsters cycling to matins has always been false. The 1930s also had the misery of mass unemployment, and a prolonged agricultural depression. For all my interest in history, I prefer my central heating, my warm beds, my Ibuprofen and my modern dentistry. Fascinating as it might be to see Shakespeare face to face, I don't think I could cope with a river of sewage in the street, plagues of boils, and dying of old age at 30. Change has always been a feature of life. You can't jump into the same river twice, or step on the same cowpat, whatever Lynda Snell and the Council for the Protection of Rural England might think:

> In my beginning is my end.
> In succession
> Houses rise and fall, crumble, are extended,
> Are removed, destroyed, restored, or in their place
> Is an open field, or a factory, or a by-pass.
> Old stone to new building, old timber to new fires,
> Old fires to ashes, and ashes to the earth
> Houses live and die: there is a time for building
> And a time for living and for generation
> And a time for the wind to break the loosened pane
> And to shake the wainscot where the field-mouse trots
> And to shake the tattered arras woven with a silent motto.

Said T. S. Eliot in *East Coker*. So therefore I have come to the conclusion that we have no choice but to engage with change: if we don't, then we may find that the future gets shaped in ways we don't like, by others who have seized the opportunity. Belloc again:

> Men do not live long without gods, but when the gods of the New Paganism come, they will not be merely insufficient, as were the gods of Greece, not merely false; they will be evil.

All that is required for evil to triumph in the elections is that good men (and women) do not vote. Who to vote for, is of course another problem. I can now think of at least one good reason not to vote for each of the people who are standing round here. I am exactly the opposite to the Sex Pistols, who sang "Don't know what I want, but I know how to get it". I know exactly what I want. I want us to build the new Jerusalem. I am just a bit hazy on the detail as yet.

30th May 2004

It has been a busy week here in the Holme Valley. And a pretty adverse one. The dismal, stop-start summer continues to be dismal, and to stop and start, with one sunny day being followed by two cold dull ones. It has apparently been the driest May since

1998 - not here, though! A storm of Biblical proportions today cleared Sainsbury's car park in minutes as people ran to get shelter anywhere and the rain bounced off the cars like a giant car-wash. If I'd seen it coming, I'd have squirted washing up liquid all over the car before I set off and saved myself £1.50 next week.

The beastlings have all been restless: they can't understand why the summer is slipping away without any of the warm days it normally brings, and we are all powerless to stop it. Dusty, Kitty and Nigel come in wet through and mew plaintively to me, as if I can do anything about the weather. I've tried telling them that if I was in charge it would be sunny all the year round, but they don't understand. Even Tig and Fred look at me quizzically, while they sit and steam by the radiator after a particularly showery "walkies".

There's nothing quite like the unpleasant effect of a soaking wet cat waking you up at 4AM by invading your space under the duvet and drying itself off on you. I sometimes struggle to remember how lucky I am in these circumstances. It has that disturbing combination of being awoken roughly in the middle of the night and being forcibly wetted by the actions of another, that is normally only available to those experiencing the English public school system.

Russell continues his recovery: we're all trying not to build too much emphasis on it 'til June 15 when the vet makes his next assessment. He seems to have regained a lot of his catty shape, at least he's not the bag of bones he was three weeks ago, but he's still a long way off the halcyon days when he weighed 6.4KG, and the vet described him as "a walking draught-excluder".

This week I have finally finished editing the galley proofs of *Hampshire at War*, amidst a positive barrage of D-Day memories everywhere you look, on all TV channels. This, and the fact that it is Whit Sunday, have had me thinking about war and its effects. I have had the quasi-traditional folk song "Dancing at Whitsun" on my brain all day, playing away on the internal juke-box, with its plaintive lyric about how the women tried to keep up the tradition of Morris dancing at Whitsun during the first world war, with all the men away in the trenches:

> The fields they stand empty, the hedges grow free
> No young men to tend them or pastures go see
> They have gone where the forests of oak trees before
> Have gone to be wasted in battle
> There's a straight row of houses in these latter days
> Are covering the downs where the sheep used to graze
> There's a field of red poppies, a wreath from the Queen
> But the ladies remember at Whitsun
> And the ladies go dancing at Whitsun

Whit Sunday was of course a significant day in the agricultural year, and is one of the days associated with the Morris: no doubt they will all be working up for the massed gathering of Morris sides at Bampton Day in June, when the rivers of ale will rival the prodigious flood of the Thames itself under Radstock Bridge. I wonder if that pub near there, with one of the best names of all English hostelries, "The Rose Reviv'd" still flourishes.

My own Whitsun memories are more Philip Larkin than Pa Larkin, going on the train to Bridlington with my dad (steam train, in those days, yes, I am very old). In those days, when I used to wear short trousers and avidly devour war comics filled with the exploits of Captain Hurricane, The Wolf of Kabul (clickey ba!) and "Tough Duff" the commando (all my secrets are coming out now) and sit on the roof of my grandma's disused air raid shelter in her garden at Welton watching the planes from Brough Flying School doing circuits and bumps, I used to dream of being a Spitfire ace, battling the evil Nazis up there in the clouds.   My dad, however, who had actually been in the war, and who had been around when some of the concentration camps were liberated, never actually spoke about it.

Gran never spoke much about her brother in law, Harry Fenwick, Royal Field Artillery, either. He had been gassed at the battle of Ypres in 1917, and it was only much, much, later, long after she had died, that I finally found his grave amongst the immaculately kept lawns and endless rows of identical Commonwealth War Graves memorials stretching away to the horizon in every direction at Etaples military cemetery.

If you have never seen one of these war cemeteries in northern France, I recommend a visit, firstly to remind you of, and make you thankful for, what you have got, and secondly to bring home the sheer enormity of the sacrifice of war. Standing there and trying to compute all of those lost lives, all those stifled hopes, broken dreams, and unfulfilled ambitions, imagining all those bad news telegrams being carried up country lanes to remote farms, or down terraced streets of back to backs, I was filled with sadness at the empty futility of it all.

> Whatever we inherit from the fortunate
> We have taken from the defeated

Says Eliot, in *Four Quartets*, and we have got our freedoms (just) in no small part because ordinary people, who would probably much rather have been at home in the pub, or playing cricket, or Morris dancing come to that, were willing to surrender theirs, sometimes permanently.

So let's enjoy our Whit Sunday, sitting outside the pub (assuming we've already been to church, if we go) and bask in what little sun there is, and reflect that although there is much that needs putting right, there is also much to be proud of here in Britain. Not in a jingoistic way, not with a flag waving "scrag Johnny Foreigner "mentality, that probably belongs in the pages of "Wizard" or "Hotspur". Let's be proud, instead, of our Morris Dancers. And pints of mild.

One day, perhaps, wars will be danced, not fought, God willing. And decided by boozy judges, floridly holding up numbers on cards. Like Eliot's rustic dancers,

> Keeping the rhythm in their dancing
> As in their living in the living seasons
> The time of the seasons and the constellations
> The time of milking and the time of harvest
> The time of the coupling of man and woman
> And that of beasts. Feet rising and falling.
> Eating and drinking.

§

6th June 2004

It has been a busy week in the Holme Valley. Summer, of a sort, has come at last, marked by one of the seasonal indicators that we country dwellers learn to mark the seasons by, the arrival of a 9 tonne skip from Holme Valley Skip Hire on the driveway. This rare seasonal migrant has been fed by us all week, usually with garden rubbish, but also with a lot of the contents of the garage, much of which has been untouched through two house moves, in some cases having been boxed up for 16 or 17 years since I moved from Chichester.

The animals have been amazed by the possibilities of the garage. Nigel, enticed no doubt by the cool concrete floor which is gradually being uncovered as we clear away the clutter of our collective lifetimes, has taken to sleeping in there. He has also managed to break the (internal) cat flap between the kitchen door and the lobby, where the cat food is. Which means that we have had to take the broken cat flap surround off. Which means there is now a hole big enough for Freddie to get through, which means that, unless closely watched, he will polish off his own food then nip through the cat flap hole and polish off the cat food too. Whoever said animals don't work things out.

Tig has taken to flopping out on the carpet instead of sleeping on the bed, Dusty and Kitty spend much of the short night out of doors, only coming in for food and departing at first light. At last, it feels like summer. Russell continues his yowling for food, but he's had a couple of setbacks this week, where he seems a bit preoccupied and quiet. In nine days time we will know the best, or worst.

I was sorting through the stuff in the garage this morning while listening to the D Day service from Arromanches, and just as I found some of my old school exercise books, coincidentally on the radio, they started singing one of the hymns that we used to hammer out in assembly. Of course, we always garbled it by singing "Immortal invisible, God, Ernie Wise" and I could never sing the line about "pavillioned in splendour and girded with praise" without thinking of Geoffrey Boycott.

In many ways, sorting through this old stuff, from school exercise books, through to my college notes, interspersed with photos of old girlfriends, hastily consigned to a separate envelope, and things like the first edition of *Chichester History* which I edited, was like looking at a re-run of my life - the sort of thing someone light put together for a memorial service, or - perhaps more pretentiously - a memorial service.

In another way, it was like looking into the past of someone else. Some bits of me have changed so much since I was that snotty nosed kid in short trousers and a duffle coat, always held out in the traditional "Vulcan" manner while I ran round the corner from Alexandra Terrace to Crowle Street Junior and Infant School (demolished in its centenary year by the philistines of Hull City Council) making the requisite machine gun noises that all kids of the 1950s were required to do in homage to war comics.

When you start to think about how you got to this particular point in your life, even without all the staggering choices that had to go right just to create the cosmos in the first place, your mind reels with the sheer improbability of it all. Suppose my grandad hadn't met and courted Granny Welgate, back in those grim days of 1919, when everyone came back from Flanders looking for a land fit for heroes. In another universe, I would probably have been someone else. But a unique concatenation of circumstances put me in that building at that time, listening to Mr Price play the piano as we all sang, in that peculiar off key rendition that only primary school children do so well, to the tune of *Waters End*:

> Glad that I live am I, That the sky is blue.
> Glad for the country lanes, and the fall of dew.
> After the sun the rain, After the rain the sun;
> This is the way of life, 'till the work be done.
> All that we need to do, be we low or high,
> Is to see that we grow, nearer the sky...

But of course the most potent memory for me is the time when Mr Price in his best Welsh Presbyterian manner, began playing the introduction to something I had not heard before. I looked around at the big plain glass windows, that had the East Hull sunlight streaming through them, complete with suspended dust-motes, the ranks of tiered desks the blackboard, the chalk dust, the bottles of turquoise ink, as he stirred the notes of Parry's music, and, right on cue, the older kids, who had done it before, came in with

> And did those feet, in ancient time ...

Today, in the garage, holding those exercise books, I was back there, forty years ago. In 1964, we were only twenty years away from the war. We lived in a terraced house where the floorboards ran with damp, and a big hole had rotted away down one side. Outside our door, the other side of Alexandra Terrace had gone, in 1941, courtesy of a Luftwaffe bomb aimer who was trying for Alexandra Dock and missed, unusually for such a militarily precise race as the Germans. On the bomb site, me and Trevor Tozer used to play at being archaeologists. Maybe he became one, I hope so.

I however, inspired by Mr Price, who probably neither knows not cares, looked around me at the Terraces, looked around me at the electricity sub stations, the gasometers, and the docks, and made a silent vow to make things better. If I couldn't build Jerusalem, I would have a damn good try.

One of the books I found in the garage today was J B Priestley's *English Journey*. Debbie had "tidied it away" - the fate of any book which is not about Jim Morrison or Michael Jackson. He describes (page 112) the children of Rusty Lane, West Bromwich, thus.

There ought to be no more of these lunches and dinners, at which political and financial and industrial gentlemen congratulate one another, until something is done about Rusty Lane, and about West Bromwich. While they still exist in their foul shape, it is idle to congratulate ourselves about anything. They make the whole pomp of government here a miserable farce. The Crown, Lords and Commons are the Crown, Lords and Commons of Rusty Lane, West Bromwich... and if there is another economic conference, let it meet there, in one of the warehouses, and be fed with bread and margarine and slabs of brawn. The delegates have seen one England, Mayfair in the season. Let them see another England next time, West Bromwich out of the season. Out of all seasons, except the winter of our discontent."

Out of the corner of my eye, just beyond the garage door, I can see a nine year old kid in a duffle coat, with a war comic protruding out of one pocket, adjusting his national health specs and saying, " Amen, Amen."

13th June 2004

It's been a busy week in the Holme Valley, with the pressure really on to get the web sites updated and let everybody (ie the entire book trade of the UK and beyond, the press and any private individuals or schools who have found their way on to our mailing list, that there will be a new Gez Walsh book in September, and a new one by Chris White as well!

All of which has seen me sitting at the computer frantically deduplicating databases and preparing mailshots while everyone else is flaked out in the sun outside. Nigel has found a patch of shade under a garden seat, Kitty seeks the cool of the spare bedroom, Tig flakes out on the decking, her and Freddy become a panting heap of dogs after even the shortest walkies.

Russell continues to hold on, and of course we're all gearing up to hear on Wednesday whether or not his kidney damage is permanent, meanwhile he occupies himself by mewing for attention, yowling for food, and walking over the keyboard in a futile attempt to help with the deduplication by deleting page after page of bookshops if he was allowed to get away with it. These days we've learned to minimise anything on screen if we are away from the keyboard, ever since the time when I cam back and found the screen saying "you have chosen to delete Windows 98, continue Y/N?" courtesy of Russell's transit over the keyboard on his way to the sunnier destination of the windowsill.

Dusty has been conspicuous by her absence. The special low calorie food which she has from the vet to stop her looking so much like a Davy Crockett hat goes untouched as she prefers the delights of that left out by Mrs Rocky. The other day I pulled up in the car and saw what I thought was Freddie coming down the road: thinking "what's he doing out here" I then did a double take and saw it was actually Dusty trotting along, and that she is now the size of a small dog. I mentioned to Deb that I was thinking of putting "Do not feed me, I get fed at home" on her collar, and she said "Good idea, I think we should put it on your collar as well." This is typical of the gay banter which passes betwixt us. I often suspect her of not paying attention to anything I say to her, so I have, on occasion, slipped the odd outrageous statement into our everyday conversation while she is watching East Enders: for example "I'm running away to join the circus dear" or, "On the way home, I was abducted by aliens and rectally probed"

Neither of these caught her out, however. Her reply to the first one was that she had "already phoned them, and they have got enough elephants", and to the latter "the flying saucer couldn't take off if you were on board"

Actually this week the banter has sometimes had an edge to it, as we are all feeling the stress of getting all this info out to the book chains before they make their crucial Christmas buying decisions. It's not been helped because we have been talking about holidays, realising that if we don't make plans to go somewhere soon, we will be into september and book launches and another year will go by holiday-less.

It's been a bitter sweet day today, sitting here doing mailshots while Joni Mitchell has been on the CD singing that "the wind is in from Africa, and last night I couldn't sleep" I know the feeling. My favourite destinations right now would be Crete, France, or Santiago de Compostella, whereas Deb wants to go to Iceland, Norway or Russia. Send me a postcard. Last night I asked her how she felt about Estonia and she gave me a funny look and wandered out of the room. It's just a gift I have.

The way the years zip round, does sort of bring it home to me how life is rushing past while I stand by and watch it like an ineffectual spectator. At its worst this is manifested by awful glimpses where the mind becomes conscious of its own mortality, and at best I often find myself wondering what, if I "went" tomorrow, I would have accomplished, would I be remembered for anything? We got talking about what I wanted at my funeral the other day, as I had been playing Geoffrey Burgon's Nunc Dimittis and said I wouldn't mind that. Then I added that what I really wanted was "Sound the Trumpets" -

"Who's that by?" she said?

"Oh come on, his first name is Henry, and he washes whiter than white" I chided "You *must* know who I mean"

"Henry Daz?"

Yes, sometimes I worry about that wife of mine. Planning your own funeral is all very fine and good. It would certainly have saved my sister and me a lot of heart searching if my dad had left some indication of what he wanted. I hope we got it about right. But it would be nice to think you had achieved something. Ten years ago, we were involved in doing a festival in Sheffield for the charity Tree Aid, that raised enough money to build a well in Ende, Mali. And we got a letter of encouragement from Joan Baez. I have still got it somewhere.

It would be good to do something like that again for this terrible Sudan thing that's going on, but I doubt we would get the people to do it for free these days, unfortunately compassion fatigue has taken hold over Africa, it's all very depressing. Not that it'll stop us trying. But if Bob Geldof and all of Live Aid couldn't sort out Africa, I think it's best to be realistic about what a fat old baldy can expect to accomplish these days.

So if I can't be remembered for saving Africa, I suppose it's going to be for inflicting "Bitey The Veggie Vampire" on an unsuspecting world. Ah well. I suppose what really counts is to feel content with yourself, not to dwell on your regrets but to give them due weight, and feel that you tried your best. That's all that we can hope for really. That, and, as Philip Larkin said, that "what will survive of us is love".

I seem to have been overtaken by these thoughts again while writing this. It's because on the compilation CD I was playing, there was an unexpected time bomb waiting for me. James Taylor singing "Carolina on My Mind", which, for me, is forever associated with all the trips I made driving up from Chichester to Hull when my mother was dying, for some reason that cassette always seemed to be in the deck, and as James Taylor sang "with a holy host of others all around me, still I'm on the dark side of the road" I always used to think about all the people in that ribbon of light that was the M1, all those lives in transit, moving towards a conclusion, trying to do their best on the way.

So I think I ought to get up, go downstairs and watch England lose nobly to France while cooking some veggie barbecue for all the beings, furry and non-furry, who I am responsible for feeding. Sometimes, when you have been to the edge and peeped over, it's nice to go back to the comfort zone of the familiar middle.

Otherwise I will end up composing my own epitaph. "He was a pain in the arse. He was always arguing with people, causing trouble, and asking awkward questions. He liked drawing and painting, mainly pictures of trees and mountains. He was sometimes good at stringing words together. He wasn't scared of hard work, but it often bored him. He liked sharing wine with people, he also liked drinking it himself, and playing the guitar. He listened to weird music though. He would always go out of his way to help an animal, but was much more choosy about people. He had a nasty temper. He was capable of bearing grudges, usually about things that many many other people would have just let go, such as what the government had done/not done about this and that. The intrays of whitehall will be the emptier for his passing. His legs often hurt" Cue: "Sound the Trumpets" by Henry Daz.

20th June 2004

It has been another busy week in the Holme Valley. Whoever decides these things (aka God the Almighty) has once more turned off the tap marked "summer", with the result that on Friday evening I was reduced to an (unsuccessful) attempt to re-light the stove, using several old newspapers which I had soaked in linseed oil (in lieu of firelighters) and the dregs of the last bag of coal from the delivery back in March. Like the summer itself so far, it flamed briefly, and was gone, leaving us once more reliant on the central heating, which I banged on at full blast. Somehow, though, it's not so romantic sitting around a blazing radiator.

The sudden change back to colder weather has of course meant that Dusty and Kitty have forsaken the solarium which they had set up on top of Mrs Rocky's shed, and are once more to be found in a tangle of cats on the spare bed. This morning I let Tig out for her early morning pooch-mooch in the garden and it promptly hailstoned on her. On midsummer's eve, no less. She was, to put it mildly, both bedraggled and unimpressed.

This week was the week when we took Russell back to the vet for what we thought was going to be the final word on whether what he has got is terminal, life threatening, or merely something that can be managed with drugs, Unfortunately, it turns out that it's too early to tell, so we now have another date to put a red ring around and worry about, July 7th. Thanks, by the way, to all the people who've sent me emails wishing him well, and posted messages here saying they are thinking about him: if wishes were fishes, he'd not only never go hungry, he'd be cured, and he'd be 10 years younger! You know who you are. And thanks again.

It's not all been doom and gloom this week, though: we've been following another tortuous saga full of tragedy and drama as each day unfolds - England's progress in Euro 2004. This came to a head for me on Thursday evening, when I arrived back home to find the house empty and in darkness. Debbie had gone round to her mother's house over the other side of the valley, to watch it on widescreen red-button interactive surroundsound digital satellite dish thingy, in the presence of her twin footer-mad brothers and no doubt several dozen cans of lager. So I turned on our own, rather more modest, set and watched the end of England's feeble attempt at beating ten not very good Swiss players, then phoned over to ask what she felt like me cooking for tea. On being given the answer, "baked potatoes", a quick visit to the veg rack revealed that we didn't have enough potatoes. Like Switzerland, we were one short. Not to be foiled, I hit the redial button. I got her mother.

Me: "Has Deb already left?"
Her: "Yes, she's just gone"
Me "Ah, I wanted to ask her to bring back a potato"
Her: [short puzzled silence] "I'll see what I can do"

It was about 15 minutes later when Deb came in, clutching a potato. Her mother had apparently erupted out of the house brandishing the said vegetable just as she was driving off, shouting "I have got a potato for you!"

Debbie, based on a conversation which they had had earlier in the day, about someone who had sent Frank Skinner a potato which looked like Wayne Rooney, and taking into account the excited way in which her mother was waving the King Edward in question, for some reason assumed that this must be a potato of such overwhelmingly staggering likeness to the said England striker, which her mother had discovered by chance at the moment of her departure, and that she could not wait til their next meeting to share her discovery. There followed a brief but confusing exchange, until Deb's mother managed to explain why it didn't look a bit like him, and was in fact destined for our oven.

The weird, zany atmosphere continued yesterday when I caught Deb trying to re-program the video.

Me: "What are you doing?"
Deb: "I want to record this film that is on BBC2"
Me: "Oh, right - what is it?"
Deb: "Well I only caught a glimpse of it but I think it's "Carve Her Name With Pride" and that's always been one of my favourites."
Me: "Oh. Right"

Much hissing (from the video) and cursing (from Deb) ensued until she finally got it to lock on to the channel in question, just as Jack Hawkins was giving the order to fire the depth charges.

"This is 'The Cruel Sea' " I said.

"Oh," she said.

Much later, carefully picking my moment, I plucked up enough courage to ask "didn't you think it was odd that the French Resistance had somehow managed to get hold of a destroyer and take part in the Battle of the Atlantic?" to which she replied "Well, there's sea round France, isn't there?"

And so we came to Midsummer's Eve, today, but it's hardly been a dream (and don't worry, I have no intention of performing with my Bottom. No energy, for one thing.) In fact it's been a day spent struggling with boxes of letterhead and unpacking the new printer we took delivery of yesterday, 30KG of chunkiness and about as portable as a one of Jack Hawkins' depth charges. I thought that computer equipment was supposed to be getting smaller and more compact. It's meant an interesting afternoon, lying in the fluff and old rubber bands under the desk, trying to work out what wire goes where. Believe me, writing this is a breath of fresh air for me, even if reading it isn't for you!

Yes, all in all it's been a crazy old week. A week in which it wouldn't actually have seemed too out of place if Violette Szabo had taken over The Compass Rose and gone on a cruise hunting U-Boats. A week where the very Lords of Misrule seem to have taken control of everything. This can be the only explanation for some of the things I have seen and heard this week. Here are only a few examples:

Some people, watching the fight break out on Big Brother on Channel 4, actually phoned the police. ("Hello officer, there are some people fighting inside my TV") I have always wondered, *inter alia*, why people phone the police when they see a UFO, as well. "Yes Madam, thank you, we'll just get Sergeant Johnson to pop up to 25,000 feet in his panda car and flag them down for a ticket". This always assumes of course that Aliens know what blue flashing lights mean. Would they want to get involved, though, in real life?

The *Daily Telegraph* reported that Scottish Natural Heritage have called off the Uist Hedgehog Cull for this year (because the Hedgehogs are assumed by now to have mated and the females to be pregnant) They have killed 250 animals this year, at a cost of £190,000, or £760 per hedgehog. You can organise an individual drive-by shooting of someone for less than that amount if you know where to go in South Yorkshire. Less, if they are unpopular. Several phone calls by us have failed to find a recipient for the free van load of superannuated computer equipment which we have outgrown and no longer need. This includes a monitor, an old laser printer, several keyboards, some miles of ethernet cabling, various mice, and our first ever colour printer, an Epson Stylus 600 which nowadays only prints when it wants to. Deb's first reaction was to try and give it all to Oxfam, but of course they are only interested in working systems with Pentium 2 chips or above (it's obviously vital in Eritrea and Somalia that people have the wherewithal to play X-Wing on-line) and no one is willing to take the stuff, apart from a recycling company in Armitage Bridge which wants to charge us money for them to crush the stuff and put it in landfill!

So if anyone knows of a suitable donor within a driving distance of Huddersfield (that wouldn't negate the idea of recycling by using yet more energy to drive there) let me know. Of course, this is all tied in somehow with some European directive about recycling waste electrical products - the biggest Lords of Misrule of the lot are often to be found within those hallowed portals, but I can't help but feel another candidate for the fool's bladder and the cap and bells must be those companies that make the consumables for a printer, more expensive than the cost of buying a new printer.

Tomorrow marks the longest day. After that, it's downhill all the way towards Christmas. A reminder, if any was needed, that time is passing relentlessly, and that we only have so long to sort out life's lunacies. Some of them, such as merchants talking to donkeys, and lovers whispering sweet nothings through party walls, can safely be consigned to the stage. So, this evening, let there be cakes and ale, and by St Anne, let ginger be hot i'the mouth too: but tomorrow, it's time for sermons and soda water and let's all try and somehow strike a blow for sanity, because this Earth, which so far has kept faith with us and has kept spinning around, from season to season, from solstice to solstice, is the only one we have got.

27ᵗʰ June 2004

It has been a rough old week in the Holme Valley. I don't know who is in charge of the weather. God or Michael Fish. But I wish to register an official complaint. This summer is dead. It has gorn to meet its maker. It's been nailed to its perch. Etc.

Kitty and Dusty of course, think it's me who's in charge. That's why they have greeted me with plaintive mews of protest each morning when we have woken to skies the colour of a zinc dustbin and drumming rain on the roof and windows. I'd really hoped that a long hot summer would allow the roof of Colin's house to dry out, but alas it looks like it's not to be.

Russell continues to use the bad weather as his excuse for staying indoors curled up in the best armchair. His special diet is in its second week, and the "KD food", as it is known, has already been christened "KD Laing" food, by us. To encourage Russ to eat it, the vet suggested that we mix a little chicken breast with the KD Laing. Unfortunately Russell has learned how to separate them again. Quite quickly. By a simple process of eating the one and leaving the other.

Nigel has continued being his stolid ginger self. It's difficult to describe Nigel. He never actually does anything, he just gets quietly on with his own little destiny, which is to be a medium sized ginger cat in the opening years of a new millennium.

Tig and Fred have been dodging the showers and interviewing a potential new member of the wolf pack, a Jack Russell called Betsy who belongs to a friend of Deb's Mum, who has had to go into hospital. I have not met Betsy. I am told the jury is still out on whether she comes to stay with us. Since our house is the sort where another couple of dogs could easily slip in and mingle unnoticed (Tia, from two houses down the lane, often saunters in through the conservatory and lies down in front of the stove with not so much as a "hi, I am your new dog") perhaps Betsy has already moved in and I simply haven't picked her out in the swirling mass of mutts.

And with the weather being so bad, our spirits have dipped too. All I have done this week to justify my existence is spend Tuesday driving to Coventry and do a powerpoint presentation which should have lasted 20 minutes but ended up taking 90 minutes, including questions. This is not necessarily a bad thing, but by the time I fought my way back up the M1, I was already feeling ropey, and not just with the early start. Wednesday, Thursday, Friday and Saturday, I spent churning out mailshots for the new books, while my head throbbed and my limbs ached. Either it was a foul bug breathed in during my exposure to Coventry, or my body telling me that I had been overdoing it rather, or both. Whatever else it was, it wasn't pleasant.

Thursday night was the nadir of the week. Not only did I feel totally wasted, in every sense of the word, but the evening was topped off by the debacle of England playing football. I have never harboured any particular animosity to the Swiss, but in my febrile state I do recall wishing that the referee's eyesight had been better, and William Tell's been worse. Some people spread joy and happiness wherever they go, others do it whenever they go, and I was definite that Mr Meier was of the latter camp. I feel better now.

It got to the stage yesterday where we decided that the only thing that would make us feel better would be to declare Sunday a holiday and go and see our good friend, who always cheers us up. Dr Keswick. So it was that at 2 o'clock today, we were Ambling into Ambleside, and at 2.45, our wheels came to rest in the car park in the middle of a strangely empty Keswick town centre. Having dropped Debbie off so she can do her thing of looking at everything in all the camping shops in the lake district twice, within twenty minutes I was continuing my watercolour of St Kentigern's church at Crosthwaite.

A very pleasant afternoon, interrupted only when the verger came out and asked me at a quarter to five is I was one of the visiting Durham bell ringers. Sadly I had to disappoint him. Obviously he had mistaken me for someone else. Perhaps my face rang a bell. Back to Ambleside, and a chance for Tig to go swimming in the stream at the White Moss National Trust site. Whatever you say about the National Trust, and I have said plenty bad about them, at least they keep that site in a presentable state, although it was wetter and colder than the last time we were there back in March. Debbie wimped out of the walk, so it was just me, Tiggy, a gnarled old walking stick known as "Harry Lauder" - I have a picture of me leaning on it next to Loch Lomond - and the two ducks splashing in a new arm of the stream which merged with the path owing to the downpour of Biblical proportions which had just taken place. Apart from that, we had the whole of White Moss to ourselves. A silence so profound you almost could reach out and touch it. On a Sunday in June in the Lakes.

And I thought how lucky I am, even with my crap life and limited mobility, to be stuck in the rain in Ambleside. "Oh mama, could this really be the end, to be stuck inside of Ambleside with a mobile phone again."

Betsy's owner, stuck in Huddersfield Royal, - and all the other people in hospital - all the people my sister looks after in Leicester Infirmary - would probably trade their last bedpan to swop places with me. People who are facing operations, or whose health is a lot worse than mine. So I paused, and sent them all a positive vibe, from White Moss National Trust site, full of rain and sun and incredible brightness and the new damp smell of everything fresh after the storm. I hope it got there.

Suitably re-charged, via a diversion through Manchester courtesy of the closed M60, we're back. Bayonets fixed for next week, and ready to go over the top. Nothing new there then!

§

4th July 2004

I am not going to mention the weather. Until the weather changes I am doing my best to ignore it, and you can safely assume that it's been a wet old week in the Holme Valley, which it has, even to the extent of having to place buckets in the garage to prevent the rain from the many leaks that the deluge forced in the roof.

Kitty and Dusty are two hacked-off cats, at their summer holidays on top of Mrs Rocky's shed being curtailed, and Nigel is a frequent fugitive, coming in soaked and bedraggled through the cat flap after yet another downpour caught him sleeping on the decking.

Russell is up one day, down the next. He had a bad couple of days in the week when he even went off chopped up pieces of cooked chicken - a hitherto sure fire way to make him take his tablets, by wrapping them in it - but he seemed brighter again by the weekend.

This week has - like last week - been hell on wheels, the printers shouting for copy for the new books, trying to get the artwork off for the reprints of the books that we have sold out of, a VAT return to do, someone having a conference wants 400 leaflets, and so it goes on, relentlessly.

So it was that, come Saturday, with Deb at work til 4pm, I found myself driving back East. Out along the M62, along the North bank of the Humber "Where sky and Lincolnshire and water meet" as Larkin described it in The Whitsun Weddings. My thoughts were not so much about Larkin, but Eliot:

> I do not know much about Gods,
> but I think that the river is a strong, brown God,
> sullen untamed and intractable ...

Eliot was thinking of the Missouri of course, and when my feeble remembering of the lines came to an end, I found them perfectly supplemented by Paul Simon on the cassette deck

> The Mississippi delta, was shining like a National guitar
> I am following the river down the highway through the cradle of the civil war

My own destination was not Graceland, however, but Spurn Point, that incredibly lonely and desolate spit of land where the Holderness coast sticks out into the Humber estuary, and apart from the sea-sound the only noises are the wind and the eerie hooting of the sirens of tankers coasters and North Sea ferries as they negotiate Immingham Roads.

Although Spurn is deserted now, it was once the site of Ravenser Odd, a bustling medieval port now washed away by the ceaseless grey grind of the North sea's longshore drift, which sometimes nibbles eight feet a year out of the edge of Holderness. It is also where Henry Bolingbroke landed. But all there is today is the deserted remains of the lighthouse and lifeboat station. And a bird sanctuary.

I quickly realised, while I was still 10 miles west of Hull, that there was no way I was ever going to make it to Spurn. Although the M62 will carry you, via Clive Sullivan way, right into the City Centre, once you have crossed the tidal surge barrier and started out along the Hedon Road, you soon realise how many miles you still have to go. You have to get past Saltend and its chemical works, and places like Patrington with its church known as the Queen of Holderness, and Winestead, where Andrew Marvell was born.

> Thou by th'Indian Ganges side should'st rubies find:
> I, by the tide of Humber, would complain ...

There was never going to be enough time for me to reach Spurn, do my painting, and get back in time to pick up Deb at 4pm. So I did what I normally hate doing. I compromised, and ended up at an alternative destination, Brough Haven. I hadn't intended to go back to Brough. I always nod towards it, if I ever do pass it on the M62, but seeing other people now living in what I still occasionally think of as "our house" isn't my favourite way of stirring up good memories (or bad ones for that matter).

After a bracing walk along the old towpath from the Haven, behind Blackburns, where I was at once amazed by how much work the council (? I assume ?) have done to make it a "proper" path, and saddened to see the old slipway from which Blackburns used to launch their flying boats to test them on the Humber had either been demolished or had finally fallen into the mud. Tig was more interested in sniffing all the new, interesting, maritime smells, with their overtones of tar and oil, and I was more interested in getting back to the car before I was blown over.

Brough was the ancient Roman settlement of Petuaria, where they forded the Humber. It's said that if you know your way over the sandbanks, and don't mind wading up to your head in freezing cold water, you can still walk across the Humber, the way the Legionaries are supposed to have done. They must have scarcely had time to tip the fish out of their armour before they were set to work building the fort, which now lies underneath the playing fields next to The Burrs, where we used to play our rag tag cricket matches and go traipsing home like the urchins we were, carrying the spacehopper that served as an auxiliary fielder (if you hit the ball and it hit the spacehopper without bouncing, you were out caught. Note to the selectors: England could do with a few fielders like that spacehopper, right now.)

The elements conspired to put on a display of their power while I sat there and painted my watercolours. The Humber changing from brown to silver and then back to brown again as the sun appeared and disappeared behind huge banks of grey and white clouds, and the wind whipped round the car and rocked it as the rain drummed on the roof, competing with Joni Mitchell, who could have been singing about me:

> I am a lonely painter, I live in a box of paints

The shapes of the clouds flitting over the hills of Lincolnshire a mile away over on the other bank, brought to mind an irreverent reference to Donne:

> Thy gown going off such beauteous state reveals,
> As when from flowery meads, th'hills' shadow steals.

And *vice versa*. Even the seagulls, normally so aerodynamic, and allegedly Reginald Mitchell's (no relation to Joni!) inspiration for the wing shape of the Spitfire, were being flung and buffeted this way and that by the raw power of the gale. As I painted away at my modest little watercolours I couldn't help but think back to when we used to live here, in the village, a mile up the road. Of the four people who occupied that little house, two - my parents - are dead and the other two now don't see each other as often as maybe they should. I started thinking about when we used to be taken to the seaside in my dad's Reliant.

Because he had a full motorcycle licence, and you could drive a Reliant three wheeler on that licence, he never bothered taking his car test, and instead drove a succession of Reliants. The ones I remember are not the later, fibreglass, "plastic rat" type, so beloved of the Trotter Independent Trading Company, but instead the earlier ones, particularly XAT540. XAT540 had perspex windows, and smelt of petrol and leather, and going for a drive in XAT540 was more like going for a flip in a biplane than driving. This effect was enhanced by the roar of the motorbike engine that powered it, making conversation quieter than a shout impossible.

Quite a lot of the times we set off for Aldbrough, Bridlington, or Kilnsea, we never actually got there. Once, when coming back from Hull, my dad had to pull up at the roadside because the driver's seat caught fire (too near the engine sump) and he had to beat it out with his hands. I thought about all the times I used to hold the torch for him while he bent over the engine, cursing while he tried to get a spanner somewhere inaccessible in XAT540's innards. Well, Dad, you passed the torch on to me in 1992, I hope I'm carrying it to your satisfaction.

As I came out of my reverie I realised that what I thought was rain on the windscreen was in part supplemented tears on the inside of my specs.

I don't know why I felt so peculiarly sad and happy simultaneously about going back - however briefly - to a place where I lived from 1965 to 1973 and again from 1976 to 1980, but they do say that "what the heart feels today, the mind understands tomorrow". Maybe I will get to the bottom of that bittersweet mix of emotions one day soon.

I know that when I talk to my young nephew Ryan about when I was young, it's obvious that the past really is another country, and they really do "do things differently there". He was amazed when I showed him Nuv-Nuv, the toy rabbit I have had since I was five, expertly repaired by having a large section of what had previously been a bri-nylon sock sewn into place. Deb says that this toy screams "deprived childhood" at her, but I can't square that, because I know I caused the hole in Nuv-Nuv by cuddling him so much that he frayed. Ryan can't understand why I never had a Play Station. Ryan has got all this stuff, and more, but I hope that as he grows up, someone will find time to cuddle him, not necessarily til he frays, just once in a while.

Tomorrow, I have to get up early and go to Manchester, of all places. A city where, if you can see the Pennines, it's going to rain, and if you can't see them, it's already raining. It may yet be sunny for the rest of the summer - who knows? But if it's going to get its act together, there is not much time. Who is that imaginary figure down there in the boggy wet field behind the piggery setting up his Anglo-Saxon barometer? Why it's our old chum, St. Swithun.

11th July 2004

It has been a busy week in the Holme Valley. However our spirits have been lifted by the endless succession of scorchingly hot days with blue skies and fluffy white clouds, reminding us what the true nature of the English summer should be. Har Har, I don't think. However, despite the rain, and the cold, that has led Dusty and Kitty to resume their wintertime impersonation of a cat lasagne under the duvet in the spare room, and led Nigel to spend his days curled up in a tight ginger ball on the duvet in our room, I do feel strangely uplifted, elevated and in touch with myself these days. It's probably to do with being happy with what small morsels life deals out on those odd occasions when someone shows you a kindness that you probably didn't expect. Being happy with your lot. If I was a troll, I could think of worse fates than spending your life underneath A Bridge and asking awkward questions.

Life has been posing us awkward questions this week. In purely technology terms, Deb's computer has developed a dicky motherboard, my mobile decided to lock itself up for over 12 hours before deciding to free itself again, the printers can't read the disk with Gez's new book on - but then the internet has only just reached Chippenham - so on all sides we are surrounded by embattled machines with attitude problems, yet despite that I do feel, like Gerard Manley Hopkins that "there lives the dearest sweetness deep down things" and maybe it will all come out right somehow which isn't immediately apparent to me yet. Which is about all you can hope for out of life in general really.

We were going to go to Grasmere today to see the Blake watercolours for Milton's *Paradise Lost* that are on display there, but sadly we rose much too late to set off. Because of the nights in the week spent fighting the machines, I guess, but the watercolours are there til October. So there's time yet. Tig was deprived of her dip in the river at White Moss though, and has had to make do with half an hour of "frisbee fetch" in Beaumont Park today, after we got back from my painting trip to Horbury this afternoon.

Tomorrow is going to be an interesting day: we get a visit from Deb's cousin Pete and his wife, who are stopping over one night, en route by motorbike from Scotland to Cornwall. Rather them than me. Tomorrow is also an interesting day because we get the results of Russell's latest lots of tests, which will either be that his kidneys are regaining function, or he's much the same, or he's worse. So depending which of those three options it is, Pete and his wife could either find us en fete or strangely subdued.

Russ himself is blissfully ignorant of his plight, mewing loudly for chopped ham and when there's nothing better on offer, deigning to eat his "K D Laing" food.

It seems almost perverse to retain an inner hope that things will suddenly magic themselves right, but at least believing in magic gives it a chance to happen. Sometimes of course, magic happens anyway, whether you want it to or not. So after this I am going to light some incense and waft it over Deb's computer. The worst that can happen is an insurance claim!

In between all the chaos this week, I have been hearing exciting reports from Maisie of how her new book on S. P. B. Mais is going. Swopping emails with the West Sussex Record Office in Chichester (where Mais's papers are deposited) brought back to me the memories of the time when I used to live there, from 1980 to 1989, when I came back to Yorkshire to start my own firm. Happy days, many of them, spent sampling the local brews (Ringwood Old Thumper I remember as particular hangover fodder, and Gales Ales of Horndean. They used to say, "if the bottom's falling out of your world, drink Gales Ales, and the world will fall out of your bottom" a truism to which I can, sadly, attest.) Sussex is a great county. If I didn't live here, I would live there. Like Hilaire Belloc

> I'll settle me down in Steyning to sing
> Of the girls I have met in my wandering

Stanmer Park, with its cricket matches in the summer, the cliffs at Rottingdean where Bob Copper and his family sang their archetypal English folk songs, Brighton which never quite goes to sleep, with its crumbling piers, its shabby-genteel air and its insanely-odd pavilion. And behind it all the majestic sweep of the South Downs. I remember sitting up on the trundle, looking out over Chichester with the distinctive spire of the Cathedral, pointing upwards like a spike on a sundial, reminding us that time is passing on our journey to heaven.

It was at Felpham, just down the Bognor road, that the redcoats came to arrest Blake for sedition, and found him and his wife naked in the garden reading Paradise Lost to each other. We laugh at this innocence, we perhaps put a cynical, knowing gloss on it, but at the end of all things, personally, I think it would be a much better world if we all sat naked in the garden reading *Paradise Lost* to each other. But what would I know? Me and Blake, we're just superannuated old hippes who believe that all you need is love and you will reach Jerusalem, and all society's problems will vanish: and you too can be a pacifist axe murderer.

Mention of hippies leads me on to the other thing that keeps me going, my dreams. I will put them down here, some of them, so you can laugh at them. But laugh softly, for you laugh at my dreams. This dream is of a long low stone farm house with dogs, cats and chickens, including all the animals we currently possess, and the people who live in the house all get on together and all look after each other and all cook each other food, and sing songs round the fire as the wine glass gets refilled and they laugh and they sing, and the dogs snooze in the glow by the hearth and the cats curl themselves up and purr and twitch as they dream, and as the embers die down, the people find their rooms and curl up under their duvets and perhaps they also purr and twitch and dream, and who knows, two or three of them might wander off and start reading Paradise Lost in the nude to each other in the woods. And would that be a bad thing? Nettles aside of course? If you think this is all hippy rubbish from the 1960s, there's nothing new under the sun. S. P. B Mais was a great advocate of nude swimming and he also turned down an offer of a job which arrived in the form of a telegram (remember them?) from Hitler of all people, because he was busy at the time playing cricket on Southwick village green. I think I may be his lost spiritual child.

It's fashionable to decry the 1960s as a drug addled slough of self-indulgence. All I can say is give me a summer of love any day. Or every day. Well, just give me a summer would be a start! So Mustardlanders, turn on tune in, drop out and find that copy of *Paradise Lost*. Or better still, find that paradise you have lost. Or at least make a start on finding it.

18th July 2004

It has been a bloody awful week in the Holme Valley, marked by computers and other electronic apparatus turning up their collective toes (not that they have toes of course, we're talking metaphorical toes here, the worst sort) left, right, and very possibly centre. We have lost a week's production time on the two new kids' books because Deb's computer has either a bad boot sector, a lacy hard disk, a problem with peripheral drivers, a problem caused by a duff network card in the server, or possibly any or all of the above, depending who you ask and what direction the wind is blowing at the time.

And of course this is the week we have heard the fantastic news that both of the new kids' books have been chosen for the Booksellers Association Christmas Catalogue this year - along side the likes of H. Potter esq. Despite this being a great honour, we still have to pay for it, and Phil now has the wonderful task of securing orders for 2000 extra copies to pay for the cost of the ad. Should be a breeze, and we are now seriously worried that the initial print runs might be too small. All good healthy problems just in case you ever felt like giving your insomnia a few additional phobias to boost it a bit.

In all the computer chaos we've hardly noticed the weather. Dusty, Kitty and Nigel have been in a lot, so I guess it's been raining. Russell got his latest set of results this Monday, he's got to have Fortekor for the rest of his days, and he's got the problem that developed with his heart getting enlarged because of the strain from his failing kidneys. Apart from that, the vets described him as "stabilised" So that's at least one stable member of the household. We're working on the others.

Monday saw a flying visit by Debbie's cousin Pete and new wife Wendy, who were wend-ing their way down from Scotland back to Cornwall, on their rather large rather impressive 1100cc motorbike. Deb was secretly hoping to get taken for a flip on the back of this, but it didn't happen. We all sat up til 2AM talking though, and much wine was caroused. That, and a couple of other nice things that happened when people were really kind to me this week even though I doubt that I deserved it, were the only nuggets of gold in a week that was otherwise unleavened problems, thick and fast, from all sides.

Finally, on Friday, Vince our computer guru arrived on his motorbike (the neighbours have probably concluded we have founded a new chapter of the Hell's Angels from the evidence this week. We could call it the publishers' chapter. Har har!) and finally got Deb's machine working again. He also said that it had the most illogically organised hard disk he had ever seen, the most icons on a desktop, and the prize for the number of files in a root directory (normal computers have about 20, Deb's has 167). So, some hard disk gardening has been in order.

Last night we had a surprise visitation from Deb's mum, who was looking after Ryan. As they stayed for tea, Ryan had his first ever pasta, which necessitated great discussions about Italy, where it was, what they did to the wheat, the Romans, different sauces, etc. Well, if he grows up into a celebrity chef, I will claim the credit.

Today would have been my Mum's 76th birthday had she lived, and I didn't feel much like working after this week, so you can probably guess what happened when we woke up this morning and found it was finally sunny. Yes, you got it in one.

Soon we were bowling along up the M6, with heavenly music floating out of the stereo deck. Lyrics by God, Music by Handel. The best ever combination, marred only by Deb not wanting me to turn it up too much.

Me: but I can't hear it properly

Deb: what's to hear? They are singing halleluia.

I don't think she has quite got the point of Handel. It reminds me of her attitude to marine archaeology, when she watched a whole programme on the raising of the Mary Rose and then damned it at the end by asking the devastating question "who cares why it sank?"

At 2pm I was dropping Deb off in Ambleside so she could continue her life's work of inspecting camping shops shelf by shelf and rail by rail, while Tig and I went on to Thirlmere, where I spent three blissful hours doing a watercolour of Hellvellyn from Dobgill. Later we went to collect Deb and all three of us had a lakeside picnic, with much frisbee throwing for Tig. A perfect evening.

On the way back we stopped off at the Bowness viewpoint to take some photos of the sunset over the lake. The opportunistic seagulls clamoured round, used to being fed with the chips of a thousand trippers.

Deb asked: do they all have black heads?

Me: only the black-headed ones.

I felt this made it one-one for Handel. What John Reid would call a score draw. Driving back, I fell to musing, as the tyres ate up the miles and Ry Cooder warbled his stuff (a compromise. I got off lightly. It might easily have been Nirvana - whoever *they* are) about how my life has changed in the eighteen years since my mum died that snowy January day in 1986. At the time it never seemed as if the gloom of that depressing winter would ever lift. It was the worst of the worst.

But it just shows that life may be bad from time to time, but it doesn't necessarily stay that way: who would have thought that eighteen years from that day I would be enjoying the sunshine beside Thirlmere with a wife I hadn't even met then, with my own publishing business, (though that may be a mixed blessing) and with a dog that hadn't even been born then.

You may be going through a crap time in your own life right now. Who knows. In eighteen years time it's going to look a lot different. Take heart - gyres run on, and every state eventually becomes its opposite.

I hope mum's having a good time in heaven. Maybe it's not like that at all. Maybe it's like Like Wordsworth said of Lucy instead:

> No motion has she now, nor force
> She neither hears nor sees
> Rolled round in Earth's diurnal course
> With rocks and stones and trees.

Personally the thought of spending eternity with Auntie Maud and several other relations is a slightly sobering one. Even with dad arriving in 1992 to hep out with passing the macaroons and putting the kettle on for another pot. But maybe it's not like that. Maybe as Eliot says, their communication is tongued in fire, and all shall be well, and all manner of things shall be well. Maybe the experience of heaven is so unknowable that it cannot, it may not, be revealed to us, except in the odd moments where the sunbeams pierce the clouds, or the odd moments where you watch the dancing silver waters of Windermere. Something whose dwelling is the light of setting suns. Long as I gaze on, Windermere sunset, I am in paradise. Good night all.

26th July 2004

It has been a busy week in the Holme Valley: St Swithun's summer limps on towards a dismal conclusion, and one thing's for sure: Colin's roof will definitely not dry out like I hoped it would, and the builders, who were supposed to come back and finish the driveway and make a start on moving the porch have, like Kipling's captains and kings, departed, at least for the time being. I've been too busy to chase them, with computers going "ping" left right and centre, and printers ringing up to chase missing image files, so it will all have to wait. Maybe even til next summer now, as book launching time draws nigh.

Kitty went missing for a couple of days - although "missing" is always an approximate term for a cat who treats the place as a bed and breakfast, as does Dusty. She's back now, probably encouraged by the rain and the "evening meal" served by this establishment she chooses to patronise, ie Whiskas big pouches for two cats which she can usually polish off in one go. No wonder both ladycats are starting to look like a house-end. Nigel, too, has been spending more time around the house than he normally does, eating Russell's KD Laing food and yowling at me about the weather. Looking out the window, sometimes I feel like yowling back.

But the big surprise has been Russell: earlier on this week he was in a bad way again, obviously not cutting it, not even interested in cut ham or chick-chick. Things were not looking good. But on Tuesday one of my friends came round and she asked how he was. When I explained, she had a go at doing some sort of alternative therapy on him. In a spirit of "try anything once" I said, why not. I have no idea what she did or said to him in the fifteen minutes she spent alone with the cat, but from Wednesday onwards he was back once more to his old, old self. Coincidence? Who knows? An unreconstructed old hippy like me always tends to think that there are more things in heaven and earth Horatio, etc - so who knows? If she could bottle it, she'd make a fortune. I owe her so much, to name but one, if the effect is permanent.

It's not been a week for knowing much, really: sometimes this week it's been like being washed along in the flood. All you can do is hope that when the waters/events eventually subside, they'll leave you somewhere nice. We all like to think we're in charge of events, in charge of our lives: sometimes we just have to acquiesce though.

There has been a lot about bells and bellringing on the boards this week, a subject about which I know zip, but which has made me think again about William Golding and *The Spire*. If you don't know the book, it's a story of a man, Dean Jocelin, who is driven to the point of obsession and insanity by his need to serve God, or, ultimately his need to feel worthy in God's sight. He demands obedience and servitude from those around him, driving them to complete his vision of a 400 ft spire above his cathedral. In the process, some will die, others will lose faith, hope, and love. Only as Jocelin comes to terms with his fallibility do we begin to care about the doomed outcome of his dream. Only as he admits his own pride and stubborn-ness do we hope for his absolution, deserved or not. Golding's book is an ode to all those who become obsessed by religion and love, who strive for something to the point of sacrificing everything of true value along the way. But finally, he finds a way to show the madness of humanity while still proffering a glimmer of hope.

One of the things that brought these thoughts to mind was looking at the ruined church at Heptonstall, during Saturday's Hebden Bridge Mustardland meeting.

Rebuilt in the 14th and 15th Centuries, the remains of the early Parish church are still a focal point in the town. Its roof was torn off by gale force winds in the mid nineteenth century, but the new

Victorian Gothic church was built close to the original site, without disturbing its ruined predecessor.

Seeing the wreck of the church, demolished by storms and left as a ruin while the Victorian fathers of Heptonstall built a new, solid, black, square, utilitarian church directly alongside the ruin, made me think of the faith of people who set off building Cathedrals not knowing what the result would be, or even if they would live to see it. I thought of the treadmill in the roof of Beverley Minster (a fine church with its distinctive bells if you ever get the chance to visit) which they built in situ to drive the ropes that hauled the stone up to build the towers. At the end, they had no option but to leave it where it was, and there it remains today, a testimony to medieval ingenuity. I also thought of the spire of Chichester cathedral, which collapsed with such dramatic terror in 1858, and was, again rebuilt by the Victorians. Of course, we couldn't leave Heptonstall without looking for the grave of Sylvia Plath with its plaintive inscription:

> Even in the midst of fierce flames
> the Golden Lotus may be planted

This quotation, which Ted Hughes attributed to the Bhagavad Ghita, actually comes from the book 'Monkey' written by Wu Ch'Eng-En in the middle of the sixteenth century. I don't know if this is the same "Monkey" that became the 1970s cult TV series, but you can bet your bottom, or even your bottom dollar, if you must, that if it is, then Sylvia is probably revolving faster than 33rpm at the thought

Hebden Bridge is a marvellous place. I just wish they had levelled the site before they had built it. Life should contain a minimal amount of 45 degree slopes, and I feel I have now done my own life quota, several times over. Arriving just in time to see QB re-enact his storming performance in the hop-scotch, we then repaired to Nelson's wine bar, where we did a passable imitation of Sir Edmund Hillary to get me and my knee down the stairs (is that Sherpa Tensing? No, he looks pretty relaxed to me)

Having visited Heptonstall, food called. And of course, in Hebden Bridge, where it is normally impossible to throw half a brick without hitting an organic vegetarian yakburger in lentil and macramé sauce, we managed to find the only carnivorous pub in Mytholmroyd, or Royston Vaisey as it must now be known:

> "Oooh, you're VEGETARIANS. I've never served a vegetarian before. How do you spell Cannelloni? Are you LOCAL?"

Simon's pub, the Fox and Goose, is alao a WONDERFUL place though, and everything a pub should be. I only wish there had been someone to drive me home. To consume Clausthaler or whatever it's called, when there is Old Nun's Twisted Shag, original gravity ABV 19.5% or the equivalent, on cask, is nothing short of a criminal act on my part. But it was great to meet everybody in real life. If I try and list everyone I am bound to forget someone, so can I just say thanks to you ALL for making me so welcome and if I didn't get to talk to everyone, hey there's always next year.

To everyone who I did manage to talk to, some at length and in my case not very coherently, thanks for what you said. It meant a lot to me. (Sad git that I am).

While I was standing there at Saturday teatime, looking out over the crazy paving of the levelled gravestones in Heptonstall's old church, I kept hearing an anthem by William Boyce that I had been playing on cassette in the car earlier on in the week (sad git that I am). Apparently it comes from the First Book of Kings, Chapter 8, verse 13.

> I have surely built thee an house to dwell in, a settled place for thee to abide in for ever.

But later on, Solomon is struck by doubt, in verse 27.

> But will God indeed dwell on the earth? behold, the heaven and heaven of heavens cannot contain thee; how much less this house that I have builded?

Like Dean Jocelin, we all set out on the objectives of life without necessarily knowing where it's leading. We all have to have faith that the tower won't fall, that things will come right in the end. We can't always see the pattern straight away, any more than the people who painfully assembled the stained glass windows of Chartres piece by piece knew what it would look like until they finally stepped back and saw the glory of the finished version. And of course, because we can't see the bigger pattern, the plan, we become despondent, we fail and we flag. A lump of stone is a heavy burden, and as Yeats said, too long a sacrifice can make a stone of the heart.

If you are feeling like that right now, that you are trying to build something and you don't know if it's going to come out right, and you're not sure you have the drawings the right way up, you might like to take heart from a notice pinned in the porch of Heptonstall church. "Do not feel totally, personally, irrevocably responsible for everything: That's my job. Love, God."
We are all building the cathedral. And "even in the midst of fierce flames the Golden Lotus may be planted". Good night.

§

1st August 2004

It has been a busy week in the Holme Valley. The sybaritic pleasures of Hebden Bridge remain dear in the memory, but this week has been very much to do with the application of various noses to various grindstones. After the Lord Mayor's parade comes the dustcart, as the saying goes.

The animals are all well, in their own way, going about their doggy and catty existences in a way which is blissfully un-self-aware. The warm weather has seen Kitty and Dusty take up residence once more in their solarium on top of Mrs Rocky's shed. Nigel seeks out a shady spot in the garden and then makes a Nigel-nest in it, and Russell has got the art of eating the bit of cooked ham while simultaneously spitting out his tablet from the corner of his mouth, down to a fine art. He's worked out that he gets twice as much cooked ham this way, rather than if he just ate the tablet at the first attempt.

The week has been dominated by the continuing battles over Deb's new computer, culminating on me putting the phone down on the would-be suppliers on Friday when they wouldn't give me their bank details to pay in the money which they demand up front before they start building the computer. Giving someone a large amount of money should not be so difficult. Grit teeth, count to ten, and start again tomorrow, I guess.

It has also been the week where it emerged in conversation that Deb thought that the number of Greenwich time signal "pips" was the same as the hour of the day, so that you got eleven pips at 11 o'clock, and so on. Mind you, I can't really gloat. For a long time, I thought Sheryl Crow and Shania Twain were the same person. (You hardly even see them together, after all).

The other thing which has been filling my thoughts this week is the massive print job we have undertaken for a major public utility which we were in serious danger of falling behind on, to the extent that we couldn't get it finished by the agreed time. Fortunately, even though the main machine it was running on kept jamming, by putting bits of it on little machines dotted around the place, eventually we found that the cumulative effect of all those little bits and bats of print runs all added up and got us out of trouble. Without wishing to trivialise the memory of those who fought there, as narrow escapes go, it really has been the printing equivalent of Dunkirk.

Sometimes the collective power of the small can make a big difference. I always say to people who complain about some injustice or other, some campaign, when they say "what difference can I make, I am just one person on ,my own", that they need only think of the awesome power of a drop of water hitting a stone, over and over again, eventually working its way right through. It was little people, after all, who tore down the Berlin Wall, hand by hand. It was the little people who cheered when, at a performance of Verdi's Nabucco in Ceaucescu's Romania, the slaves' chorus formed the outline of the Romanian borders on stage. Ceaucescu and his entourage, watching from their fine seats in the front row, had no idea what was causing the standing ovation. But the poop people in the cheap seats in the balcony and circle could see the shape of their country and picked up the music and sang along. They knew then that the government couldn't put them all in jail. There weren't enough jails in Romania.

I've especially been thinking of the collective power of individual people of conscience this week in view of the government's decision to stigmatise people who care about animal welfare as "terrorists." I accept that there is a lunatic fringe, and in no way condone their actions, people should be free to carry out their work, free of intimidation and harassment, but equally, with freedom comes responsibility. People who want to kill animals, or blind them in order to test household cleaners, should be forced to defend their actions, not hide behind the mechanism of an increasingly paranoid state. Do people want household cleaners that have been dripped into the eyes of rabbits? Holy-stoning the step was good enough for my grandma and I'd be happy to get down and do it if it meant no more rabbits in labs, but we aren't given the choice.

You have to look at the disease, not just the symptoms. People act like they do out of a sense of frustration, our of a sense of disenfranchisement. The government promised a Royal Commission on Vivisection in 1997. We're still waiting. But this is a government that refuses to engage in the argument, because animals have no votes. It prefers, instead, to brand all those who disagree with it as terrorists. I suppose, having written this, I should expect the men in black and the knock on the door. If there's no Epilogue next week, you will know why!

This isn't intended to be a thread about the rights and wrongs of animal testing. So often this case is presented as "well if it meant we got the cure for <insert name of any deadly disease> then isn't that worth the lives of a few monkeys/beagles/ kittens, or whatever." But of course that's a false choice. I lost both my parents to cancer. Genetically, it's probably going to be what gets me in the end. But you see, I don't think that some of those who control the big research programmes, the ones run by the universities and the drug companies, actually want to find the cure. If they did, they'd all be out of a job! No more funding! No more Nobel prizes! No more learned papers, no more international conferences in swish hotels, no more being able to insist that the third world pays full whack for branded drugs. OK, I accept that may be an extreme statement of the case, but there is definitely a feeling that, when it comes to animal testing, nobody wants to be the first scientist to point out that the emperor is naked.

People often say I am too quick to criticise, that I never offer a constructive alternative for my dream of the new Jerusalem. Well, just to prove that I can come up with ideas, here are just a few of my wackier ones for making things better for everyone. As Groucho Marx (the only Marxist I ever listened to) said, these are my principles, if you don't like them, I have others.

Give collectives of homeless people loans to help them clear selected brown field sites and build timber framed kit homes on them that they can then inhabit at affordable rents, which are used first to repay the loans and then after that to fund the loans for new projects. It worked for the Diggers.

The Vatican should market inflatable life-size Popes to liven up parties and other social occasions

There should be a facility for declaring a non-statutory voluntary public holiday for the remainder of the day when the temperature reaches a certain point on any day in June, July or August

Let's have a referendum on animal testing. Let's actually have the argument the government is ducking. Let them read Andrew Linzey on *Animal Theology*, where he comprehensively states the argument, (p110) that animals are not to be sacrificed for humans, that they must not be seen as lesser beings which, while valuable, can be traded in for some kind of greater advantage to humans. For the more religiously minded, see Matthew 10: 28-31

> Do not fear those who kill the body but are unable to kill the soul; but rather fear Him who is able to destroy both soul and body in hell. Are not

> two sparrows sold for a cent? And yet not one of them will fall to the ground apart from your Father

If that is so for sparrows, how much is it also true for the lab rats, and the apes in cages at places like Huntingdon Life Science.

And finally, those of us who care about animal welfare and oppose the government's anti-libertarian stance should all wear purple ribbons. A short length of purple ribbon, pinned to the coat, or fluttering from your car aerial, or tied through your lapel. Start tomorrow. Purple ribbon is cheap and easy to obtain. It was the way in which the mourners at the funeral of Jill Phipps showed their solidarity with each other, when she died ten years ago, falling beneath the wheels of a lorry at Coventry airport while trying to stop the export of live veal calves.

Of course, at the start, there will only be one or two of us. As Ghandi said "first they ignore you, then they laugh at you, then they fight you, then you win."

But as the word spreads, and people ask why you are wearing your purple ribbon, and then some of them adopt it themselves as a non violent symbol of their objection to the government's stance on animal welfare, it will grow. It will grow to the stage where one day, the government will look around them and see purple everywhere they look. Then they will know, in their own black hearts, in the same way that the dictators of East Germany knew, in the same way that Ceaucescu knew, that the game is up.

8th August 2004

It has been a busy week in the Holme Valley, as ever. All of the animals are making the most of summer, especially the ladycats, who are missing for days at a time, grilling themselves in the unaccustomed sunshine, on the roof of Mrs Rocky's shed. Nigel has now taken to meowing plaintively about the heat (formerly it was the rain) while Russell continues to go from strength to strength, thanks to all the people who wished him well and prayed for him.

This week has zipped by. It's been a challenging week, with quite a lot of problems to be met, dealt with and seen off. It's been the sort of week when, if you're still upright at the end of it, you think you've come out even.

This week my thoughts have been turning to holidays. Next week - next Friday (the 13th) we take delivery of Gez's new book, and you could say that marks the official start of Christmas. Which is very depressing. The more so when you ring up someone you know who lives by the seaside, hear the seagulls outside their window, and wish that you were there. In that one simple sound the whole summer is encapsulated: the shingle, the blue sea, the decrepit piers, the streets laid out when the resort was just a smugglers' village, the artists, the folk clubs, the pubs with their desperate attempts to be nautical... oh, how I miss it all.

By the time Friday came around, I was definitely in holiday mood. Which is fortunate, considering that I ended up hosting an impromptu birthday party for Debbie's mother (61 years and counting) Despite having her suitcase packed to depart for Becky and Adrian's at the behest of the phone call saying labour has commenced (New Labour, new danger) she had agreed to be taken out for a meal by Sam and Chris. But Sam and Chris couldn't get a baby sitter for Ryan at short notice, so she ended up coming round to ours instead. Panic.

However, a couple of quick salad bowls later and I had the basics of a meal. In addition, I managed to construct, at very short notice, a punch (incorporating large quantities of Pimms and Cinzano) of the "guide Harold back to the punch, he's on his third glass of aquarium water" variety.

So all were merry, and possibly bright. At least until this morning, when I woke up with a hangover the size of Tibet. Apparently I announced to the assembled company that I was going to sniff the air in the spare room, then anoint myself with lavender massage oil. Hmm. Needless to say I did neither, falling instead into an intensely drunken sleep. Which lasted until this lunchtime

By the time the Ibuprofen kicked in today, it was too late to do anything meaningful. So, instead, I made a Quixotic gesture:

we finally made it to Spurn Point, in lieu of doing anything more useful. The heat was incredible. All the way through Thorngumbald, Welwick, and Skeffling, the windows were down and the blowers were on. I was really looking forward to finally getting back to somewhere I last went on holiday when I was 9, and seeing if it really was the magical place I remembered - rock pools with glistening pebbles, the caravan site with the long grass full of dragonflies and grasshoppers, and flying my balsa-wood gliders in the ever-present East coast wind.

Sadly, lots seemed to have happened in the intervening almost 40 years. There was now a car park at the end of the road, together with a toilet block. The road to the beach was now concreted. Even the beach itself looked smaller. Surely that pathetic slab of concrete couldn't be the remains of the blockhouse where I played "I'm the king of the castle?"

The road down Spurn Point, which I remembered as a wild and lonely place, now has a toll bar administered by the Yorkshire Wildlife Trust at the price of £2.50 per car, and STRICTLY NO DOGS are admitted. Which I found difficult to explain to Tig. It is still a heartstoppingly beautiful place though, in some respects, with mile and miles of shining mud flats.

Debbie of course didn't hesitate to pour additional scorn on what was already becoming a disaster - dubbing Kilnsea as exactly the sort of place someone having a deprived childhood which included rabbits made of bri-nylon socks, would come on holiday. Maybe she's right. One thing's for sure. Never go back.

It's not the place that makes the memory, it's the people. I could go back to the seaside now, go back to my life on the South Coast, but it wouldn't be the same. It would be lacking the people who made it what it was. Who knows, I may have new good times, with new people. But those days are gone. Let them go. I can't walk back to Springfield Avenue, open the door and expect to find the kettle has just boiled. However much I might cry hot and unexpected tears at that revelation, I have, ultimately, to come to terms with it. Life doesn't have a reverse gear. So if you are feeling like you need to go on holiday next week, go. Go while the going is good. And if you live in a seaside resort, go an sniff the ozone for me, and think on how lucky you are.

I realise that there are people on this board who feel threatened by me exploring my feelings every week in this piece of self-examination. It concerns me that these people are so in denial of their own feelings that they seek to ridicule other people when they are trying to get in touch with their emotions and work out their lives.

I have to say, if they think that their comments are going to stop me writing about what I am thinking and feeling, then they are sadly mistaken. You may think it's your board, and the church clock stands still at ten to three. But the times they are a changin'. Never go back, you'll only be disappointed. The way lies ahead. Even if you can't see the path properly right now.

15th August 2004

It has probably been a busy week in the Holme Valley. By all accounts, it's been a wet one. But here in the Lakes, it's been quiet. Possibly the most energetic thing I have done all week is evict three spiders from the bath. With Russell continuing to be "on the mend", and therefore able to be left in the care of Deb's mum now his condition has stabilised, and the others all relatively settled, the simple provision of a hastily-written sheet of "cat-feeding instructions" covering the complicated ritual of ensuring that Russ the Puss eats his tablet as well as the chopped ham meant that we were able to pull out of the driveway with a clear conscience and into a rain storm of biblical proportions. One that almost made me feel that we should, instead, be departing in an Ark, with all the animals safely aboard. Our holiday had begun. It was official, It was raining.

The road journey to the Lake District from our house can either be fast and tedious, via the motorway, or slow and tedious, the backroads version. This time, we chose fast and tedious. Dodging through the flying spray on the M6, with Tracy Chapman blasting out of the tape deck, we were attempting to avoid caravans and truckers alike, the latter stonking along at a rate of knots, aiming for the ferries at Heysham or Cairnryan, probably.

Arriving at our destination, just north of Keswick, we found the whole enterprise deserted. This isn't unusual. The family who run it also far, teach, paint, and one of the is a noted fell runner. So they were probably busy elsewhere. No problem, "our" little cottage had the key in the door and was unlocked. It's that sort of place. There have been one or two changes since we visited last, at Christmas: a new wooden gate across the path, presumably to demarkate the boundary between the communal approach, the cottage and the house. And a new hen-coop, inhabited by a few wary chickens. These seemed to be the main alterations, apart from the Buddlea which had grown another 50 feet or so!

Other than that, once we were unloaded, we settled gratefully into familiar armchairs, put the kettle on, and set up the small TV set wittering in the corner (noting that the reception was still as bad as ever - the brooding presence of Skiddaw reduces all TV in this area to a snowstorm, through which you can occasionally glimpse the better-known presenters on BBC Scotland (whoever they might be!) Later, we set about the business of getting "loaded" again. Corks were pulled, and the grainy old farm table where I wrote this in longhand was laid with an improbably inter-racial mixture of French bread, salad with an improvised vinaigrette, onion bhajis, coleslaw, and tapenade.

I'm keeping this place a secret: not because of the fear of a drive-by shooting or physical violence from those who object to my writing, but simply, and selfishly, because I don't want too many people to find out about it and ruin it. We only chanced on it by accident, and this is the best way. The Lake District is under tremendous pressure. On the one hand, it needs its income from tourists like us. On the other, it's being eroded by the sheer grinding weight of the tourists it entices each year. You can now not only get Focaccia Bread in Booth's Supermarket in Windermere, you have a choice of two different types. And, surprisingly, as well as a 1995 Cotes de Luberon (for those with the money) they also sell Cotes De Bergerac, which seems to have vanished elsewhere. Cotes de Bergerac does not, despite its name, make you grow a long nose and be the finest swordsman in all France. Nor does it make you want to move to Jersey and start solving crimes, in the company of Charlie Hungerford and "Diamante Lil". But it does make you drunk. And if you drink enough of it, it can bring on drunken adaptations of Ralph McTell's classic song [John] Nettle[s] Wine:

> In My country garden
> Underneath the mountain…

Followed by much snoring and the soundest sleep you have had in many a week.

It's not been the right weather for sitting naked in the garden reading *Paradise Lost* but it has been my only chance to see Blake#s original illustrations for it, which are on show at the Wordsworth Museum, attached to Dove Cottage at Grasmere, for the first time in many years, and probably the last time in my lifetime, as they are soon due to return to their sterile, humidity-controlled conditions in California's Henry E Huntington library. What struck me about them was how modern Blake's style was. Done in the 1770s. they looked for all the world like 1920s Wyndham Lewis.

I said as much to Deb, who had just been round Dove Cottage and seen Wordsworth's ice skates. She gave me a funny look. The other gem is a manuscript letter from Blake asking if it might be possible to do the illustrations for the Book of Job on a press which he has already got set up in his kitchen, as it is light enough and it will save a considerable time in taking down and setting up the press. Something which gives me heart, since I am still producing books at my kitchen table, 200 years on.

Deb couldn't let a week in the Lakes pass without conquering Scafell Pike, which she and Sherpa Tiggy achieved at about 4pm on Saturday, just as I was finishing a watercolour of Wastdale Head, approx. 3200 feet nearer sea level. I was slightly concerned that someone who has difficulty remembering the cardinal points of the compass without chanting "Never Eat Shredded Wheat" to her self under her breath, should be let loose on a mountain as important as this one, but, as it turned out, all was well. It's one of life's little ironies that, because of my time in the Boys' Brigade, I know how to use a compass and find my position on the map by taking a bearing on two different objects, but because of my knee, I have no way now of ever putting that to practical use. Whereas Deb clambers off up Scafell knowing nothing of it and all my attempts to teach her how to give a six figure reference were met with the usual levels of scorn and derision.

I am not looking forward to next week. With commendable planning, Gez's new book and Debbie's new computer arrive simultaneously. I am still slightly concerned (and foxed) to find that Deb's new computer has, apparently, a "Prescott" chip in it. Garbled logic and meandering sentences are supposed to be my forte, without her joining in. Speaking of the redoubtable amateur pugilist, Mr Prescott, reminds me of his comments about "plates shifting". Many others have already - and unkindly - commented that he looks like a man who has shifted a few, but, possibly uniquely in my existence, I can set down these momentous words: I know what John Prescott is on about.

There is undoubtedly a feeling of change afoot, in my life and in the country at large. Finding myself reading Bernard Crick's excellent book on George Orwell, I can't help but remark on the many resonances between the pre-war England of the 1930s and ours today. "Preparing for Emergencies" has a very 1930s ring to it. The bomber will always get through.

> Nothing is likely to save us except the emergence within the next two years of a real mass party whose first pledges are to refuse war and to right imperial injustice. But if any such party exists at present, it is only as a possibility, a few tiny germs lying here and there in unwatered soil.

Or as Tracy Chapman put it, perhaps more succinctly:

> Finally the tables are starting to turn
> Talking 'bout a revolution sounds,
> Like a whisper

Next week will be my own personal "Paradise Lost". By the time you read these words we will have been driven out of Eden and be back amongst the "Dark Satanic Mills". It will also be the official end of summer and the start of autumn, which can only mean one thing, the irreversible commercial logic of Christmas. Like the Lake District, that which nourishes me, destroys me.

The old order changeth, and giveth way to the new, and "the full fed beast shall kick the empty stall". As the blind forces of the cycle of the year propel us headlong towards 2005, and the ancient of days marks another tick in his perpetual calendar.

22nd August 2004

It has been a busy week in the Holme Valley, but then we always knew it would be. Like I said last week, after the Lord Mayor's parade, after the bunting comes down, all that is left is the grey, utilitarian efforts of the clearing-up squads. Likewise, after last week's holiday, we were back down to earth with a bump.

This week is the first week where this Epilogue is appearing in more than one place. It's also being published, with permission, in the community forum pages of I-church, in pastoral group 20. (One day you will log on and *every* page on the internet will be written by me. It's coming, and you cannot escape!)

Arriving back on Sunday night late, with Deb and Tiggy still nursing (between them) six aching legs from their ascent of Scafell Pike, it was all too soon Monday morning. Monday brought the rain, and with it the news that Colin's roof was leaking, over above the office. We worked on, keeping half an ear open for the drip, drip, dropping to stop. Whoever was responsible in the Bible for the saying that "it is better to dwell in the corner of the housetop, than with a brawling woman and in a wide house" has obviously never seen Debbie in the attic looking for a roof leak with a torch. On the other hand, since the same passage goes on to say "a continual dropping in a very rainy day and a contentious woman are alike" maybe I ought to revise that observation

While we were away, Dusty has been annoying the neighbours again, invading their barbecue and leaving her pawmark on history by walking across their newly-laid tarmac path. So she's currently grounded, shut in with the cat flap firmly locked til tomorrow morning. Kitty has been showing sisterly solidarity with her by lying in a pile of cats on the spare bed and fixing me with an evil glare whenever I put my head round the door.

Other than that, the week has been pretty much as expected. The stock of *Mum The Dog's Drunk Again* turned up from the printers on Friday and on Monday I began the dreary business of putting together press and review packs and getting them round to the post office, since the Royal Mail helpfully closed the PPI account on the grounds that our spending £4000 per year was not enough for their accounts department to be bothered with. So we're back to licking stamps for the time being. In fact, I should be typing press releases instead of writing this, but everybody needs some light relief. Meanwhile, Deb's new computer which arrived on Wednesday, is still stacked up in the corner, awaiting Vince to plumb it in to the network.

Russell continues to be stable. Nigel continues to be unstable, still spending nights out in his catty hideyholes and SAS style bivouacs in the hedge bottoms where the shrews and mice can be found. However, with the coming of the colder nights, I expect that we shall soon have to light the stove in the kitchen (note to self - ring the coal yard next week) and that will bring him in.

I sometimes think laying a fire is almost a religious observance. In fact, as I have said before in this series, like George Herbert I often mutter to myself, when doing scut-work,

> A servant with this clause
> Makes drudgery divine
> Who sweeps a room, as to thy laws
> Makes that and the action fine.

But when you lay a fire, you first have to do all the sweeping out and cleansing and preparation of the grate, then you make these tiny little screws of newsprint, which in their own way are as intricate as any favours showered on the crowd during Semana Santa. And of course you are laying the wooden sticks in crosses, something I am now incapable of doing without thinking of that fragment of the true cross that they have in Holy Cross Abbey in Tipperary, which I saw during our Irish trip in 2000. It was a great holiday, we were in Ireland for a week and it only rained twice, once for three days and once for four.

Then of course there's the coal. Theologically more problematical, since it brings with it ideas of compressed ferns that were once munched by dinosaurs. However, I am minded to observe that if God can create a whole universe, a few minor details of geological - and genealogical - dating that we quite properly worked out yet, haven't worked out yet shouldn't be beyond his scope. Finally you add the divine spark of Promethean fire itself. Before you all think this is getting a tad pagan, I can also cite a Biblical reference from Isiah "- Behold, all ye that kindle a fire, that compass yourselves about with sparks: walk in the light of your fire, and in the sparks that ye have kindled."

If lighting the stove is a religious service, I admit it's a bit of a strange one, with only two cats as Altar Boys, but at least I suppose the fact that they are both eunuchs might help them to be more spiritual and less focused on worldly matters! Anyway, no doubt in a couple of weeks it will be lit, and then will stay to keep us warm and safe. God willing, through the dark time of the year.

I don't do autumn well. It's my least favourite time of the year. I know for some there is the satisfaction of a harvest gathered, a year coming round to its conclusion. For me, autumn means only one thing. Roll on Spring. At this time of year, I tend to try and focus on the eternal renewal of the yearly cycle. Winter punishes, Spring redeems, but listening to the Pope's astronomer, Brother Guy Consolmagno, on Radio 4 this week, in his programme *A Brief History of the End of Everything*, it seems that eventually the sun will flare up and take us all with it. But not til at least as much time as has elapsed from the start of the universe to now, has elapsed again. So it will probably see me out.

Coincidentally, the day I heard this programme, I also found out that my Uncle George, who I had lost touch with after my Dad died in 1992, had in fact, died himself in 1998, at the age of 91. So another possible source of information on my Dad's early life and the unanswered questions about it, comes to nothing. Pity. Uncle George was a good bloke, her served on the Atlantic Convoys during the war, was torpedoed and spent 14 days adrift, so I suppose making it to 91 was quite an achievement really.

I don't know why the Pope needs an astronomer, and if they ever want to cut costs, they could probably make do with an inflatable replica, but for the moment, Brother Guy has got the gig. Sometimes thinking about cosmic distances and time scales makes my head hurt. Sometimes, it brings with it such a sense of the hugeness and endlessness of eternity that the only response of the brain is to quail, numbly and staggeringly at the concept if infinity and eternity. This is probably akin to what happens in Zen when you go into a state of *Satori*.

But the most comforting thing for me, is the increasing congruence between the findings of modern physics, and the tenets of religion. Instead of disproving the existence of God and of immaterial things and states, theories like string theory and m theory, with their tales of new dimensions and alternative worlds only go towards reinforcing my conviction that the scale, magnificence, grandeur and planning of the universe means that, in the words of "Desiderata", "Whether or not it is apparent to me, no doubt the universe is unfolding as it should."

And that somewhere there may be an alternative and everlasting dimension called heaven where once again we will see those who we cared for, whole and entire, not ill, wrecked, or in pain, and where all the wrongs of this dimension, from war to animal cruelty to the Post Office, are righted. I hope I catch up with Uncle George there, and he's got the kettle on. But just don't make me share eternity with Alastair Cooke. Good evening.

29th August 2004

It has been a busy week in the Holme Valley. The year moves inexorably towards autumn, with the last bank holiday of the year. For us, though, there is no bank holiday, with a VAT return to do and a new computer with lots of programs to install or re-install, Shark in the Toilet needing to go to press, not to mention a book launch next Saturday at WH Smith in Huddersfield to organise, it has been very much a case of business as usual. Or, as we sometimes refer to it "holiday? what holiday?"

With the turning in the weather to cooler, cloudier days, the cats have been around the house a lot more this week, Nigel, Dusty, Kitty and Russbags seeking out warm beds, windowsills that magnify the weak remnants of summer's light, and armchairs where they are assured of a purr-laced cuddle if a human happens to want to share with them. Russell has even started his winter habit of invading the duvet in the middle of the night.

Dusty has managed to exercise her talent for self injury by hurting one of her toes, possibly as a legacy of her encounter with the hot tarmac last week, necessitating a quick trip to Donaldsons, the best vets in the universe I have found so far, on Friday, for a quick nail clipping and a shot of antibiotics. The more I see of Donaldsons, the more I am thinking of signing off from the NHS altogether and giving myself up entirely to their care. They could sort out my diet, deal with my coat, inject me with various antibiotics and worm me if necessary. They could even microchip me for those odd occasions when I have been out to the pub and find it difficult to remember where I live.

With us all too busy to do proper walkies some days, Tiggy has been out running with Freddie and Grandad. Grandad really is a Grandad now, in the week that saw Debbie's mother become a real Granny, Deb become an Auntie, and me become and Uncle. When I described Katie Elizabeth as an oven-ready chicken in my original posting, I did her a disservice. In the pictures which have been emailed to me, she looks disconcertingly human. And more grown up than she should be, given her age. Perhaps it's another sign that I am getting on in years: the policemen look younger, the babies look older.

So it's been a week largely devoted to family matters, when we haven't had our heads stuck in a book. I've been thinking a lot about family matters. In the same week that I saw the pictures of Katie Elizabeth for the first time, I have been delving into my Granny's photo album, which we inherited, trying to find photos to scan in and send to my cousin Marion in time for Aunite Eileen's eightieth birthday on Tuesday. So I have seen both ends of the spectrum. Many of the pictures in the album are of people of my mother's generation as young children in the 20s and 30s.

And of course, behind them into the distance are the many women of each generation of the Fenwick clan, with their war cry of "A Fenwick" (in the words of the Roman Soldier in the late, lamented, never since repeated, *Chelmsford 123*, "Yes, that says war cry to me" So much better than the Rudd's family creed, which speaks of "giving assistance" and "standing forward" and "We will do what we can do"). I suppose standing on the quayside waiting for trawlers to come back makes you more stoical than a gang of mad Northumbrians and Scottish lowlanders who spent all their time stealing cattle and organising rebellions against the Hanoverian upstarts!

Little did they know, those Fenwick and Walker girls in the 1930s, what lay in store for them, in those perpetual summers where they pose awkwardly, clutching unwilling farm cats scooped up for the purpose of being photographed, squinting into the sun outside Elloughton Dale Cottages, with their cloche hats and best dresses. All too soon, for that generation, to be traded for the uniform of the ATS or the WAAFs, all too soon to be found in the porch of Elloughton Church in hastily posed pictures with their wartime soldier husbands, who were only later Uncle Ted, Uncle Frank, and Uncle Dick to me, buyers of treats and bowlers of googlies to the scrofulous kid I was.

I wonder what lies ahead for Katie Elizabeth. As the child of a teacher and an air traffic controller, I am pretty sure she won't want for much, materially. I hope that she also discovers the holiness of the heart's affections and the indomitable nature of the human spirit. And a love of animals. As well as the Philip Larkin poem "Born Yesterday" I have been wandering round singing "Little Green" by that other seminal poet of the 20th Century, Joni Mitchell, (who also found time in a very busy musical career to design the Spitfire - or so I am told!)

> Born with the moon in Cancer
> Choose her a name she will answer to
>
> Call her green and the winters cannot fade her
> Call her green for the children who've made her
> Little green, be a gypsy dancer

> Just a little green
> Like the colour when the spring is born
> There'll be crocuses to bring to school tomorrow
> Just a little green,
> like the nights when the northern lights perform
> There'll be icicles and birthday clothes,
> And sometimes there'll be sorrow

Yes, sometimes there'll be sorrow. I hope Katie finds love and is loved, and comes to realise that if she must go through any things which hurt, these have to be endured as a part of making you stronger, like for the Fenwick girls: as Hilaire Belloc said:

> Fortitude is the virtue of the menaced of the beleaguered ... it is the converse to and the opposite of aggressive flamboyant courage, yet it is the greater of the two, though often it lacks action. Fortitude wears armour and holds a sword. It stands ready rather than thrusts forward ... it is replenished of its own substance - sometimes fortitude will earn fame but not often. Always however, it will bring reward. Fortitude is primarily Endurance, That character which we need most in the dark business of life.

Because life is not unalloyed joy and pleasure. I hope Katie will be spared a year like 1992, where I lost a parent, a partner, and two loved pets, and almost a business, all in the space of 12 months, but life itself does have the habit of bowling googlies: in the week where Katie was born, Roger, from the Archers board, has lost his Dad to a heart attack, and David's nephew has been tragically killed in Kenya. No words I can say about the cycles of life and death will make the rawness of their sorrow any less keen, right now, even though everyone on the Archers board rushed to give their usual brilliant and generous and heartfelt feelings of sympathy, no matter how much I can write about Death not being the end and how they could only be in the next room. (Even though, if you believe M theory and string theory, they could be - or at least in the next dimension, which may be even nearer, if we could but see it) All we can do for Roger and David is pray for them and their families in whatever way, and for anyone else in here who is facing adversity.

As Belloc said " A man is a fool who says he is not afraid of death" and of course Larkin has also written chillingly on the subject. But at the same time, for me more hopefully, Shakespeare can say

>We are such stuff as dreams are made on
>And our little life is rounded with a sleep.

If there is any consolation in these thoughts, it lies for me in the sort of thoughts set out in Nigel Mazlyn Jones' (writer of the remarkable "Ship To Shore") "Wave on Wave" where he sings about how one day you can be happy, "and then a wave comes" that finds you "driving miles and miles alone" and then "another-nother wave comes" that reverses the direction of the first wave and restores you to happiness. Life is made up of waves of joy and sadness, which gives you the consolation at least that however bad it is right now, and for Roger and David it must be, it will eventually get better - maybe not back to how it was in the old days - but at least you will be happy again in some way. And it is that which gives us the courage to keep on jumping the waves. So we sail on, this evening, in this strangely shaped boat called Britain, with

>the moving waters at their priest-like task,
>of pure ablution round earth's human shores.

I haven't heard the shipping forecast for today, but here's mine. Sorrows, decreasing, westerly. Good. Happiness, four miles away and closing fast, improving. Good. Memories, good, regrets, nil. Those we have lost, happy, though, visibility, currently, poor. Dreams, and Hopes, rising. Good. Companions, good, some new. Help, available, direction, often unexpected.

Or as Nigel Mazlyn Jones would probably say, if you asked him for a signal from ship to shore:

>Papa Echo Alpha Charlie Echo.

§

5th September 2004

It has been a busy week in the Holme Valley, running up to yesterday's book launch, doing the VAT return, and churning out mailshots galore. All in a week when the weather has decided that it's going to be even more like summer than summer was.

Despite the warmer weather, Dusty and Kitty have resumed their attempts to create a "cat lasagne" using the duvet in the spare room. Deb put a cotton throw over the whole bed to safeguard the duvet and one night last week, in cross section downwards from the top, it went throw, cat. Duvet, cat, sheet, mattress. Dusty has, however, briefly relented to rolling over on her back and allowing me to look at her damaged toe, which seems to be healing up well. The timing is critical because like all cats which lie on their back and let you furfle their tummies, in a millisecond she can switch from being cute, charming and compliant to become a savage bundle of teeth and claws. I know some people like that, too.

Russell has learned that if he "bargains" with us when taking his tablet, he gets a better deal. For a long while he's been OK with his daily tablet and his KD laing food if we chopped the tablet up and gave him it in three or four bits wrapped in some cut ham or chicken roll. Now he's realised that if he refuses this offering, we will bring out ever more exotic and cat-yummy fare in an attempt to tempt him. So far this week he's upped the stakes to Philadelphia cheese and Edam slices.

Once he had extracted these from us and necked his tablet wrapped in a variety of exotic morsels, he then goes and polishes off all the previous bits of ham and chicken from the earlier, failed attempts. Yes, he is spoilt, but never let it be said that cats can't work things out. If he had an opposable thumb, knew how to work a can opener and could open the fridge on his own, he'd probably be figuring out how to push me downstairs so he could cash in the insurance policy. He probably already knows how much Felix £42,000 could buy.

With the late warm weather, Nigel has taken to spending his nights in the hedge-bottom again, stalking unsuspecting rodents and coming in, in the morning looking like he's been dragged through a hedge backwards, which he probably has.

Debbie has been clinging to the remnants of summer by reading holiday brochures for next year, her latest wheeze being "Elk watching in Sweden". The Elk watching people even have a web site complete with photographs and sound effect clips, a few of which I have downloaded, mainly because I liked the titles: "Irrtiated Elk", to name but one, and my own personal favourite, "Elk making an irrational noise in a dispute over food". I especially like the latter because it seems to imply that Elk can also make rational contributions - presumably along the lines of "I say old chap, would you mind if I nibbled that fallen branch, redolent with delicious pine cones?" (Only in Swedish of course. I imagine a rational Elk could sound a lot like Sven-Goran Erickson)

Needless to say this has raised some of the tensions that always creep into our marriage whenever holidays are discussed: the other morning I left the top off the washing basket with one of my socks protruding, which earned me a "You're not going to leave that like that, are you?"

On balance, my reply to the effect that I was hoping for an Arts Council grant to make it a permanent installation, was probably unwise in the circumstances, judging by the length of time it took her to speak to me in a civilized tone again, but it did take me back to the three years I spent studying Anglo-Saxon at university.

The weather seems to have galvanised our local farmers as well. Suddenly almost every field along the road I travel most mornings from here to Rotherham has become full with giant lumbering farm machinery, blowing chaff and creating these wonderful mosaics of yellow green and brown that so characterise the English countryside at the back end of summer. I thought we wouldn't see it this year, last week they were talking about the harvest being so bad they were going to plough it in, but they seem to have decided it's worth a shot.

The fields that are not currently razed to stubble are full of sheep, or so it seems, bringing to mind Keats's lines from the Ode to Autumn, about "full grown lambs loud bleat from hilly bourn"

> Then in a wailful choir the small gnats mourn
> Above the river sallows borne aloft

In such a landscape, it is not too fanciful to think of shepherds holding eclogues with each other was they pipe their "oaten reed", those characters, Batt and Gorbo, Colin and Hobbinol, who have played their part in every pastoral verse from Spenser, through Milton, Dryden and Marvell, to Louis McNiece. Coming back at night, watching the sun set over the stubble, I am reminded of Eliot's pastiche description of the rustic dancers in the *East Coker* section of *Four Quartets:*

> In that open field
> If you do not come too close, if you do not come too close,
> On a summer midnight, you can hear the music
> Of the weak pipe and the little drum
> And see them dancing around the bonfire
> The association of man and woman
> In daunsinge, signifying matrimonie —
> A dignified and commodiois sacrament.
> Two and two, necessarye coniunction
> ,Holding eche other by the hand or the arm
> Whiche betokeneth concorde.

I even managed a half-decent watercolour of some harvest fields, in a sort of sub Van Gogh manner, the other day. I doubt that I could ever earn my living by forging though. Van Gogh might be OK but Canaletto could be a problem - all those little bods in fancy hats and cloaks wandering about on the Rialto.

For us, however, a more reliable harbinger of autumn is the first book launch of the year, heralded this time by Gez being interviewed on BBC Radio Leeds yesterday morning then dashing through the streets of West Yorkshire back to Huddersfield in an attempt to reach WH Smith by the advertised start time. Even though he made it, there was a queue, which was a good sign. Let's hope WHS were impressed. The launch went off OK - at least, this time, no one asked me where the Bibles were. I obviously look like someone who knows where the Bibles are kept in WH Smith. It must be the beard. (Actually it's not just WH Smith. Last time I was on Doncaster station waiting for a train to London, someone asked me where they could catch the trains for Sheffield. I thought briefly of advising them to stand on the tracks and flag it down as it came in, but in the end the good angel won, and I directed them over the footbridge.

The crowds of kids who clustered round the books with their parents on Saturday, and chatted to Gez about the times when he had been to their school, also brought to my mind how lucky we have been so far in the UK, to have avoided something as bad as the current Russian siege atBeslan, and also what we have had to give up, in order to do so.

It's also been the 65th anniversary, this week, of the day the second world war broke out, a sobering thought when you consider how little in some ways we seem to have advanced since the defeat of Nazism. I remember in the 1960s, as a child, being taken to York on a day out that also happened to be Battle of Britain day, and seeing a real Spitfire (no more Joni Mitchell jokes please) parked in the courtyard in front of Clifford's Tower. To me, as a child, of course, it was an incredible symbol, a living embodiment of the stories in the war comics I devoured every week. To my father, who had seen action in real life, I imagine the experience had different connotations.

By the 1960s, our parents' generation had come back from winning the war, founded the Welfare State, and set up the conditions for social progress. With the technological advances of the 1960s and the space programme, and the explosion of universal love in the philosophy of the hippies, it seemed to me, on the verge of adulthood at the start of the 1970s, (although I could not have articulated it thus at the time) that there was nothing we couldn't do. Disease and poverty would vanish. War and famine would end. Where did it all go wrong? Didn't Jesus say something about loving your neighbour?

Reading people like Orwell, writing about the paranoia and fear of 1930s society, living in the shadow of the threat of mass aerial bombing campaigns, in Guernica for instance, I am struck by the similarity to what we are all being forced to endure in today's "war against terror", especially given the horrible scenes being played out in Russia.

So we "officially" enter autumn, by my calculations at least, and much sobered by events in the world at large, and wondering where it is all going to lead. Resolved, though, in my case at least, to carry on insisting that - however much we need to alter our ways to protect ourselves from danger - we still need a world where there are book launches, sheep, harvests, and Elk-watching holidays. A world where sheep may safely graze, where shepherds watch their flocks by night, hold their eclogues, and wait patiently for the fast-approaching star that marks Christmas, and perhaps a turning point in this dark tunnel we are about to enter.

12th September 2004

It has been a busy week in the Holme Valley. The warm late summer continued, at least up til today, giving sunny vistas of harvest fields now reduced to stubble, alongside the road through High Flatts and Birdsedge. Today has seen a real change to autumn, however, with cooler, breezier weather and rain, albeit as yet only in showers. There is a real feel of what my granny used to call "back-endishness" about the year now. The evening is setting in outside the office window as I write this, and there is a sense of the trees gathering in the darkness around them like blankets.

We have an extra guest here this week. Freddie is staying here full time, while Granny continues her ministrations to Becky and Adrian and, of course, Katie Elizabeth, down in Southampton. Fred adapts well to any change in circumstances, once he's got past his "no one loves me I am an abandoned orphan" phase of curling up in one of the armchairs and ignoring all comers. This week he has been doing boisterous things, and going out through the cat flap into the porch to refuel on the cat food whenever his own supplies are exhausted. I asked the vet once, why cat food tastes nice to dogs and he basically said a lot of dog food is rather bland and boring whereas cat food has lots of interesting flavours. This caused me to ponder still further: why don't the people who make dog food just use the ingredients from cat food? And, possibly more unsettlingly, how did the vet know this, unless he had once eaten both?

Tig has been ignoring Freddie as much as she can and giving forth deep and heavy sighs as much as to say "I don't know, kids today etc etc" She has obviously forgotten her own wild young days back in 1997, when she ate my CD of *John Wesley Harding* and chewed through the speaker surround-sound wire.

Nigel, Kits and Dusty continue to go about their catty business, and Russell has now upped the ante on the bargaining for food with which he will eat his tablet. We are now at the "mature cheddar" level, which seems to be working well. There is only "smoked salmon" and "truffles" to go.

We have suffered a loss this week though, Deb's mum's old cat, Bonnie, who has been ill and old and doddery for so long that her death has been daily expected for most of the summer. Unfortunately, this week she declined still further and had to be put to sleep. The other half of the pair, Clyde, has apparently been wandering round looking for her. Living right by the A616, it was quite an achievement for Bonnie to have died of old age, and I cracked open a five year old Rioja last night and we drank a few glasses to her memory, and that of all the cats who have gone on "into the world of light", as Henry Vaughan might have put it.

The mad rush for publication of the two new kids' books goes on apace, but this week I have been getting a lot of earache. Real earache, I mean, of the sort that has led me to conclude I need to pay a visit to Almondbury surgery soon. If I don't, and I lose much more sleep, I run the risk of having to spend even longer trying to recover from something even worse, so it's best to zap it now. I was discussing this with Deb and I happened to quote "Quis dociet ipsum doctorum " to which she replied "Who are you calling dozy?"

Sometimes I do *worry* about that girl. Normally, this weekend, we would have lit the stove, and in fact we drove all the way down into Huddersfield yesterday to visit the coal yard and make our order to last til Christmas, and take a couple of bags away with us to get it going. Over the summer, the coal yard has obviously decided to start shutting at 1p.m. on Saturdays, as we discovered at 3.45 when we arrived to find it locked and deserted. Oh well, I will have to try and sort it out in the week.

Other than that the only glimmers of humour in a pretty mundane week have been the call I got from a woman from Toucan Telecom telling me about some special offers they have got for BT customers. Since we are not a BT customer, I started to tell her this, only to be interrupted by her having phone trouble and not being able to hear me properly. They really should change their hardware. And their name, if it comes to that. Two-can telecom is, indeed what it was. Marred, at her end, by a bad string.

And just to complete the week's wackiness, I give you the saga of Psychic Elaine, who rang on Wednesday to ask for a quotation for printing some leaflets to advertise her services. (How come she didn't already know the price? I know, I know) Anyway, I said I would email her a quotation, and what was her email address. There was a long pause. "I don't know." she said. She turned to speak to someone else at her end of the phone. "What's my email address…?" and the guy in the background said "Psychic Elaine at …."

Oh dear. Oh dear. There is also a Spiritualist church in Barnsley somewhere that has a weekly raffle, which has also struck me as being slightly biased towards church members as opposed to those who don't have a direct line to the great hereafter. But maybe that's just me being flippant.

The growth in that sort of thing (psychics and spiritualism) seems to go hand in hand with periods of uncertainty in the world. The great spiritualist boom of the 1920s and 30s was fuelled by people seeking consolation in trying to contact loved ones lost in the carnage of the First World War. In an equally uncertain age, when three thousand people can die in a morning because someone flies an aeroplane into a skyscraper, perhaps we shouldn't be too surprised if their next of kin, the ones that don't belong to an organised religion, were to seek alternate ways of assuaging their grief.

9/11 has been on everyone's mind this week. One of our authors was on holiday in New York when it happened, and saw the fall of the second tower from outside his hotel. I remember our frantic - and futile - efforts to send a text message to his mobile to see if he and his girlfriend were OK. They had been due to go up the WTC the next day. I remember watching it on TV here in the UK, and turning to Deb and saying "That's it. We are all Americans now."

Since then, much of the support which everyone felt, not that specifically for the victims, which has remained largely undiminished, but for America as a whole, has turned to frustration with the idea of "The War on Terror", which has become the sort of potentially never-ending struggle that Orwell, writing in his 1948 essay "The Prevention of Literature" from the remote cottage on Jura (where he was also hammering out 1984) seemed to prefigure, when he wrote:

> This seems to me the worst possibility of all. It would mean the division of the world among two or three vast super states, unable to conquer one another and unable to be overthrown by an internal rebellion ... and the crushing out of liberty would exceed anything that the world has yet seen. Within each state the necessary psychological atmosphere would be kept up ... by a continuous phony war against rival states.

Of course that is all very much on the macro scale. On the micro scale of individual human behaviour (ie mine) there's plenty of evidence of the fallen nature of the universe! I seem to leave it wherever I go, and whatever I turn my ham-fisted hands to. This week I have had a perfect example of losing my rag with someone who I thought deserved it, and at the same time upsetting, annoying, and permanently alienating someone else, who I didn't even know. You could always say that I am trying to hide my own inadequacy by blaming the fallen nature of the universe for things like this. But we do all have personality flaws. Mine is quickness to anger, a vicious and snarling tongue (but then even Andrew Marvell was said to swear like a bargee) and an unwillingness to forgive and forget: it is like that crack of imperfection in the Chinese vase of which Eric Mascall writes on the fall from grace

> like a microscopic crack in a china vase it initiated a process of disintegration and corruption whose consequence spread far beyond the area of their origin and affected the whole subsequent history of the human race and the material realm"

And of course, it's always the on the day when you try and flail away the attentions of an unwelcome wasp, that you knock the vase off the shelf and it breaks. It's the day you try and move the TV aerial to make reception better, that you knock the last of the good wine glasses off the desk and it shatters, as also happened to me last week.

It's potentially much easier to forgive and forget the individual idiosyncrasies and arguments of one or two human beings of course, than to forgive an entire terrorist atrocity. But ultimately the process still involves sorrow and contrition, on one side, and at least a willingness to take a step towards conciliation on the other. I note, in this context, the words of Hanabeth Luke, whose boyfriend was killed in the Bali nightclub bombing. Asked for her feelings when the bombers were convicted, she said:

> I see them as very lost and pretty bloody nasty people, but I do not hate them. Hate is not going to make me feel any better.

Last night we gathered round the not-lit fire, put the central heating on instead, watched the "Last Night of the Proms" and, fuelled no doubt by the Bonnie-induced Rioja-induced maudlin feelings, I found myself once more profoundly affected by the singing of "Jerusalem". Those radicals like the Digger, Winstanley, or Blake, believed in the perfectability of human nature. I am not so sure, because I have so often fallen short of even my own poor idea of perfection. But if there is to be perfection, if there is to be a Jerusalem, then maybe it starts by saying sorry.

So, I am sorry to anyone I have upset or insulted by my foul tongue lashing, or ridiculed in the last week, however inadvertantly. Sorry, Mrs Toucan, Sorry, Psychic Elaine (but you knew that anyway.) You may not have been my target, but like the innocent victims of terror, it hurts just as much if it's inadvertant. Sorry. And I will try and do better.

19th September 2004

It has been a busy week in the Holme Valley. A week where everything I have touched to do with computers has either locked up, burst into flames, or both. The upgrade of our systems has stalled with the inability of Phil's new computer, which used to be Debbie's old computer, to run Sage properly. At the same time, the rust on Phil's van, which is already held together by chip fat, gunge, string, and the power of prayer, has got worse, making a replacement inevitable with all the book signings coming up for Gez and for Chris White. So, all in all, not a good week, but nothing that a new van and yet another new computer wouldn't solve!

My standing with the animal kingdom, however, has improved drastically, or at least my standing with those representatives of it who share the shelter of our roof. Following my visit to the coal yard and the purchase of twenty-two bags of Solarbrite, two of which I brought back in the tailgate of the car, much to the detriment of the suspension, the stove has been lit, in response to this Michelmas-y, autumn-y weather, and immediately Freddie and Russell claimed the two nearest chairs and slept there all night, resisting all blandishments to relinquish these cosy spots. Tig sprawled on the rug, only turning over when she was done on that side, and even Nigel - who had probably only come in to see what the fuss was about - ended up spending an hour or so toasting his whiskers.

Dusty and Kitty had their own little treat, as I switched on the central heating in Colin's side of the house. My reasons for doing this were more to do with drying out the roof space after the recent heavy rainstorms than kindness to the cats, but in any event the way they sprawled on the spare bed with all their legs going in different directions meant they, too, obviously found my actions favourable.

For light relief this week, I have been reading the treatise of St John Chrysostom. Well, the alternative was doing the VAT return, so that sort of puts it in context. I have not exposed myself to St John Chrysostom before (or to anybody much, your Honour!) but I have occasionally taken St John's Wort, the herbal remedy to ward off depression. I suspect, however, that the "wort" is named after a different St John, possibly the one that gave us "in the beginning was the word", another passage that has left me possibly terminally confused.

St John Chrysostom was apparently known as "golden tongue" and was one of the best orators of the early Christian church. I can only assume that he was having an off day when he did the treatise. Deb caught me reading it:

"What's that?"

"It's a treatise by St John Chrysostom: he sets out to prove that no one can harm the man who does not injure himself."

She thought for a moment:

"Huh! I could disprove that right now, by smacking you in the gob!"

"I rather think that St John Chrysostom would say I brought that on myself by marrying you, dear."

She had no answer to this. Thankfully. I was tempted to add that I thought he was getting at the idea of "what you put in is what you get out", which is what I always think of at this time of the year, now the harvest has been gathered. But St John contends that "each thing is subject to one evil which ruins it" He even gives a list:

> ...ears of corn are ruined by mildew and droughts, and the fruit and leaves, and branches of vines by the mischievous hosts of locusts.

I am still not sure what he is getting at here: leaves could, for instance, be ruined by being munched by an Elk (rational or irrational, it doesn't matter.)

As if anticipating my puzzlement, the treatise continues by establishing that if we can establish the virtue of a man (he means mankind as a whole, I think) we can then look at the one injury alone which is destructive to it.

> What then is the virtue of man? Not riches, that thou shouldest fear poverty; nor health of body, that thou shouldest dread sickness; nor the opinion of the public, that thou shouldest view an evil reputation with alarm; nor life simply to its own sake, that death should be terrible to thee; nor liberty, that thou shouldest avoid servitude; but carefulness in holding true doctrine, and rectitude in life. Of these things not even the devil himself will be able to rob a man ...

At that point I had to call a truce. The VAT return won out: but I will return to St John Chrysostom. I feel at the moment like we have both had the first round of a prolonged wrestling match, and I am back in my corner, sweating heavily and sloshing buckets of water over my brain, while he has barely broken into a healthy glow.

I like the idea of "true doctrine and rectitude in life" - if only I could work out what "true doctrine" was meant to be, bearing in mind that my brain is like an unsorted scrapbook of clippings from the Methodist tradition (from my time in the Boy's Brigade, where they taught me how to do various things including how to fire guns in a truly Christian manner!) the Roman Catholics (from the years I went out with a catholic girl at University) from my own reading about Buddhism and eastern religion, and from the radical Quaker/Nonconformist tradition of English social history. It's all there, St John, could you kindly indicate the true bits. I could do with some alleviation of the terror of death.

Death is, of course, I suppose, another harvest, and a reaping. You get out what you put in, and you hope that spring will follow and result in rebirth. I hate this time of year, between when the clocks go back and the shortest day: it's like a long black tunnel with a pinprick of light at the end, called Christmas.

So, it was in a spirit of contemplating St John's assertion that no one can harm you if you don't injure yourself, that I found myself driving over to Barnsley last night to pick up Debbie, who had been out for a drink with some friends of hers from her social worker job, Gail and Carol.

Prior to setting off, Deb had vouchsafed to me, that she wasn't thinking of "making a night of it". Unfortunately, where alcohol and social workers is concerned, any announcement of that intention is a bit like the Titanic saying that it didn't intend to "make a voyage of it".

Barnsley, as well, is the drinking capital of South Yorkshire. The pubs in Barnsley town centre are separated from each other by other pubs, and the people make withdrawals from bottle banks. Barnsley is full of pubs with grim-faced doormen who ask you "have you got any offensive weapons on you?" and when you say no, they say "Tek this then, you'll need it!" So I expected Deb to end her "girls' night out" completely sozzled.

And so it proved, when I pulled up outside the pub to collect her, and saw she was obviously having trouble with small particles of blood in her alcohol stream. All was resolved, however, when, after we had been going only ten minutes, she turned a strange green colour, and groaned at me to pull over, which I duly did, in a deserted country layby near Darton. As I said before, you get out what you put in, and there is some corner of a Darton field, that is now forever Stella Artois, possibly mingled with spicy parsnip soup from earlier on. I didn't investigate too closely. Wiping her face with the proffered baby wipe, when she pulled her head back inside the window, she observed:

"Ooh, I feel quite hungry now. I could murder some chips".

You can take the girl out of Huddersfield, but you can't take Huddersfield out of the girl! So, today has been a muted affair. I bought a teapot at Homebase, and some batteries. Then I put the car through a car wash, to remove any lingering shreds of carrot. Freddie liked the car wash, and hurled himself against each window in turn in a paroxysm of foam-related fury. Actually, I also thought the car wash was probably the best entertainment available in Huddersfield at that time. It was either that, or watching the traffic lights change. Deb nursed a hangover the size of Latvia. No one can injure you if you don't injure yourself, by imbibing too many pints of Stella. Meanwhile, St John Chrysostom brooded in the background, like a disapproving yet strangely bearded Uncle.

26th September 2004

It has been a busy week here in the Holme Valley. Once more it has been the sort of week when very little went right, which seems to be par for the course these days. Phil is back to using his old computer and to mend what is truly wrong with Debbie's old computer (which was, in my master plan for universal domination, destined for Phil) it would cost almost three hundred pounds. Considering you can get a new IBM clone for about the same money, with a lot bigger hard disk and a faster chip, it seems our efforts to recycle and re-use and harvest scarce resources must once more fall victim to planned obsolescence.

We have lost another old friend to planned obsolescence this week, Phil's van. He will deny it, but when he came back from the garage, with the radio from it under his arm and his personal maps and bits and bobs in a carrier bag, there were tears in his eyes. Actually I was pretty choked too, since, before Phil inherited it, it used to be my van. I remember the day Debbie drove it at 110mph past a police car on the A1. I have never been able to work out why they never chased us: it was either because they thought the van would be produced in evidence and the case laughed out of court, or they thought they were hallucinating.

Anyway, it was already suffering from terminal rust and when the cam belt went on Wednesday, it instantly became nothing more than a very large, very heavy, very useless paperweight. Still, it went down fighting, returning from a trip to deliver the proof of the jacket of *Shark in the Toilet*, and it finally conked only 200 yards from Phil's house. Near enough to be pushed to its last resting place on the local garage forecourt. It could almost make you believe in an underlying purpose to the way things work out.

The animals have been reacting in predictable ways to the succession of crisp sharp mornings which we seem to have had this week, and the other signs of autumn such as the starlings writing their improbable musical notation on the telegraph-wires. Are they crotchety, or merely quavering? Who knows.

The colder nights have caused Tiglet to invade the bed and curl up on the duvet next to Debbie. So much so that on occasions I feel two pairs of accusing eyes looking at me with the air of "I don't know why he wants to sleep here, he has got a perfectly good basket in the kitchen"

This means that in the morning these days I look across the pillow and see those appealing eyes and cold wet nose and slobbering tongue and think, "she almost understands every word I say". But that's enough about Debbie. The dog, of course, is usually snoring.

Russell's brinkmanship (brink-cat-ship?) over what he will and won't eat his tablet reached new and potentially ridiculous heights this week, with - at different times - both scrambled egg and Genoa cake being used as the medium to introduce the drug to his innards. Thankfully, sanity prevailed and following my last trip to the supermarket, chicken roll is once again his "chaser" of choice. Nigel and Kits have both spent long hours on their respective fluffy cat beds and Dusty has discovered a warm pipe that runs under the bathroom floor to the heated-towel rail, which means she spends the night curled up smack in the middle of the bathroom floor, a furry-davy-crockett-hat-shaped hazard to the unwary bathroom visitor in the middle of the night.

Deb has been struggling with embedding sound files in the National Poetry Day press release today: her reaction to any computer problem is to play something called "Smells Like Teen Spirit" at just below pain threshold, on repeat. I would certainly like to see that file embedded, preferably in industrial strength lead-lined concrete, to prevent it annoying me further. She was very impressed that the coal yard stacked twenty 20KG bags of Solarbrite across the drive rather than along it on Friday, and she had to re-stack them before she could get in the house.

With the VAT return to finish, the accountants hassling me

for last year's figures as the filing date approaches, and the constant struggle over getting the mailshots out and seeing "Shark" through the press, I really could do to be in two places at once sometimes. If there really are multiple universes, then of course I already am in two places at once, which is a disconcerting thought considering how little work I have got done in this one. In this universe at least, St John Chrysostom has gone unread this week.

Bilocation is an interesting idea of course, and one which still occupies Catholic theologians, as in the case of St Padre Pio. In a universe that can encompass string theory and M theory, perhaps bilocation should not seem such a difficult concept. You could say, for instance, that science is disproving the basic tenets of religion, one by one. That would be the basic idea of science, after all, a rational process that disproves all of those old uncertainties based on superstition. Yet the more scientists look at the structure of the universe, especially in quantum mechanics, the more it becomes apparent that there is no such thing as objective reality. What seems like a solid door, I could walk straight through, if it happened that the gaps in my atoms coincided with those of the door. And the atoms which make up the door, and those which make up me, can either have a place, or an electrical charge, but not both. As with Schrodinger's cat, all experiments are influenced by their observers.

Two hundred years ago, if I had suggested that it would be possible to transmit a piece of paper so that a facsimile of it simultaneously appeared in Australia, I would probably have been burnt at the stake as a witch. Yet today, the fax is a technology which has not only come, but come and gone, being largely replaced by email. Who knows what discoveries may come in the next two hundred? And will these discoveries deny or confirm the existence of God, the ghost in the machine? Call it synchronicity but there is undoubtedly a force that brings these coincidences to our attention. If you ask me, my bet is, the more we look at the warp and weft of life the more we will see the evidence of the hand of the weaver.

§

3rd October 2004

It has been a busy week in the Holme Valley. It would be nice to think that we had had our fill of mishaps for a while, but no: this week the email server went "ping" and had to be re-set, leaving us cut off from the internet and *ipso facto*, the known universe for almost a day. Still, at least it also stopped me getting spam about the tooth whitening of the stars and debt consolidation with a Christian perspective, so it wasn't all bad. Then Tony the warehouseman decided to celebrate the return of online access by pinging one of the water pipes coming into the warehouse with the forks of his fork lift, fracturing a joint and creating his very own Diana Memorial Fountain, until we were able to get to the stop tap and turn off the supply from the road. Yorkshire Water answered the emergency leaks hotline in a dizzyingly fast 8 minutes 13 seconds. I was tempted to say "glug glug glug, too late" when they finally put me through. No wonder we always have hosepipe bans.

Russell has been stable this week, continuing his campaign to get to know the lady-cats better by invading Colin's house through the cat flap and eating their food in front of Dusty and Kits while they stand by and hiss at him like the very devils at the end of Faustus, tails like bog-brushes and eyes popping. Next Thursday he goes back to the vet again and we find out just how stable is "stable". I can't believe it's two months since he last went, but it is. Two months that have passed in a whirl of book-related tasks. Nigel has taken up a new perch, high up amongst the accounts filing in the office, which is nice and warm and only disturbed at the year end. Descending to ground level from this latest Nigel-hole today, he knocked a stack of 500 compliments slips off a shelf, thereby creating his very own tickertape parade, and sauntered off leaving chaos in his wake with all the insouciance of someone whose motto is "cat fur for everyone!"

October has come to both field and fold all around, with words like "fallow" and "dun" springing to mind. The fields next to the office have already been ploughed over, and the nights drawing in mean that frequently, this last week, I have left the office and drove home under dramatic autumn skies, looking across bare fields to the horizon. These days always make me think of "Heavy Horses", the Jethro Tull track:

> Standing like tanks on the brow of the hill
> Up into the cold wind facing
> In stiff battle harness, chained to the world
> Against the low sun racing
> Bring me a wheel of oaken wood
> A rein of polished leather
> A heavy horse and a tumbling sky
> Brewing heavy weather.

Ah, the heavy horses! Once the powerhouse of all these farms round here, under which the coal-seams ran. Before the pit ponies, there were the heavy horses. Their very names read like a list of ships of the line, like a litany of dreadnaughts: The Suffolk, the Clydesdale, the Percheron, the Shire. Harking back to the days when Britannia truly ruled the waves. The Edwardian countryside has been very much in my mind over the last few days as I have been trying to help Debbie's mum with some genealogical research, particularly a specific branch of her ancestors who were drawn in from the flat fields of East Anglia by the bright lights of the big city, in this case Wisbech, in this case changing from red, through amber, to green, then back again. In the words of the folk song, "Home Lads Home"

> Oh Captain, Boxer, Traveller, I see them all so plain,
> with tasselled ear caps nodding, all along the leafy lane.
> Somewhere a bird is calling, and the swallows flying low,
> and the lads are sitting sideways, and singing as they go.

Of course, the golden Edwardian age was never so golden as was made out, and the Heavy Horses soon found themselves shipped out to Flanders: perhaps William Evans, Private, of the 1st Btn, the Suffolk Regiment, who put aside his horses and his Deal-carrying, and who died of gangrene in 1915 and lies in Wisbech cemetery, and who also happens to be Deb's great-grandfather, would have seen the horse-teams on the Western Front.

> Well, gone is many a lad now, and many a horse gone too.
> Of all the lads and horses, in those old fields I knew.
> Oh, Dick fell at Givenchy, and Prince beside the guns,
> on that red road of glory, a mile or two from Mons.

> Dead lads and shadowy horses, I see them still the same,
> I see them and I know them, and I call them each by name.
> Riding down through Swanmore, when all the west's aglow,
> and the lads are sitting sideways, and singing as they go.

In many ways, the First World War was the defining moment for the countryside: the loss of manpower represented in the slaughter on the Western Front, the agricultural depressions of the 1930s, briefly checked by the need to "Dig for Victory" in World War Two, the transfiguring effects of the 1960s and 70s style "prairie" farming, and the advent of the EU, have all conspired to give us the countryside we see today. A patchwork wrought by change. Change is inevitable, but sometimes at dusk it is possible to wonder what, for instance, the lost gardeners of Helligan would have thought had they been able to return from war and see their efforts, eighty years on. Perhaps they would have been surprised at their "organic" methods, coming back into vogue.

Change is all around us. As both Heracletius and David Archer reminded us, it is not possible to jump into the same river twice. Sometimes, though, change brings unexpected results for the good. Not all change is bad. In my end is my beginning. Russ was ill, now he's better, he may get ill again, he may get well again: plans get laid then thwarted, then come to fruition in unexpected ways. Very seldom does the beginning accord to the end, as the Gawain-poet says. And if you keep something long enough, it becomes valuable again.

> I noticed tonight, that the world has been turning,

This is why we don't slit our wrists, when faced with the human condition: we know that every state eventually becomes its opposite. The unemployed become employed. Today's problem, the dead email server, gives way to tomorrow's, the burst water main. A generation of harvests using heavy horses gives way to tractors. Then the world turns, and circumstances change:

> And one day when the oil barons have all dripped dry
> And the nights are seen to draw colder
> They'll beg for your strength, your gentle power
> Your noble grace and your bearing
> And you'll strain once again to the sound of the gulls
> In the wake of the deep plough, sharing.

"To every thing there is a season, and a time to every purpose under heaven" : we have to endure our time, and hope for better days, which will come. We may be out of fashion now, but, like the Heavy Horses, they will want us one day.

10th October 2004

It has been a busy week in the Holme Valley. Once or twice a year, small publishers get the chance of an extra few sales, with the advent of special events and "days" geared towards books and literacy. This was one such week, as it contained National Poetry Day! No sooner had Chris White's new book "Shark in the Toilet" turned up on Tuesday from the printers, than we were plunged into a whirlwind of activity: press releases, review copies, advance information sheets; in short, a blizzard of paper.

"Look North" phoned from BBC Leeds to see if they could send a camera crew to film Gez doing his act at Royston High School near Barnsley. Various answers were considered briefly, mainly involving the Pope's religion and the defecatory habits of bears, but in the end we settled for a simple "yes, of course". So they did, and in addition they had him back to the studio at 6.30pm, for another piece in the local news bulletin.

In order to capture this straight on to digital video, Debbie arrived back from B and Q at tea time, armed with a huge coil of coaxial aerial cable and various tools for wire stripping. She had conceived a daring plan which involved tapping in to the incoming aerial signal downstairs in our house, splitting the co-ax, and running a separate co-ax cable through our house, into Colin's, up the stairs, into this office, and into the back of her computer, to allow her to run the video capture software. It failed, but I had to admire the single-minded way in which she set about wiring it up. Later that night, we were discussing the analogue video which we had recorded of Gez, and the uses to which it could be put, when Gez himself rang. The BBC had just called him back (it was about 9pm by this time) saying they were sending a car for him and could he go back to Leeds, this time to do a live radio link up with Matthew Bannister's programme on Five Live. Which he did. So that must be some kind of record, though I am not quite sure what.

In some ways then, Thursday was a triumph, but I wasn't feeling particularly triumphant, because it was also the day when Russ the Puss went back to the vets for his two month check up. The vet's a bit concerned that his heart problem doesn't seem to be getting better, also that he's only "holding his own" weight-wise with the kidney thing. He's changed his diet yet again - this time to *tinned* KD food. Russ polished off half a tin of this, immediately on his return, so I don't think there'll be any problem getting him to eat the stuff. For the first time, though, the vet admitted the seriousness of the situation, saying that if we hadn't taken Russ there when we did, he wouldn't be alive now: he seemed to be heading me towards "managing my expectations" about the outcome of this current process. Basically, we talked a lot about the options if Baggis *isn't* any better when he goes back in a month's time. They can, reluctantly, then admit that it's more than just a kidney problem and start to look for other stuff that could be wrong. This includes scary stuff like tumours. We spoke about the options: they can do wonderful things with surgery, but there's also the consideration of putting Russ through the mill, with procedure after procedure - there's also the question of Russell's "quality of life".

Anyway, we wait to see what happens. I was left feeling a bit down and blue after this setback (more so than Russ, who fell blissfully asleep in the chair by the stove after polishing off his KD Laing). The only thing to banish the mood was music, which I employed to its fullest extent, in the form of Chumbawumba, singing it for Russell and for me:

>I get knocked down, but I get up again
>You're never gonna keep me down…

The others have all been well enough this week, Nigel curled up in one or other of his Nigel-holes, Kitty and Dusty under the duvet in the spare room, Dusty only venturing out to play with the middle of an empty loo roll on the landing, skittering it downstairs, chasing after it, carrying it back up and then repeating the proccess. It must be nice to have spare time, though I suppose to a cat, all time is spare. Tig's been feeling the cold, too, curling up on the sofa in the conservatory with her nose in her tail.

And so we got to the weekend, and Chris's book launch in Derby. A couple of years ago, I was in Derby launching "Wang Foo, The Kung Fu Shrew" and happened to catch a rehearsal of Elgar's "The Dream of Gerontius" in Derby Cathedral. Derby Cathedral is an eighteenth-century wedding-cake of white and pink, confident as iron, square as the mason's square, gold-leafed, its buttery flags, diamond crossed, laid down, were all brought there by rails of Derby iron.

The faded colours of local Yeomanry hung, shot through with blood and moths, Their embroidery bearing names such as "Polygon Wood", "The Dardenelles" and other battles now only the dead remember. "In a vault near this tablet lie the remains" of the ironmasters, the magistrates, the founders of almshouses, squire and gentry, where masons' chisels have numbered their noble deeds in stone, with marble skulls and weepers, and hands that once stretched out in charity to the poor of the parish, are now crossed for ever in sleep.

That day, I paused by Bess of Hardwick's tomb, and read the coffin-plates of reasoned scientists and (oddly, in a place so "Protestant") I saw candles, lit for the fallen Polish airmen: bright pinpricks of light, they flickered a flare-path for the souls of the last war. And, as I turned to resume, the orchestra played Elgar once again, strings lush as the green fields of England, green under blue skies beside slow rivers; chalk dust in summer's roads; white cottages, sheep in snow-rutted fields and spring gales off coastal cliffs.

Sadly, on Saturday, there was no repeat of such an experience, no such respite. Navigating my way along the A52, hoping the tyre would stay inflated, trying to find the Eagle Centre car park, I was humming the company song to myself. The company song? I hear you ask, in a quizzical tone: yes, it's "No retreat, baby, no, surrender", by that well known corporate management expert, B. Springsteen.

Every time we have set out to do an event, book launch or book fair, or for a tough meeting, I have always sung it to myself, sometimes out loud, watching the dawn break over the A1, sometimes under my breath:

> Now on the street tonight the lights grow dim
> The walls of my room are closing in
>
> There's a war outside still raging
> You say it ain't ours anymore to win
> I want to sleep beneath peaceful skies in my lover's bed
> With a wide open country in my eyes and these romantic dreams in my head
> We made a promise we swore we'd always remember

> No retreat, baby, no surrender
> Like soldiers in the winter's night with a vow to defend:
> No retreat, baby, no surrender.

It's one of my touchstones, that song. Maybe in future epilogues, I can drivel on about the others! The book signing went well, Chris sold 58 books, signed all the rest, did 91 drawings, on the spot, of cartoons and characters from his books for various kids, and went home happy (presumably to dunk his arm in a bucket of ice cubes). The Eagle Centre has all of the shops you find everywhere in the UK these days, and was incredibly busy with people bustling back and forth. It reminded me a lot of Saturdays in Hull when I was a kid, described by Larkin in the lines

> A cut-price crowd, urban yet simple
> Pushing through plate-glass doors to their desires

Last night, we got back from Derby and I cooked a curry of less-than-oriental splendour, and we watched the programme on TV about the women who were parachuted into Europe with the SOE during the war. Regular readers will recall Debbie's previous confusion of "Carve her Name with Pride" with "The Cruel Sea".

I could see Debbie, had she been born at the right time, as being part of the Maquis, with her penchant for sabotage and demolition. However, given her recent expertise with co-axial cable, she'd probably wire it up wrong and blow up Noel Coward and Jack Hawkins instead.

Today we have been playing catch-up, with two days' worth of email to read, lots of mailshots to laser, and the accountants hassling me for things about last year before the 31 October filing deadline.

It has been an odd week, this week, an unrelenting, unsettling, week, and one where I have been hard put to find one phrase to sum up how I feel about it. It would be easy to be depressed about this week. Although there has been good news - on the publicity and book sales fronts - there's also been uncertainty over

Russell, and tidings of other friends having trouble of various kinds, with officialdom in its various guises. And of course, on the world stage, the murder of Ken Bigley.

In all of these cases, it would be easy to ask why suffering is allowed in the world. What good can possibly come out of Russell being ill, or people being hassled by the authorities, or fanatics murdering someone who said in his last speech "I am not a difficult person. I am a simple man who just wants to live a simple life with his family"? Those words struck home to me, because they sum up all that many of us want. Ultimately, there is no logical explanation of why these things happen, because no-one can know the mind of God. Perhaps, as Raymond Chandler writes in "The Big Sleep", it is a case of:

> Is God happy with the poisoned cat dying behind the billboard? All we can say is that maybe, like us, God has off-days, and some of God's days are very long indeed.

The only "answers" come from illogical things like faith: illogical faith that out of the suffering we will all be able to draw strength. We can draw some strength from the fortitude of victims, such as Ken Bigley or Violette Szabo, who fall into the hands of fanatics, murderers and torturers, and resist with courage and dignity. But I have no idea what lesson I am supposed to learn from the potential loss of a loved family pet; I cannot tell what will ultimately happen in my friend's battle with officialdom, which is wearing her down and causing her anguish: all I can do is to be like Luther and say "Here I stand; I can do no more".

You can run and run and run, and duck and weave, but eventually there comes a point where you have to turn and make a stand. You either believe that everything that happens ultimately happens for a purpose, or not. You have to believe that if you make a stand, perhaps a greater evil can be averted, even if you are the only one left standing. No retreat, baby, no surrender.

17th October 2004

It has been a busy week in the Holme Valley. Busy enough to keep me off the internet. Now, that is busy. Everyone is as well as they could be, no one has done anything particularly startling, or funny. Russell's latest preferred medium to ingest his tablets is organic feta cheese, but no doubt that will change and change again. The other cats have been seeking warm places to keep out of the rain and to avoid the keen edge that seems to be creeping in to autumn's nights. Whenever Tig gets on the sofa in the conservatory and curls her nose into her tail, these days she is more than likely to find Nigel or Russ joining her in a quest to share body warmth.

There have been some brighter days. Weather-wise at least. Driving to the office on Tuesday morning in the sun, on a whim, I stopped briefly by the side of the road just after Birdsedge, and got out of the car to look out over the valley (I was trying to memorise it to do a painting later) towards Emley Moor TV mast, still wraith-wreathed in mist, and all of a sudden I was aware of a strange whistling motion disturbing the air overhead, as a skein of geese appeared seemingly from nowhere and passed almost silently over me, heading south. I watched them dwindle to specks, til they were indistinguishable from the horizon and the mist, and almost wished myself flying with them, to somewhere warmer, nicer, and generally less fraught. I hope they made it. For me, it was back into the car, start up the engine, and drop down Silkstone hill to sidle through the traffic thronging the wet streets under grey dawn over Barnsley. Application of nose to grindstone. Application of shoulder to wheel.

The big victory of the week, came about almost by accident. A large chain of bookshops, not entirely unconnected with the letters W, H, and S, had managed to double-book Chris White to sign copies of *Shark in the Toilet* in the Victoria Centre in Nottingham, at the same time as Stan Collymore. Stan Collymore is not a bloke to argue with, allegedly at any rate. Two words spring to mind, Ulrika, and Jonsson. However at the last minute, we heard that Stan's publishers had rearranged *their* session, to avoid it clashing! Thus depriving me of issuing what would have been one of my best-ever press releases - "come along to the Victoria Centre and see one of the masters of his art, an acknowledged favourite with the crowd, with many fans in the East midlands and beyond - oh, and Stan Collymore will be there as well." There's only one Chris White (as they no doubt chant at Pride Park every Saturday).

Yesterday, Owen Jordan called by, on his way from Wales to Hessle, to tell me that he was 35,000 words in to *Jordan's Guide to British Castles and Fortifications*, but he won't be able to do any more serious writing on it til a lot of the sites open up in the spring again. And he has a new cat, called Gandalf. We all (apart from Gandalf, who was at home in Wales) repaired to the Balooshai, Huddersfield's - and possibly the UK's - best curry house, and a good time was had for once, to round off the working week with the best Vegetable Dansak this side of the Euphrates.

For light relief (!) this week, I have once more been helping Debbie's mum with her family tree research. As regular readers know, Debbie comes from an extended family, who put the "fun" into "dysfunctional". As far as the family tree goes, some of them still live in it. The currently discovered earliest scion of the line is the improbably-named Friend Boothroyd, a power loom tuner (no less) of Honley, born in 1846, who fathered fourteen children with two wives (consecutively rather than concurrently) and lived to the age of eighty, being finally laid to his rest in Honley churchyard in 1926.

The Boothroyds still inhabit the area in great numbers, but the mills are mostly gone, and with them the innumerable trades which are recorded in the Boothroyd family's records: the loom tuner, the woollen fettlers, the pieceners, the bobbin reelers, the rug-cutters, gone, all gone. It's almost impossible for me to think on all the mills that used to dominate the skyline of this area without starting to hum Keith Marsden's great anthem naming all the mills of Morley, his home town when the "buzzers sang their chorus through the day":

> Prospect, Providence, Perseverance, Albert, Valley and Crank.
> I worked me time in the dust and grime, with never a word of thanks
> Oh the hours were long and the wages low,
> and the gaffers was hard, lads, hard:
> But the last time's coming, thank God, coming soon,
> when I'll walk up that damned mill yard.

(or as we used to sing it, rather irreverently, Prospect, Providence, Perseverance, Albert Finney's a crank!) Huddersfield, too, had - indeed still has - its own Albert Mill, not half a mile from where I sit typing this. But perhaps the grandest of them all, Folly Hall Mill, which saw the confrontation between the Luddites and the Yeomanry in 1817, still stands empty and derelict as it has for the last twenty-two years, a monument to civic stupidity and commercial indecision.

At the end of the war with Napoleon the country was left with heavy taxation, debt and the markets were glutted with unsaleable goods. Thus the mills were brought to a standstill. This gave cause for the Luddites to rally and on June 8th 1817 hundreds of men assembled at Folly Hall, and there awaited reinforcements that were rumoured to be on their way from outside the area. The Yeomanry were called for, and a few shots were fired before the soldiers retreated and the mob dispersed.

There was a plan to turn Folly Hall Mill into luxury flats, something which happened all across the country in the 1980s. (In fact, in Hull, some of the local yobbos are busy turning luxury flats back into disused warehouses, but that's another story.) But, derelict Folly Hall Mill remains. Bradford has its Saltaire, while Huddersfield has an eyesore.

I have been out of tune with the world of work this week. Well out of tune. I know I chose this crazy life, but it doesn't stop it getting me down. At one time I harboured thoughts of retiring at 55: now, because the government appears to have spent our pensions provision on illegal wars, we are being told to work til we drop. Time for the Luddites to rally again, perhaps.

Surely, our life ought to be better than the life of a Boothroyd, better than the little piecers who had to get up at dawn, trudge to the mill, and "pay t'mill owner for permission to work" as the Monty Python sketch puts it. But are we spiritually any better? Materially, we have our TV and our phone and the internet, we have our Ipods and our takeaways, we go out for a curry, whereas they had their motor charabancs to the seaside at Wakes Week, their Sunday school and chapel picnics, singing "Messiah", cricket, and tramping over Harden Moss to the sheepdog trials. Medically, we have a better chance of beating some of the things that saw off two of Friend's children before the age of 1. And before anyone says we can thank animal testing for this state of affairs, where was the effort to attain the same end by a different means?

But I repeat, in a larger sense, are we any better off? If you start asking questions like how come most people in the 21st century still have to work all their lives and wear out their bodies and minds for little reward, and how come people in the 21st century still die, from violence and from basic diseases, in the Sudan and Palestine and Israel and Iraq, people start asking if you are some kind of communist. If you dare to suggest that we ought to forgive people and love our neighbours, they write you off as a religious loony, and if you venture the opinion that not all human beings are intrinsically worth more than animals, they call for the cops.
Terence Blacker, writing in the *Independent*, this week, takes issue with the people who desecrated the grave of the Staffordshire woman whose family had been involved in breeding animals for medical research. He says of the people who carried out the act "when they believe that, in some cases, human life is worth less than that of animals, they become socially dangerous". While I have no time for people who desecrate graves on whatever grounds, I cannot agree with Mr Blacker's wider assumption. There are several human beings I can think of who, if it came to a choice between their continued existence and that of a well-loved pet, I would choose the pet. I do not think this makes me "socially dangerous". I just happen to believe that not all human beings are inherently better than all animals. I am afraid I am a bit of a "Mrs Malone" in that respect:

> Come Thursday a donkey stepped in off the road
> With sores on his withers from bearing a load.
> Come Friday when icicles pierced the white air
> Down from the mountainside lumbered a bear.
> For each she had something, if little, to give —
> 'Lord knows, the poor critters must all of 'em live.'
> She gave them her sacking, her hood and her shawl,
> Her loaf and her teapot — she gave them her all.

Or perhaps here my touchstone should be Eddi of Manhood End, celebrated in Kipling's poem:

> Eddi, priest of St. Wilfrid, in his chapel at Manhood End,
> Ordered a midnight service, for such as cared to attend.
> But the Saxons were keeping Christmas, and the night was stormy as well.
> Nobody came to service, though Eddi rang the bell.
> 'Wicked weather for walking," said Eddi of Manhood End.
> "But I must go on with the service for such as care to attend."
> The altar-lamps were lighted, - an old marsh-donkey came,
> Bold as a guest invited, and stared at the guttering flame.
> The storm beat on at the windows, the water splashed on the floor,
> And a wet, yoke-weary bullock pushed in through the open door.
> "How do I know what is greatest, how do I know what is least?
> That is My Father's business," said Eddi, Wilfrid's priest.
> "But — three are gathered together — listen to me and attend.
> I bring good news, my brethren!" said Eddi of Manhood End.
> And he told the Ox of a Manger and a stall in Bethlehem,
> And he spoke to the Ass of a rider, that rode to Jerusalem.
> They steamed and dripped in the chancel, they listened and never stirred,
> While, just as though they were Bishops, Eddi preached them the Word,
> Till the gale blew off on the marshes and the windows showed the day,
> And the Ox and the Ass together wheeled and clattered away.
> And when the Saxons mocked him, said Eddi of Manhood End,
> "I dare not shut His chapel on such as care to attend."

Whatever I think, though, it is the blind, arrogant belief, held by Mr Blacker and others like him, that man is automatically at the top of the tree, lord of all he surveys, and can take from nature at will without replacing, that is causing us such problems ecologically. Let me give you an example: the factory ships hoover up everything in the sea bigger than a stickleback. The seals are suddenly then short of fish, so they start eating sand eels, depriving the sea birds of their food. The seabird population crashes, mankind mistakenly assumes this is because the hedgehogs are eating their eggs, and embarks on killing hedgehogs.

Others say we should club the seals as well. Some fools in Norway are even trying to make a holiday of it. Scroll back up a bit to find the real culprit: man, who started the whole chain of catastrophe by assuming he has the right to strip the sea of everything bigger than a tiddler, probably to produce fertiliser to bolster up an intensive farming system that produces surpluses in one part of the world, allowing us to push our plates to one side, switch on the TV, and see people dying for want of a handful of rice.

> And man, proud man, dressed in a little brief authority, plays such fantastic tricks before high heaven, as makes the angels weep.

It is all very well to say God will make everything right in the world to come. For all I know, this may be true. But I tend to line up with the Christian Aid slogan. I believe in life *before* Death. Something we are unlikely to achieve while we continue trying to squeeze the last drops of life out of the bounty that should surround us into the rapacious maw of capitalism red in tooth and claw.

So I am giving notice. This is officially the beginning of my campaign to start a donkey sanctuary. I am pinning it on my dream board. I was a free man in Paris, I was unfettered and alive. And I'd rather be a Luddite than a snail, to misquote Simon and Garfunkel. There's room for another, says Mrs Malone.

Easy as falling off a "logue"
[posted in the week between these two Epliogues.]

As some of you may know, Keri Davies has been exchanging emails with me this week about how the "Epilogues" are not "in the spirit" of the Archers' boards. My contention is that the "spirit" of the boards is defined by those who use them. Left to some people on this board, the "spirit of the board" would be a pretty mean one.

My last email to Keri Davies pointed out several reasons why I thought he was wrong. As it was quite a lengthy email, covering off several of the points I mentioned in my previous thread about why people should be able to post on the boards, provided they didn't break the rules, I was a bit surprised when I received an answer only five minutes later, which showed he had not read further than point one.

So, as I said to him, he is the boss, and his decision, however arbitrary, illogical and unfair it might seem to anyone else.

Anyway, as our Quaker friends would say, the "spirit" has moved me. From this week as well as on i-church, and my own site, the Epilogue is now going to be available on H2G2. Simply search there for me under my new "researcher" name Slightly-Foxed. To be honest, the delicious thought of it still taking up space on a BBC server (albeit a different one to this) was too tempting to resist. No doubt, sooner or later, the Einsatzgruppen will track me down there as well, but since every H2G2 page comes with a section entitled "my journal" which you are supposed to fill in with news of your doings, warping logic far enough to chuck me off there could be difficult.

Thanks, by the way, to all the people who spoke up in my defence in the "Epilogue banned" thread. I deliberately haven't intervened in that thread because I thought it important to let the principle speak for itself - that anyone can post anything on these boards provided it doesn't break the rules. To the people who saw the Epilogues as "egotistical", I can only say that if being egotistical was a reason to get banned, several posters I can think of would not have reached double figures, let alone four. And to say that the Epilogues might inspire others to do likewise is a bit of a strange reason to advance, when six months or more of postings have not produced a single "logalike" apart from a few individual posts.

I am not going to stop posting on these boards. In fact I feel rather liberated by the experience. Time to come down off the moral high ground and bayonet a few survivors I might as well. Being reasonable hasn't got me anywhere.

For now though, I leave you with the most valuable lesson I learned from a detailed study of the life of Mother Teresa of Calcutta - you gotta moisturize!

24th October 2004

It has been a busy week here in the Holme Valley. Still time to glimpse the sun, perhaps, but no time to stop and sniff the flowers. Work, as usual, predominates.

We are still arguing, as well, about holidays: Elk watching (rational and irrational) is now on the back burner. Last night, the admirable Bettany Hughes presented a very interesting TV programme on the ancient customs of the Minoans. I ventured an opinion to Deb:

"I would like to go to Crete, it's full of ancient ruins."
"Send me a postcard, I am married to one."

Subject closed. For now.

Last night we had a really "winter" meal: baked potatoes. In my case, this was accompanied by some white Port, which I had procured of Messrs Sainsbury after reading about it in A. N. Wilson's book on Hilaire Belloc. It was, apparently, his favourite tipple (Belloc, not A. N. Wilson, I have no idea what he drinks!) It's always amused me the way some drinks are associated with certain writers: Hock-and-seltzer with Byron. Grappa with Hemingway. Anything with alcohol in it, with Dylan Thomas. Having drunk Grappa myself, I now understand why Hemingway only ever wrote in short sentences. And having drunk white Port, I can understand why some of Hilaire's output was Bellocs.

Talking of back burners, Russell, Nigel, Dusty and Kitty all had their comfortable domestic arrangements disrupted by a major fault with the stove, this week which meant we had to let the fire go out in order to fix it. Cue for much yowling, and a tablet-taking strike on the part of Russell which was only broken when I quartered his Fortekor pill and stuck it in some extremely pongy Shropshire Blue cheese. Tig accepted the creeping chill which settled over the house more philosophically, curling up as always with her nose in her tail, on her favourite settee.

Anyway, a quick visit to the people who sold us the stove, the improbably-named "Batley Barless Fire Company" (forever known to us, in honour of Charlie Dimmock, as the Batley *Bra-less* Fire Company) soon secured the bits we needed, and a half hour or so with a rat-tail file widening the hole on one of them, followed by a similar length of time grovelling on the kitchen floor with my arm up the ash pan aperture, this meant that we were able to adapt it to fit on the end of the bit where the previous pan had burnt completely away, then re-assemble all the parts we had disassembled, and re-light it. Peace, warmth and harmony were restored.

In a bizarre twist of events, the office nearly "caught fire" the day after. This is the "office" office, not my "home" office where I am typing this. I was sitting working away when the fire alarm started going off. After telling everyone to get out, I went to investigate, only to meet Terry coming the other way who said it was a false alarm. Because it is on a "redcare" system, they automatically send the Fire Brigade unless you phone the alarm company's "central station" and tell them it's not for real. Terry did just that, only to be connected, instead of to the usual live operator, to their call centre queueing system. I looked out of the window to see two fire engines pulling in to the courtyard, and went to put the kettle on for fourteen cups of tea.

We spent the rest of the day making up bogus call centre recorded messages on behalf of the alarm company: if you are dying of smoke inhalation, press 1; if you are being fried to a crisp, press 2, please continue to burn, your call is important to us, and so on. There's not that much to do in South Yorkshire.

Actually, that line about putting the kettle on for fourteen cups of tea used to be one of my mother's favourites whenever my dad was trying to light their fire by holding up a news paper in front of it. Always a perilous exercise if you were a child of nervous disposition, as I was.

This week is the run-up to Halloween, a festival now almost completely taken over by Hollywood-inspired dross, and rampant children-targeting commercialism second only to Christmas. The true meaning of All Souls Day, of which the precursor is Halloween, of course, is to remember the dead. People sometimes get the idea that remembering the dead is morbid, but scarcely a day goes by without me thinking of the voices of my parents, as above, and the comments they would have made, as I go about my daily tasks. This week would have been my dad's eighty-third birthday. In the end, we are all going to live only in other people's memories of us. As Larkin says at the end of "An Arundel Tomb"

> What will survive of us, is love.

Originally, All Souls Day was the day when Christians remembered the dead. Those endless ranks of people who had gone on ahead, as Vaughan puts it, into the "World of Light", and left us "lingering here". A time when the unknown and unknowable membrane that separates this world from the next dimension might be stretched so thin that you might be able to glimpse, tantalisingly, a shadowy figure or two. Maybe heaven itself could be glimpsed, as a bright warm light, like the glow of a welcoming fire seen through a held-up sheet of newspaper. Mind you, that might be a bit theologically unsound: perhaps flames are better kept for t'other place. Either way, I'd like to think there would be a cosy celestial fireside waiting in heaven, and a cup of tea for me while I catch up on the gossip and stroke, for the first time in many years, Ginger, Silvo, and Halibut, who have all gone before.

Sometimes, when I am driving to the office in a ruminative mood, I ask for a sign that heaven exists. Dangerous territory, really: you shouldn't provoke God, assuming you believe in him of course. Last week, on Wednesday morning, I rounded the penultimate bend before my destination and there, hanging in the sky ahead, were two perfect contrails, in the shape of a cross. If only I had asked for a sign that morning. Or is it that the signs only come when you stop asking, like remembering where your keys are, when you have finally, exhausted, and exasperated, given up looking? Perhaps the souls of heaven operate to a different timescale to the rest of us down here, it being eternal and everything.

My Grandma, who was the oldest inhabitant of Welton at the time when she died in 1980, could remember the children skipping down the lanes when she was young, the urchins and ragamuffins of Edwardian England, singing the "souling" songs:

> A soul, a soul, a soul-cake
> Please good missus a soul-cake
> An apple a pear a plum a cherry
> Or any good thing to make us merry
> One for Peter, one for Paul
> One for Him that made us all

I am not sure if I believe in ghosts. Certainly not the clanking, head carrying, spectres which feature in horror stories. Why should ghosts mean us harm, if they exist? And presumably, if a ghost thumped you, its arm would go straight through you, or vice versa. So the worst you might get is a nasty chill.

If ghosts do exist, maybe there is cause for sadness about some hauntings. I can appreciate the theory that some cataclysmic events do leave some sort of psychic impression of terror or another strong emotion on their surroundings, which in some way replays itself to people who can see it, but even then, we should, perhaps, rejoice, and seize on this as further proof of an existence outside of our three solid dimensions.

We should be embracing ghosts. Except of course, our arms would meet in the middle if we did. Why should ghosts be a source of terror? Wonder should be nearer the mark. Seeing an apparition should be not a trick, but a treat.

31st October 2004

It has been a busy week in the Holme Valley. With the two new children's books now out and in the world, and only seven weeks to Christmas, the publicity campaign has been stepped up even further. If possible.

Nigel, Dusty and Kitty have been their usual catty selves and are all well. Kitty still keeps up her unique dialogue with me every time I feed her.

"What was the name of that revolutionary leader again?"
"Mao!"
"Do you want feeding later, Kitty, or now?"
"Naow!"

And so it goes on. A small idiocy, but mine own. Little things please little minds. Tig has been reluctant to go out in the garden especially as the mornings have been getting darker. I hold the conservatory door open for her and she stands there looking at me with her head on one side as much as to say "if you think for one minute that I am going out there in that rain and dark and cold, you must be out of your tiny little Chinese mind!"

Russell has not been so good this week, he has been off his food and what my late mother would have called "wowy", an adjective reserved exclusively in her vocabulary for poorly cats. So, I don't know. He spends a lot of time curled up in the chair nearest the stove, maybe the warmth helps him, I don't know. In her book, *The Cat Whisperer*, Claire Besant says that older cats like warmth.

Russell's tablet-taking has now entered a new dimension, with "Bernard Maffews" American fried chicken now being used as the medium of choice.

With Christmas so close, we've started already working towards books which are due early in 2005, including the delayed "Hampshire at War 1939-45, an Oral History". Pat, the author, and her husband John, very kindly drove up to Huddersfield and we spent the weekend in a Travelodge in Mirfield going through the manuscript on a lap top computer. Having spent two days closeted in a Travelodge, now I know what it feels like to be a terrorist. Anyway, came Sunday and the task was, if not finished, as near finished as makes no difference. With Pat and John safely ensconced watching "Foyles War" (enough war, already!) Debbie and I decided that the only solution to our hunger was a takeaway.

We toasted "Hampshire at War" with a dry red Portuguese table wine, which tasted as if it had been made from dry red Portuguese tables, or at least used to strip the varnish off them. Fortunately, the secret mix of oriental herbs and spices in the takeaway from The Balooshai was enough to numb the palate and save it from the full effect of the vino collapso.

It is a strange coincidence that I have been working on "Hampshire at War" in the weeks running up to Armistice Day. I guess it is just one of those unanswerable questions like what do occasional tables do the rest of the time, and why can you never find your camouflage net. One of the things that has struck me about this book, where ordinary people tell of their experiences of wartime life, is just how much heroism there was in ordinary, everyday life. The story of the Wren whose father sent her his favourite rosary, in the post, with no explanation: she assumed the worst when she received it and phoned her home, asking her mother "Is father dead?"

With commendable sang froid, the mother replied "I don't *think* so dear, I have just cooked his breakfast, but I will check" returning later to the phone to say "no, he is not dead, he's just finished his egg". Ah, the unflappable nature of the British stiff upper lip.

In the second world war, about 55 million people died. Roughly equivalent to the population of the British Isles. The statistics of war are quite startling, when you view them like that. A whole country-worth of people, many in their teens or early twenties, scattered like leaves on the wind, all those unfulfilled hopes and dreams, all those unkept promises. In 55 million people there would undoubtedly have been some villains, some who we wouldn't miss; Hitler for one; but who knows but that just one of those people whose life was tragically cut short, might not have, in other circumstances, had events ran differently, been the person to discover the cure for cancer, or some other dread disease. All that waste.

This week, it has been reported that 100,000 Iraquis have died under the current misguided attempt to bring "democracy" to Iraq. If this is true, it is a crushing blow to both George Bush and Tony Blair. No one knows for sure how many people Hussein killed, of course, and any attempt to get to the bottom of the figures founders on the rock that the idea of "responsibility" in a totalitarian state, is a very complex one. If someone murders a prisoner because they think that is what the dictator wanted, is the dictator responsible, even if he had no idea it was going on?

This week, America, currently still bitterly engaged in a massive undeclared war in Iraq, will probably make one final attempt to raze Fallujah to the ground, at the same time as George Bush makes one final attempt to cling to power. George Bush is of course, supported in his idea of a never-ending, unwinnable (in pure military terms) war against "terror" by various people in the US and elsewhere who refer to themselves as Christians, and who specifically see their mission as being to evangelise.

I love America and many of the things it stands for, but I am unable in my heart to reconcile these paradoxes: people who purport to represent religion urging on a destructive conflict on what many believe to be the wrong target, led in the name of democracy by someone who may not even have been democratically elected. As Joni Mitchell wrote, about a different war, Vietnam, in 1969,

> And so once again
> Oh, America my friend
> And so once again
> You are fighting us all
> And when we ask you why
> You raise your sticks and cry and we fall
> Oh, my friend
> How did you come
> To trade the fiddle for the drum

Would Jesus recognise the idea of a just war? Who has the power, the moral authority, to claim they have God on their side? The Christians I most admire from the last war are people like Bishop

Bell and Dietrich Bonhoeffer, who are both about as far away from Billy Graham as you can get without actually leaving the planet. We are back to those unanswerable questions again.

I recommend a detailed study, especially for people like George W Bush and Tony Blair, of a seminal religious tract; Bob Dylan's "With God on our Side". The whole song exposes the fallacy of the concept of politicians manipulating the concept of "the just war" but I can only squeeze in the last verse.

> So now as I'm leavin'
> I'm weary as Hell
> The confusion I'm feelin'
> Ain't no tongue can tell
> The words fill my head
> And fall to the floor
> If God's on our side
> He'll stop the next war.

God of course only works through man, or so we are told. Let's hope he moves the hearts of many Americans to turn their country away from the road that leads to four more years of carnage. It is time to take the fiddle from the wall, dust it off, and play the tunes of liberty and freedom once again.

§

7th November 2004

It has been a busy week in the Holme Valley, and one that has seen me laid low with the first really foul bug of 2004. The firebricks in the stove have partially collapsed, which means that a) we have to let it go out again and b) another trip to the Batley Braless Fire Company. No one has yet broken it to Nigel, Kitty, Dusty, Russell, or Tig that we will have to do with the ineffectual central heating until the firebricks can once more be screwed into place.

Work continues on books, on publicising books, and when we aren't doing either of the former, adding up the books - though not, yet, so far, cooking them. No stove anyway.

I managed to make it to the "office" office on Friday morning despite already feeling wretched. With the accent on the retch. My trouble is that simultaneously I hate being ill and will literally try to go on until I drop in my tracks, but at the same time, I am a terrific hypocondriac. I have had to stop watching medical programmes on TV because I immediately assume that I have got whatever it is that they are showcasing - from conjoined twins to ectopic pregnancy.

By mid afternoon Friday, I knew there was something seriously amiss in the alimentary dept, and bogarted some Kaolin and Morphine mixture off Phil - this got me to the stage where I felt able to drive home, and I staggered in at 4pm and settled myself by what was left of the stove (we'd already decided to let it go out) and dozed fitfully for two more hours before dragging myself bedwards.

Whatever it was peaked during Friday night, my temperature shot up, I was alternatively boiling and shivering, and somehow started thinking about what would happen to the business if I died. What would the succession be. Moose face would be OK, because the extremely expensive Keyman insurance we pay Barclays for would kick in, and pay off any debts. She might have to go and get a real job once the ashes were settled and the dust was scattered, but that wouldn't hurt her. Then I started thinking (remember I was semi delerious at this time) about Guy Fawkes and his attempts to alter the succession, and about Yasser Arafat, and what it must have been like for him, lying there ill and hearing bangs going off all around him, just like I was, only his bangs were RPGs and tank shells. Then I started thinking about George Bush, and how unlikely it seemed that we had to suffer four more years of bangs going off all round, then back to Guy Fawkes, then back to Arafat, I tell you, that Kaolin and Morphine is strong stuff, man. I didn't see any giant pink spiders though.

At this point Deb put her head round the door to check on me.

"What do you think will happen when Arafat dies?" I croaked, weakly.
"His wife will finally be able to do the drying up".

So much for the compassion of the caring professions. Anyway, having slept (on and off) for 24 hours or more, and risen finally briefly last night, I seem to have burnt it out of me, whatever it was, and I feel much better. We have reached Sunday. St Willibrod's day, apparently, according to my dictionary of Saints. I need to go and look him up properly because all I really know about him at the moment is that he had a very silly name. Sunday: as Stanford would say, and Katherine Ferrier is currently singing about on the CD as I type this - "A soft day, at last, thank God"

While I was lying ill, Tig and Nigel both joined me on the bed, so every time I came out of my reverie I saw two glittering gold eyes and two sad brown ones anxiously fixed on me, no doubt wondering if I would survive ever to open another tin. Russell studiously ignored me, but he's got illness problems of his own, so I will let him off.

Anyway, last night the only thing I had the intellectual chutzpah for was watching the John Peel tribute on the Beeb. Lots of clips of groups (Medicine Head) that I had forgotten I had ever heard, let alone liked. It almost made me want to pick up a guitar again, or get my old Banjo out.

In the years when I lived alone in Barnsley, I used to play the banjo a great deal more than I do today. It's not a social instrument: in fact I once got rid of some double glazing salesmen by getting out the banjo and starting to double thumb frail "Little Birdie" in a lilting appalachian yodel. Nigel, who never shows any reaction to human music, (apart from for some strange reason best known only to him, Tanita Tikaram - perhaps she hits notes only cats can hear) was always strangely enervated by the banjo and tried to get between me and it, either because he thought I was having sex with it and wanted to join in, or he thought I was fighting it and he was trying to save me, or he recognised some of his relatives in the strings and wanted to effect a reunion beyond the grave.

I don't know what will happen about John Peel's succession, but here's an idea from the Slightly Foxed Bank of Good Ideas (the people who brought you cockney assonance slang: apples and pears = fears) that the BBC should institute John Peel memorial sessions for new bands.

They are all going, this year, all the old touchstones - John Peel, Alistair Cooke, and even Fred Dibnah. I will miss Fred Dibnah, especially because he tried to reconstruct a fully working Victorian mine-shaft in his garden in Bolton. Well, someone's got to do something about property prices rising out of control.

John Peel actually called us once on the phone, in person. It was when he was in The Archers, as a walk-on part, playing himself. I wrote a stupid little letter to the *Guardian* saying that the credibility of the real characters in the Archers was being undermined by imaginary people like John Peel appearing in it. It must have been a slow news day because the *Guardian* printed it, and in those days, the *Guardian* had a policy of printing the full name and address under letters and Peel must've looked up our number in directory enquiries, he rang to berate us - albeit in a friendly way - for referring to him as "imaginary".

I was pretty overawed - after all, this was the bloke I had listened to on a whistly transistor as a 15 year old in Hull, trying to be blacker, older, and more like Howlin' Wolf than any of my contemporaries.

Looking at him on the TV programme last night, I was very jealous of his lifestyle - nice house, garden, cats and dogs wandering about, big farmhouse kitchen, big table to sit around having breakfast, or dinner, red wine a-plenty. The only downside - for me at any rate - would be the bin-bags of stuff which arrived every day, containing tapes and CDs from aspiring musicians. As a recipient of unsolicited manuscripts, I can sympathise. I was a free man in Paris, nobody calling me up for favours, no one's future to decide.

I am not one of those people who goes all "Candle in the Wind" whenever a celebrity dies, and I don't think that John Peel was God.

I do, however, think that God, if he exists as a sentient force or being, is probably a lot like John Peel. Bumbling, curmudgeonly, occasionally forgetful, loving of his family, occasionally disappointed, but always willing to give something new a try, and speaking directly to people who are tuned in. Sifting through the bin bags of our offerings and alternately smiling and crying at their contents, as he takes upon himself all the sins of the world.

14th November 2004

It has been a busy week in the Holme Valley, but much of it has raged on around me, while I continued to be laid low by the foulest of bugs. Foolishly, last week, I thought I was on the mend and tried to get back to my desk too early: result, by Tuesday, I was not at my desk, but at the doctor's desk, watching her sign a prescription for anti-biotics following an emergency appointment. I managed briefly to visit my "office" office for about half an afternoon, before once more giving up and heading for home, and bed.

At some point on Wednesday, I became convinced that there was a large black squirrel on the roof, and that this was a bad omen. I began reciting George Herbert's "The Harbingers" to Deb, who was unimpressed by the drug-fuelled arguments I was putting forward.

> The harbingers are come. See, see their mark;
> White is their colour, and behold my head.
> But must they have my brain? must they dispark
> Those sparkling notions, which therein were bred?
> Must dulnesse turn me to a clod?
> Yet have they left me, *Thou art still my God.*

Once I was fully awake again, I could see that the squirrel (or at least what I took to be its nose) was, in reality, one of the brackets holding on the guttering outside the window.

Having weathered the squirrel crisis, I drifted off again, only to be wakened a couple of hours later by the sound of African harmonies and a choir singing "The Lord is My Shepherd". This time, I thought, they really are coming for me, but eventually I worked out what it was: Lockwood Cemetery, which is across the way from us, is a favourite burial place for the local West Indian community, and they must have been having one of their spectacular funerals that they hold from time to time: the angels I thought were coming for me, were actually the voices of the graveside choir, borne on the wind.

The animals continue to be bemused by my plight. Tig spends hours looking at me propped up in bed, just willing me to get up and open a packet of dogfood. She had an unexpected treat during the week when, in one of my shuffling and incoherent rambles downstairs, I noticed an opened packet of pressed ham in the fridge. Thinking that Debbie must've bought it as a treat for Tig, and feeling guilty that I had been neglecting her, I made her sit and give paw, while I fed her the remaining slices. Much licking of chops and tail-swishing ensued. Later, Debbie came into the bedroom: "Have you seen that ham my Mum left in our fridge for Jonathan's tea?" Tig and I shook heads simultaneously, and I pretended to be more delerious than I was.

Nigel, too, has been spending time with me, his favourite method of ensuring he has my attention being to claw the duvet next to my ear, having first watched me go to sleep. It's no fun if the subject's awake, apparently. With the advent of the frosty weather, I have banged the heating on in Colin's side of the house, which of course has had the result of luring Kitty and Dusty back to the bathroom, particularly Dusty, who has now been renamed "Bogpuss" by Debbie's mother, on account of her general size, shape, and continual inhabitation of that place. In fact, Dusty's life mostly consists of staying in the bathroom all the time with only brief forays outside to have a crap. Exactly the opposite of the way the majority of us do it!

Dusty virtually living in the bathroom full-time means of course that one now has to share one's, er, more intimate ablutions, motions and solutions, with an audience of not one, but sometimes two cats, watching intently. I fully expect them to start holding up scorecards one day, after the manner of Olympic judges.

Russell, virtual cat of I-church, went back for his check up appointment with the vet this week, and this was the crunch one: the vet was to weigh him, to see if he had gained or lost weight since last time - lost weight would indicate potential causes other than just his kidneys for his plight. In a week of struggle and disaster though, this was to be good news: he had actually put on a bit. Maybe, just maybe, we can start to be cautiously optimistic about the longer term. A soft day, thank God. Russell celebrated with some fish I managed to get up and cook for him. He also discovered the potential perils of a vegetarian diet when a large chunk of frozen veg curry in a freezer bag fell out of the top tray of the freezer and crashed onto the kitchen tiles just next to his head. Curiosity and cat's don't mix. One more life down, I think he's still got about four left though.

The only other "news" as such this week concerns the stove. We finally had to let it go out and clean the whole of it out, in an attempt to solve the firebrick problem. A trip over to Batley Braless resulted in Deb returning not only with a new set of firebricks, but also a new baffle-plate. The baffle plate sits over the top of the firebricks and holds them all in place, and our previous baffle-plate had burnt away, leading to the bricks collapsing and getting cracks in them. True to its name, the baffle-plate defeated Deb's attempts to fit it, and it was left to me to come down like a *Deus Ex Machina* and whack it with a poker until it slid into place.

As you can see, it has been a week which has been by turns aimless, feckless and witless, and I have got absolutely no work done. I have been trying to come to some decision about what spiritual lesson the week held for me, and the nearest I can come at the moment is that I have treated this week like a retreat. I have withdrawn from the real world and spent a long time looking and thinking. In that respect, maybe my head is better, even if my guts are worse. Lying in a sick bed and hearing the angels (or the squirrels) coming for you does tend to make you concentrate on the more fundamental questions: as does listening to the Remembrance Day parade here in the UK this morning. (Sadly, in bed, so no standing to attention with a cat on my shoulder this year.)

Retreat, of course, in military terms, can be synonymous with defeat, but it does not have to be. A retreat is different to a rout. Sometimes, as I hope I am doing, all you are achieving by retreating is to gather strength, hold the line, and consolidate your position in anticipation of a future advance. So, if I chose to momentarily forsake the external world of telegrams and anger, I should use that space to strengthen myself from within, and concentrate on what is important. "On a huge hill, cragg'd and steep, Truth stands, and he that will find it, about must, and about must go..."

Retreat can also be finding your way back to a place of safety, as in Henry Vaughan's "The Retreate"

> Happy those early days, when I
> Shin'd in my Angel-infancy!
> Before I understood this place
> Appointed for my second race,

> Or taught my soul to fancy aught
> But a white celestial thought:
>
> When yet I had not walk'd above
> A mile or two from my first Love,
> And looking back — at that short space —
> Could see a glimpse of His bright face:
> When on some gilded cloud, or flow'r,
> My gazing soul would dwell an hour.

Maybe my illness is big G telling me to slow down, and sniff the flowers. At least one of the questions posed in last week's Epilogue got answered this week, about the succession of Yasser Arafat. Debbie came in and told me that the BBC late night news was reporting that all of the shops in the Gaza Strip were closed out of respect, apart from one which was selling Yasser Arafat "memorabilia."

"Yasser Arafat Memorabilia" just struck me as one of the more unlikely phrases, a bit like "German humorous literature", "Spanish animal rights protestors", "gourmet motorway services food", or possibly, "interesting Swedish furniture". I fell to musing what a collection of Yasser Arafat memorabilia would consist of. There's obviously a big market. I can just imagine men all over the world announcing they were going out to the shed to polish their Yasser Arafat memorabilia, and their wives handing them the teatowel with which to do it…

Sunday has been a quiet day so far, at which I have gradually picked at stuff on my desk. It's really tomorrow's problem, though. I have left undone those things which I ought to have done, and I have done those things which I ought not to have done, and there is no health in me. I am sorry I can't think of any more spiritual messages this week. However, it's probably just as well, we don't want people looking for hidden meanings in these rambling witterings and then going out and killing celebrities. [Though if you do feel the urge, could I suggest Celine Dion, Bono, Robbie Williams and any of Busted.]

21st November 2004

It has been a busy week in the Holme Valley now that I am back on what passes for my feet, with mountains of undone work everywhere I look. There's nothing like spending a week in bed for making your in-tray look like an explosion in a paper factory. This week we have seen the first snow of the winter, as well, much to the chagrin of the cats, who have glared balefully at me every morning as if I am personally responsible for the stuff. If only they knew that my first reaction to snow is to reach for my flame-thrower!

With the coming of the cold weather, Colin's central heating has been blasting out with renewed vigour, making the spare bedroom the warmest place in the whole house, which probably explains why Debbie found Nigel, Russell and Dusty all sharing the spare bed the other morning. A true triumph for central heating as a force for reconciliation. Only Kitty was missing from the lineup, probably because she was demolishing a dish of cat food downstairs at the time.

Tig and Fred love the snow of course, and go plunging down between the trees behind the house, barking excitedly and rolling in the stuff, chasing snowballs and generally coming back glowing, panting, with their tongues lolling. As does Debbie, whose ideal day in the snow, as a responsible 39 year old residential social worker, is to try and interest the dogs in tobogganing.

To me, the snow - or rather the ice that comes with it - is just another obstacle. If I fall over and break my ankle, two businesses go down the tubes quite rapidly, so I have to be extra careful when it snows. Snow has a habit of reminding me of my limitations. In fact, pretty much in the same way as illness does. It's not so much the illness, as the boredom, and the way in which it forces you to admit your humanity. This was brought home to me when the doctor asked me to submit a sample, on the conclusion of my antibiotics run, to make sure I really was cured. There is little in life more humiliating than "doing a sample", except possibly, handing it in. So it was on Friday that I did my duty, watched by an attentive audience of Dusty and Kitty (wow, how did he manage that?) and bore my burden back into the office. I was looking for an envelope - after all, I couldn't just hand the thing in. I wondered what the correct protocol was: should I do a covering letter, ending with "enc". In the end, I settled for a comp slip, on which I scrawled "as discussed".

I can only hope that Dr Spencer took it in the spirit in which it was intended. No word has come back, so for all I know, it is still sitting on a shelf somewhere, or lying in an in-tray. Oh, the shame of being mortal.

I suppose, actually, that lots of people have to endure much more humiliating things, experiences in the course of an illness, and I shouldn't be so squeamish about the body and its functions: but I cannot help but feel, like Yeats, that my heart is "fastened to a dying animal", and at times like this I have to make a special effort to remember that mortality may not be everything, even though

> An aged man is but a paltry thing
> A tattered coat upon a stick,
> Unless soul clap its hands and sing
> And louder sing for every tatter in the mortal dress...

So, I have spent the week looking for intimations of immortality, not easy in a month like November, devoted to death and decay. In the pre-Christian Celtic calendar, November was Samhain, the month of death, when the cattle were slaughtered and their bones burnt to scare off the evil spirits. These bone-fires were eventually taken over by Guy Fawkes and his cronies, but their origins are a lot older, and they lie in the very understandable fears of mortals who feared the monsters, Grendel and the rest, who lived "out there", outside of the warm circle of the camp fire around which they huddled in their mead-halls and villages.

Bede likens the life of a man to a sparrow flying through the mead-hall: it comes in at one end, out of the darkness, flies through the warm lighted hall, and then back out the other end, back into the blackness and rain. Not much comfort there, for those seeking a more comforting view of the relationship between life and eternity.

So what can I take comfort in, as I sit at the top of the house, listening to the dark trees whispering and the rain falling? What can I point to, that makes us more than just a hamburger on legs, with a limited sell-by date? Art, I suppose. And the occasional flickering flame of decency and civilization, such as the banning this week of fox-hunting (even though Tony Blair had to be virtually anaesthetised to agree to it). So another cruel inequality goes the same way as bear-baiting and shoving kids up chimneys. Yet at the same time, for every good deed in the world, I could name a dozen naughty ones.

> We think that Paradise and Calvary,
> Christ's cross and Adam's tree, stood in one place;
> Look, Lord, and find both Adams met in me;
> As the first Adam's sweat surrounds my face,
> May the last Adam's blood my soul embrace

Twenty years on, we are still having to make charity records in an attempt to feed everybody in Africa, yet we can always find seemingly bottomless pits of money to fund wars. Wouldn't it be nice for once, as Mark Steel has pointed out, if the warmongers had to make a record and sell it to raise funds to start a war, while the feeding of Africa and the ending of wars was taken as read as the natural task of governments? And how many people will stop at buying Band Aid 20 feeling that they have done their bit to stop famine in Darfur, making it a Band Aid by nature as well as by name?

I am out of sorts with the world this week, more so than any week this year. It feels like a week for pulling up the drawbridge and letting the world sort itself out. But that won't make me feel any better, because like all humanity, I carry with me the seeds of my own destruction. You can run, but you can't hide, eventually, you have to turn and face your own beastliness. I am fallen, like all humanity, I am reduced to the sum total of what I can consume and excrete.

The only hope, the only way out of this, is Christmas. In four weeks' time the wavering spark of light at the end of winter's tunnel starts to grow (and glow) stronger again, as we contemplate the impossible possibility of redemption. I don't feel in the least bit

Christmassy, I have taken to shouting at Christmas adverts on the TV, and asking people why it can't be Christmas every day (and getting lots of funny looks for my trouble). But underneath all the tinsel and the crap, is there a glimmer of hope? Sometimes you have to just blindly carry on, even when there is no hope, like the Magi in T. S. Eliot's poem:

> Then the camel men cursing and grumbling
> And running away, and wanting their liquor and women,
> And the night-fires going out, and the lack of shelters,
> And the cities hostile and the towns unfriendly
> And the villages dirty and charging high prices:
> A hard time we had of it.
> At the end we preferred to travel all night,
> Sleeping in snatches,
> With the voices singing in our ears, saying
> That this was all folly.

Give me the blind faith to keep on driving forward when all seems folly. Give me a star to follow. We are all human, mortal, we are in the gutter, but (said Oscar) some of us are looking for the stars.

28th November 2004

It has been a busy week in the Holme Valley, running out of time on all projects as Christmas approaches with the speed (and charm) of an oncoming express train. November is really beginning to bite now, with day after day of dullness and greyness, dampness and coldness, the browns and greys of death. It seems almost impossible that in as little as three or four weeks, the tide will have turned, and we will be once more looking forward, with longing, to lengthening days.

Many times this week, I have found myself alternately wishing I hadn't been ill, and yet wanting to pull the duvet back over my head and hibernate until what is left of this dreary, dreadful month has been banished. In fact, if I could set my alarm for April, I think perhaps I would. Russell has also been complaining long and lod each morning about the cold while I feed him his tablet wrapped in cooked chicken breast, Like me, he's a child of the sun.

But, there are those who depend on me, so on we go. This week we ran out of dog food, and almost ran out of coal. Like I said, everything has got completely out of kilter since I lost my grip on the list of tasks and allowed it to rampage unchecked for ten days or so while I lay groaning in bed. The dog food was easily solved, with a trip to Sainsburys. I called Deb on the mobile to see what else we needed, since I was conscious that the cupboards and the fridge and the freezer were all looking rather empty since I had been ill.

"We just need the essentials" she said.
"Like what?"
"Crumpets"
"Crumpets?"
"Yes, Crumpets."

OK, so it's now official. Crumpets are essential emergency food and I look forward to seeing the UN dropping crumpets on the scene of any natural disaster. God knows, they could do with a few in Darfur. The coal was more problematic, we got down to two bags before I finally remembered to call the coal yard and ask for another 20 bags of Solarbrite. Fortunately, the coal yard is clued up to take orders by phone using switch cards, and thus, as if by magic, twenty bags duly appeared, stacked neatly against the side wall of the house beside the gas meter, last Friday. This was a great improvement on the last delivery, which they merrily stacked across the drive instead of along it, and which Deb had had to move, single handed, so she could drive the camper van into the drive. As John Betjeman put it

>The bells of waiting advent ring
>The tortoise stove is lit again

Despite the coal, and the stove stonking out heat left right and centre, the house has still been cold this week. The cats have been seeking out the warmest bits of the rooms they customarily inhabit, and then curling round on themselves in tight, heat-conserving balls of fur. Tonight I cooked tea (Shepherd's pie with pretend soya mince and beans) wearing a fleece, a woolly hat, and a scarf. Tig has been curled up on her sofa with her nose in her tail.

The worst problem, though, has been that we have lost all the heat and had to turn off all the water in Colin's side of the house, because of a problem with the shower not wanting to turn itself off. While we wait for the plumber to call us back (presumably next week) we freeze, and don't wash.

We have to get this fixed because next week, Becky, Adrian and little Katie Elizabeth are coming, and you can't have a young baby in a house where half of it has no heat and no water, especially if it's the half that encompasses the guest room. So, it's all hands to the pumps tomorrow.

This will be the first time I have seen Katie Elizabeth, and it has actually been a week for new babies: this week Leah came into the office with little Lucy, now all of four weeks old, and passed her around so we could all hold her, while she gurgled, burped and chuckled to herself. I was struck by two things - how small, yet how perfect, her little hands were, and that she weighed a lot less than three of our four cats.

And just yesterday, Amy posted on the Archers' web site message board that her friend Jo has had a child. Not that I know them from Adam, or Eve, but yet another manifestation of new life. All these kids coming into the world, sometimes makes the creation of a world fit for them to live in, a heavy responsibility. For Lucy, and for Katie Elizabeth, and for Jo's unnamed baby, it will be their first ever Christmas, not that they will notice much this year. But that won't stop their families trying to make it their best ever. I hope they all grow up to be loved, and come to realise, over the course of many happy Christmases, that the best presents of all are those that have no price tag.

I have a lot of trouble with the commercial aspects of Christmas. And I haven't even started Christmas shopping! On the one hand, we are part of it, we need Christmas to sell our books. But does Christmas really have to be like this? Today, for something to do to break up what would otherwise have been a day of tedious work in front of a computer, we went over to a very large garden centre near Bradford. It was a dreary drive, and the garden centre is very difficult to find (despite having, according to its adverts, "parking for over 1000 cars") and my manic singing of the "Ying Tong Song" while driving round the outskirts of Bradford did nothing to alleviate the tension. It was only when we got there that I realised the true extent of my ghastly mistake. The whole place has been entirely given over to an enormous display of Christmas tat, from giant illuminated larger-than-life-size Santas, to fibre optic trees that play "Winter Wonderland". And tat sells, it would seem, if the milling crowds of Yorkshire folk are anything to go by. The tills were definitely jing-jing-jingling while the PA system blared out a soupy, midwest, tenor's rendition of "Hark the Herald Angels Sing".

The place wasn't entirely devoid of religious context: there was a nearly life size crib, with "realistic" resin figures, a snip at £999.99, complete with a bemused looking stray plastic rabbit in one corner. Not being an expert on the fauna of first century Palestine, I can't say whether this rabbit was meant to be there, whether it was historically accurate (which I would certainly demand if I was contemplating spending £1000 on a crib) or whether it was an unfortunate carry over from a previous display (?Snow White) but at that price, I am unlikely to carry out a more exhaustive investigation. I found myself wondering who spends all this money on Christmas, and why? Parents who want "the best" for their children, I suppose, and who think that "the best" = "the most expensive". Personally, the experience made me want to behave like Jesus with the moneylenders, or George Fox shouting "woe unto the bloody city of Lichfield" (or Bradford, in this case, obviously).

Then I thought of U. A. Fanthorpe's poem, "What the Donkey Saw" where the donkey in the manger muses, looking down on the baby Jesus:

> Still, in spite of the overcrowding,
> I did my best to make them feel wanted.
> I could see the baby and I
> Would be going places together.

This week, I have spent a lot of time listening to Thomas *Tallis' Spem in Alium*, and trying to keep focused on the idea of hope in everything. In four weeks or so, the year will turn, and summer will be on its unstoppable way, however much it still snows, rains, or freezes. The idea of faith is that you have to believe in "the spark in the dark", that it is always darkest and most depressing at the point just before the light makes its comeback. You have to believe that, despite all the evidence to the contrary, things will get better. Maybe Katie Elizabeth, Lucy, and Jo's unnamed sprog are all little sparks in the dark. They weren't born in a manger, but in bright, technological, well-lit hospitals. They have been born at the best of all possible times, from the point of view of opportunity, and the worst of all possible times, from the point of view of the way the world could go. Maybe, instead of us making Christmas better for them, they will be the ones, together with others of their generation, born to see wonders which we can only dream of, ultimately, who both ask and answer the question which keeps bugging me - "Why can't it be like Christmas every day?" Maybe Katie Elizabeth will be the one who opens all the cages, and sets the turkeys free.

§

5th December 2004

It has been a busy week in the Holme Valley, work is as unrelenting as ever, but at least we can celebrate the end of the dreary month of November. We really are counting down the days to Christmas now, when we can give up hanging on by our fingernails, turn off the computers, and have a rest for a couple of days. I am so tired some mornings that I just lie there too tired to sleep, waiting for the alarm to go off, and amusing myself by going through a sort of damage-check exercise like they do on warships after they have been in battle. (Ankle - check, knee, check, wind direction and strength...)

This week has been marked by the visit of my new-born little niece, Katie Elizabeth, and her sleep-deprived parents, as part of their royal progress through the North of England to show her off to both sets of grans and grandads, prior to returning to the warmer climes of the South coast for what will be her first ever Christmas. In the last Epilogue, I suggested that her career might be in freeing turkeys. I wish to revise this. Seeing her sturdy little frame, and having heard her practising her arias at regular intervals through the early hours of the morning, I know now that she is definitely going to be an opera singer when she grows up! Talk about *Nessum Dorma*.

We managed to get the plumbing fixed temporarily - pending another visit on 10th December or thereabouts - so at least Katie

Elizabeth, Becky and Adrian had water (hot and cold) and heating. No sooner had they left though, on Thursday morning, than the stove decided to go out. This new coal is very prone to clinker and I dug out a huge nugget of the stuff, which had choked off all the air supply to the fire. I was loath to throw it away, but since the demise of *That's Life*, the market for vaguely amusing pictures of odd shaped domestic objects has declined somewhat. Perhaps I could put it in for the Turner Prize. Anyway, this episode led to my kneeling on a freezing cold floor in the ghostly pre-dawn light of a frosty Thursday morning, cursing and trying to re-light it, while Tig and Russell looked on with an air of, "Hurry up, we're cold. And you still haven't fed us yet".

Russell is still taking the tablets, provided they come liberally wrapped in chicken breast, and seems to be livelier than of late. Just as well, as he goes back to the vet to be jabbed, checked and weighed again, this week. His one setback came during Wednesday, when he did a spectacular bout of projectile vomiting, accompanied by the sort of disgusting heaving noises only puking cats can make, all over my guitar. I don't know if you have ever tried fishing gobbets of cat-sick out of the sound hole of your acoustic guitar with chunks of kitchen roll. I would imagine few people have. Debbie suggested I leave them in there, that my playing would sound better with some muffling and, as they eventually dried out and hardened, it would add a pleasant percussion effect, not unlike marraccas. I was reminded of that old joke about "what do you call a drunken Spanish guitarist? - Segovia Carpet!"

Dusty, Kitty and Nigel have all been vying for the coveted spots in the bathroom on Colin's side of the house where the hot pipes go under the floorboards to the heated towel-rail. By coincidence I heard this week that Holly Hunter, no less, is to star in a play in the West End called "By the Bog of Cats". I could give her plenty of tips. (In passing, I also heard that her attempt at an Irish accent is off the Dick-Van-Dyke scale of awfulness. Let's hope she doesn't get savaged by the critics in the same way as Pia Zadora did when she played Anne Frank. Her performance was universally adjudged to be so dismal that it is said that in act II, when the Nazi stormtroopers burst in to search the house, several people in the audience shouted "She's in the attic!")

I've been immersed in the literature of the 1930s and 40s this week, working frantically on *Hampshire at War*, reading with delight the final draft of the biography of S. P. B. Mais which we are publishing next spring, including his epic battle with the Southwick Urban District Council to allow cricket on Southwick Green, and listening to Patrick Stewart reading J. B. Priestley's wartime "Postscripts" on BBC Radio 4, which in turn drove me back to re-read "English Journey". Just before I go out and order some plus fours, spats, and a bakelite radio I should also point out, though, that I have been working on the update for the web site as well. So it's not all "2LO Writtle, this is Daventry calling."

I have also been looking at 19th century censuses, because we have had another breakthrough on the tracing Debbie's Mum's family history front. What a marvellous source these documents are: all of Victorian society laid out for all to see, the rich man in his castle, the poor man at the gate. Once every ten years, since 1841 and with the exception of wartime, the whole of our society has been counted and listed, in the same way that the Romans wanted to count everybody in Judea, as it says in the Gospel of St Luke: "A decree went out from Caesar Augustus, that a census be taken of all the inhabited earth. This was the first census taken while Quirinius was governor of Syria" I could not help but contrast this rather bumbling, paternalistic approach with the sinister developments currently surrounding ID cards in this country. Of course, there are plenty of people who do see the advent of ID cards as pretty small potatoes, including the Vicar who wrote to "The Independent" this week, pointing out that if you have nothing to hide, you have nothing to fear, and citing in support of this, John 8:32, "And the truth shall set you free". I wonder if anybody has told him yet that those words are also the motto of the US Central Intelligence Agency!

I am not particularly interested in debating the politics of this in this forum. In any case, I am writing more in a church mode than a state mode right now. There's a time and a place, etc. My own views are well enough known anyway, but the situation has been brought home to me this week because I have been corresponding with a very dear friend who is an American citizen whose leave to remain in this country is under question by the Home Office even though she wants to make the UK her home, and I could not help but contrast the bitter and prolonged struggle which has been causing her stress all this year, with the nineteen days in which applications on which Mr Blunkett's flunkies sprinkle their fairy dust seem to sail through the system. The truth shall set you free. But what is truth? said jesting Blunkett.

Freedom and responsibility is always a difficult balancing act. God knows everything that is going to happen - allegedly - but has decided to stand by and watch, in order that we might learn, and progress, and he can see what a fist we make of it. Freedom in society needs to be tempered with wariness, in the climate we find ourselves. There are, undoubtedly, seriously unbalanced people out there who would dearly love to disrupt our systems, kill our loved ones at random, and thus make their point about how much they hate us. As Orwell said: "Men sleep peacefully in their beds at night because rough men stand ready to do violence on their behalf."

But equally, we need to be wary of going too far in the other direction, of creating a climate which sacrifices the very freedoms we cherish, in the name of some form of spurious idea of security. A society like 1930s Germany, as described by Pastor Martin Niemoller:

> First they came for the Jews
> and I did not speak out, because I was not a Jew.
> Then they came for the Communists
> and I did not speak out, because I was not a Communist.
> Then they came for the trade unionists
> and I did not speak out, because I was not a trade unionist
> Then they came for me
> and there was no one left to speak out for me.

I wonder what would have happened in Palestine a millennium or so ago, if the Romans had had ID cards. Herod would certainly have found his task a lot easier.

The unfairness of the situation with my friend possibly being deported, brought to my mind the passage on the "Two Englands" from Arthur Mee's "Who Giveth Us The Victory" in 1918:

> Two Englands there are, the heavenly England that leads the world in liberty and humanity and good government, the England of Alfred and Drake and Cromwell and Gladstone; and the appalling England at our doors, with a hundred thousand taprooms thriving on misery and ruin and disease, with landlords growing rich on slums, with children creeping hungrily to school. It is for the nobler England that our armies fight and die; the baser England is not fit to die for. It is the England of our vision that we live for; but about us everywhere is that other England, established in conceit and selfishness, strengthened and stimulated by the bitter mockery of our social system, tolerated and sustained by the cynical indifference of the masses of the people.

Or, as Alan Hull wrote in "Winter Song"

> The turkey's in the oven, and the presents are all bought
> And Santa's in his capsule, he's an American astronaut
> Will you spare a thought for Jesus, who had nothing but his thoughts
> Who got busted for just talking, and befriending the wrong sorts

For centuries, England and its ideals of liberty, humanity, and good government have been both a beacon of hope and a shelter for people who were disadvantaged elsewhere and allowed to come here and flourish and contribute to the greater whole. Whatever the whys and wherefores of how we now come to be so hated, Christmas is no time to be saying there is "no room at the inn".

12th December 2004

It has been a busy week in the Holme Valley. Christmas is looming still (the commercial aspects of it, the "arrangements" which have to be arranged) casting a dismal shadow over everything, while the spiritual aspects of it seem about as far away as ever. This is without doubt the darkest time of the year, a time for looking back and seeing how little you have achieved in return for another year that has vanished like smoke before your gaze. Today, having been dragooned into going to MFI to argue about a piece of furniture that has arrived with the instructions for another, different, piece of furniture inside the box (a long story, and a boring one) I was also dragged into Matalan, which happens to be next door, and which has an even bigger collection of mindless Christmas tat than the garden centre I mentioned two weeks ago. Including a singing karaoke Christmas moose. (I am not sure if it was rational or irrational, but by the time I escaped, I was definitely the latter).

Still, we plod on. There is, in all honesty, little alternative. This week Russell went back to the vet, and had his blood tests done again. He's gone back down to his previous weight, but, as the vet said, you can also look on this as him being "stabilised", so it's not necessarily bad news, and he's obviously not deteriorating as such, in fact he is just as much of a pain as he always was, wandering around yowling for food, scrapping with the other cats, and invading the bed when he comes in freezing cold and/or wet through from the garden. Also in refusing anything less than sliced chicken to wrap round his tablet, so much so that I fear he may be contemplating holding out for an even greater delicacy. Quail in Aspic perhaps, or Swan in Caper Sauce.

Whoever invented the term "herding cats" as a euphemism for pointless and repetitive behaviour obviously got it dead right, if the cat feeding arrangements in our house are anything to go by. To understand what I am about to say, you need to know that the house is essentially two separate houses that used to abut up to each other, which have now been knocked into one. There are still two separate front doors and in essence it can still be divided into two houses, "ours" and "Colins". Colin was the old man who lived in what we now call "Colin's" until he died in 2000. Dusty and Kitty, formerly Colin's cats, now ours, still live there, and are fed there, especially as they don't mix with Russell and Nigel - well, not without much growling and many hissy-fits. Russ and Nige get fed in the porch to our house. New readers start here.

All this domestic harmony which has served us well in the feeding of cats for the last four years, is starting to break down, or so it seemed this week. I put down Russell and Nigel's food in our front porch, but instead of eating it, Russell followed me through into Colin's where Kitty was waiting for her grub. I went through the usual ritual:

"Morning, Kitty, do you want feeding later or now?"
"Naow"
" And what was the name of the Chinese leader who destabilised Chiang Kai Shek and started the Long March?"
"Maow"

Having satisfied the requirements, I filled the dishes for her and Dusty with food. Kitty immediately started munching away, but there was no sign of Dusty. Instead, however, Russell started on the other dish. They both managed to eat side-by-side, while simultaneously growling at each other, until finally Kitty gave up and exited through her cat flap with a final hiss at Russell. Owing to the fact that Russell had now eaten the food meant for Dusty, I had to go back into "our" house to get another sachet.

As I entered the kitchen, I noted that Tiggy had managed to get through the hole where the cat flap used to be, into the porch, and had demolished the cat food which I had intended for Russell and Nigel. I scolded her, brought her back in and put some dog food into her bowl, which she ignored. Nigel wandered in, sniffed at it, and also ignored it, instead choosing to follow me back into Colin's and eat what was left of Kitty's food, before exiting through their cat flap, while I was replacing Dusty's which Russell had eaten. Dusty was nowhere to be seen. Aaarrrgh! Outwitted by four small furry animals with brains the size of walnuts, and still a full day at the office to endure.

Actually I have often thought it would be amusing if cat table manners were adopted as the standard for human meals. Especially the ones you have to dress up for. I could imagine being at a formal dinner and thinking to myself "hmm, I quite like the look of Princess Anne's sprouts", going over to her and growling at her before barging her off her plate, knocking a few sprouts onto the floor and then proceeding to chase them under the sideboard and eat them covered in nice fresh fluff. Bleugh!

Other than such musings, I haven't had a lot of time for noticing what has been going on in the world this week, but I did see a couple of news stories that gave me food for thought.

A British philosophy professor who has been a leading champion of atheism for more than a half-century has changed his mind. He now believes in God, more or less based on scientific evidence, and said so on a video released last Thursday.

At the age of 81, after decades of insisting belief is a mistake, Antony Flew has concluded that some sort of intelligence or first cause must have created the universe. A super-intelligence is the only good explanation for the origin of life and the complexity of nature, Flew said in a telephone interview. Apparently he was influenced in his thinking by some of the discoveries of the new physics. Things like the search for the Higgs Bozon having led him to the conclusion that the way the universe is constructed is just too complex to be random.

However, Professor Flew thinks that this is a far cry from the sort of God who is sentient and judgemental, and who is in charge of redemption, human behaviour, and miracles and the like. Yet in the same paper, another story points out that miracles, or at least something like them, do happen.

A medieval limestone slab which for years has been used as a gravestone for a dead cat called Winkle has fetched more than £200,000 at auction. The stone has a carved image of St Peter on it and dates from the early 10th century. It was found originally in a salvage yard by a man who took it to his home in Somerset and put it at the bottom of his garden to mark the spot where Winkle was buried.

It was only when the stone was spotted by local potter and historian Chris Brewchorne that its value became apparent. "At first I thought it was Roman but I noticed the chap's head on the carving was tonsured, which suggested it was Saxon. I don't think it's an exaggeration to describe it as the finest mid-Saxon carving in the country."

The carving went under the hammer at auctioneers Sothebys on Friday. They had expected it to fetch between £40,000 and £60,000 but a private collector bought it for £201,600. The man who found it sadly died last year before it could be sold, but the money will go to his widow, a former farmer. As for Winkle, an adopted stray who, according to Mr Brewchorne "spent most of her life hanging around the local cider mills," she will be getting a new headstone.

"I'll be making one for her," he said.

Ah, England, land of miracles and recanting atheist Professors. Land of frost and fire, land of midwinter spring beings its own season ... For all its faults, and they are many, fundamentally can there be anything ultimately and incurably wrong in a country where a stray cat has a priceless Saxon carving marking its last resting place? As Arthur Mee said "every signpost points you to its wonders."

And thank God there are still enough people around with the decency and humanity to adopt a stray cat in the first place, feed it, (with its own food) and give it a decent burial when it eventually passes on (not, perhaps, to sit at God's right hand, which was my first, and possibly blasphemous, thought, but maybe on some angelic knee, purring in contentment for all eternity).

And thank God for atheists, who recognise the complexity of the incredible web of synchronicty that surrounds us. Physicists may have opened the box which constitutes the universe and found what seems to be the wrong set of instructions inside, but hey, the very fact that there are instructions means that someone/thing wrote them in the first place. As J. B. Priestley says in "An English Journey"

> To see Beverley Minster suddenly hanging in the sky is as astonishing as hearing a great voice intoning some noble line of verse. I am no Catholic, no medievalist, no Merrie Englander, - though I have seen things on this journey that have come nearer to converting me than all their books - but I cannot help asking myself and you why our own age, which boasts of its conquest of material things, never seems to offer us here any of these superb aethetic surprises. You go up and down this country and what makes you jump with astonishment and delight is something that has been there for at least five hundred years ... if you want to know the difference between working for the glory of God and working for the benefit of debenture holders, simply take a journey and keep your eyes open.

19th December 2004

It has been a busy week in the Holme Valley. It is the year's deep midnight and it is the day's, as Donne said of St Lucy's day (who "scarce seven hours herself unmasks".) Actually, unbeknown to John Donne (rave on, John Donne) Lucy - the one that I know - hasn't been "unmasking" herself at all, but has been very sensibly curled up in front of the fire with Freddie, across the valley at Berry Brow.

So, this is the week when we have nearly reached the turning point - the "still point of the turning world", as Eliot put it. In the words of the song "I noticed tonight that the world had been turning". The ascent towards Christmas has been like toiling up a rocky pass between two mountains, and finally we have reached that flat shoulder at the top of the climb where you can look down in to the valley beyond, the valley called 2005. At the top of the pass is an inn called Christmas, where we will spend a few days resting and carousing and where we hope there will be room for everyone, before we have to press on.

Russell has been keeping a low profile this week, indeed all of the cats have. The tide of cold air that seeps through the house has left them stranded high and dry in odd places where there are isolated pockets of heat - under the heated towel rail in the bathroom, in a box of gone away envelopes in the office and, most usually, curled up in the armchairs nearest the kitchen stove. Russell had a bad "do" during the week, when the paroxsyms of his coughing and heaving were giving cause for concern, but he calmed down again and went to sleep in the chair, on top of my fleece. Like Mohammed with the tabby cat, I didn't have the heart to move him.

Tig has spent her time dozing with her nose in her tail, waiting, like the rest of us. Do they know it's Christmas? Probably not, their lives are like a permanent Christmas anyway.

From my vantage point at the top of this imaginary Christmas pass, I can look both forwards and backwards, backwards over the past week and forwards into next year. The past week has actually had little to comment it. At one point I was in a meeting during which someone broke off to take a mobile phone call from a graphic designer in Hungary, called Attilla (I kid you not) which was mainly about inflatable guitars. Debbie's Christmas "do" on Tuesday night was the usual volatile mix of alcohol and social workers, which inevitably continued into early Wednesday morning. While driving into town to pick her up, a group of drunken young male revellers - or, as I prefer to call them, prats in Santa hats, spilled into the road in front of me, trying to stop me and flag me down under the mistaken assumption that I was a taxi. I am ashamed to say that it was only the thought of the paperwork, and how bad prison food can be, that made me finally decide to swerve and miss them.

Arriving at the joint just as they were tipping out, I found little to report, except that someone had apparently tried to pick up Gail, one of Debbie's co-workers, with the immortal chat-up line "Scuse me luv, are you normal?" Ah, Huddersfield, Verona of the North.

Then on Thursday the windscreen wipers packed up on the car, which meant much chuffing about with batteries and fuses, only to discover the motor has burnt itself out. This is probably my punishment from on high for having bad thoughts about winging drunken yobs the night before. On my way to the garage, I drove past a house which had outside it an 8 foot high illuminated inflatable Homer Simpson in a Santa suit. Please, Lord, I have suffered enough.

One way or another, Santa Claus has been present in the background a lot this week. We watched the programme on TV on Saturday about the real St Nicholas. His bones were stolen from the Turkish shrine which contained them, by the fishermen of the Italian port of Bari, where most of them now lie (give or take the odd jawbone and bit of the true cross) in the basilica there, where every year the priests draw off a mysterious liquid (known as "manna" that seeps from them. Urgh.) The programme used reconstructive computer technology to build up a 3-D picture of what he must have looked like, based on a detailed survey done when the tomb was last opened in 1953. They even lowered a camera on a stick down a crevice into the tomb, to see if he was still there.

Debbie then pointed out to me that it can't be the real St Nicholas, because "where are the bones of all the reindeer?" This led us on to a detailed discussion of the names of the reindeer, and the following exhaustive canonical list: Rudolph, Dasher, Prancer, Donner, Kebab, Blitzen, Dave Dee, Dozy, Beaky, Mick and Titch. It's like the four horsemen of the Apocalypse, you can only ever remember three of them at any given time.

Sunday I spent fixing Debbie's mother's emails, and proving conclusively that it was working by sending her a test email which popped up straight away on her machine a mile away across the valley. I phoned her to see if she had got it. "Yes, well, I seem to be getting yours anyway. At least if you've fixed it so I can get local emails, that's better than nothing." I suggested she send her friend in Canada an email asking her to reply as a test, so we could see how far "local" extended!

Then in the afternoon, I ferried Deb to Meadowhall. I didn't particularly want to go, as I thought I had already seen enough of the commercial bits of Christmas, but I did venture into Past Times, which had a large display of statues of the Buddha, under a notice which proclaimed "The perfect gift for Christmas". Do they know it's Christmas time at all?

I have been waiting for the turning point of the year, for Christmas with all its miracles, for what seems like such a long time, that now it's finally in sight I feel rather numb. The world seems drab, dreary and full of bad things at large. Gyres run on - and what rough beast, its hour come round at last slouches towards Bethlehem to be born? The chinese Book of Changes, the I Ching, (probably what the Buddha will be getting for Christmas, in a special Past Times edition) talks of the passes between the mountains being sealed at the solstices, so that no one could travel. Back again to the idea of the point of stillness. So maybe what I need to do this week (and this may only work for me, I am not saying it's OK for you too) is to concentrate on the idea of the stillness. Forget the inflatable guitars and the mobile phones and the windscreen wipers and the Homer Simpsons and the karaoke Moose (rational and irrational) and sit still and enjoy the rest while I can. Listening for the quiet voice that says it's finally, OK to celebrate.

26th December 2004

It has been a busy week in the Holme Valley. Frost, snow, wind , raid, and then frost again, and finally snow. As I sit typing this, on Boxing Day, in my little office at the top of the house, we have the central heating on both sides, Colin's and ours, plus the stove going full blast, and I am still wearing a poncho, an alpaca woolly hat, and on top of that a fleece bobble hat, and I have at my elbow a warming nip of Talisker. And I am STILL cold. I must look like Chris Bonington crossed with Clint Eastwood.

The animals have all made the most of Christmas. All of the cats have got new collars and Tig has got a personalised dog blanket and a squeaky goose toy. Russell refused to take his tablet on Christmas morning, even when it was wrapped in chicken breast, but what he didn't reckon on was that Deb's mother (aka the Neigbourhood Witch) was coming round, and that he would be sized by strong women, rolled in a towel, and have his pill popped down him with one of those thingies from the vet specially crafted for giving cats tablet without getting yourself clawed to shreds. His dignity ruffled, he retreated behind a chair, unnoticed until he made a daring comeback, three quarters of the way through Christmas dinner, when he leapt onto the table, nicked a chunk of Brie, clingfilm and all, and was off under the kitchen units with it clamped in his jaws before anyone could move a muscle to stop him. We all froze, sprouts on forks half way to our open mouths, aghast, and I uttered a silent and heartfelt prayer of thanks that he was well enough to do commit that theft, bearing in mind the year he's had. Needless to say, he didn't appear again until the Brie was all gone, apart from the remnants on his paws that he proceeded to smear over his head. This is another cats' eating habit that it would be amusing if humans adopted, I can just see us all dipping our hands into the gravy and plastering it across our hair.

There were eight of us for Christmas lunch, which is why I was up and prepping veg at 7.30am. Alan, who Deb has spent a lot of time looking after but who she has rather lost touch with since he moved out, turned up unexpectedly but was a most welcome guest. Last Christmas, it was just me, Alan and Deb for Christmas dinner in the Lake District, so this year was a grander affair. And I didn't manage to set myself on fire this year either! The others were Debbie's family, apart from Damion and Paul, who are two of Deb's other charges. Both of them use wheelchairs, but because of the difficult access to the house, they were both "walked" in by Deb and her mother.

When they left, John came to collect them in the official car, and to save time, he and Deb actually carried Paul, who was helpless with laughter, out to the car, one under his arms, one holding his feet. God along knows what the neighbours must've thought, if any of them had been looking out at that time and seeing what must have looked like a very paralytic guest being poured back into a taxi!

It was great to see everybody round the table in the candlelight, tucking into festive fare, and I did try and give thanks, both to St Padre Pio and to Big G himself, that we'd made it to Christmas. Yes, 2005 is going to be a tough year, full of all sorts of challenges, but that is NEXT year's problem. For now, let's just rejoice in each other and the season, and be glad.

This must have been how it felt on the Western Front in 1914, when the British trenches heard the sound of "Stille Nacht, Heilige Nacht" floating across no-man's land. What a tragedy that the truce didn't spread far enough and fast enough to stop the war in its tracks. Instead, it became like Christmas will be to us, a brief island of peace in a world that is soon going to be back to its normal self, the world of "telegrams and anger."

But for now, I have achieved a strange type of peace. I sang *Stille Nacht* myself, to myself in the car, driving back in the rain and wind, with the motor overheating. All the verses. In German. Well done, Frau Graham, wherever you are now, you were an excellent teacher. And then I topped it off with "In the Bleak Midwinter"

> What can I give him, poor as I am
> If I were a shepherd, I would bring a lamb

> If I were a wise man, I would do my part
> But what I have I give him - give my heart

My own taste in carols tends towards the bolshie though. I am a great fan of the traditional "Withy Carol" where Mary sends Jesus out to play, and he meets three rich young lords. He asks them to play with him, and they refuse, saying:

> For you are nothing but a Jew's child, born in an oxen stall

So he does what any self respecting saviour who has been "dissed" would do - he builds a bridge out of the beams of the sun, and dances over the river. The rich young lords follow after him, and are all drowned. Their mothers naturally complain to Mary, who thrashes Jesus with a bundle of withy twigs - he then curses the willow and says it will be the very first tree to perish each winter. Not a very forgiving saviour, but one that appealed to my left-wing tendencies when I first heard that carol, over two decades ago. I have to say, in those two decades, Christmas as a whole has got a lot less spiritual. A lot less connected.

When we were going round Sainsburys on Thursday night, buying our own modest Christmas shopping list, I couldn't help but feel amazed at the amount of consumption going on all around us. While the speakers blared "I wish it could be Christmas every day" the tills were adding their own descants of joy for Sainsburys' shareholders. I bet they DO wish it could be Christmas every day. Me I would like to see a stall set up in the car park, taxing people 10% of their Christmas shopping bill and sending the money to Darfur, or even to one of those estates in the North of England where the trainers get handed down through the brothers in the family until they are so old and warn out that all there is to do is to burn them on the fire to try and keep warm, because coal costs too much. Or to the homeless, making the most of their week in the Dome that costs £250,000 of our taxes a month to keep empty. Because in seven days time, they will be back out in the cold, and I bet they wish it could be Christmas every day, too. Where is that bridge made out of sunbeams when you need it?

I wish it could be Christmas every day. I wish that we could keep that spirit and pay it forward through 2005. If I require anything of 2005, I would settle for reports of truces breaking out all over the world, of hungry people being fed, of sad people being given a meal, a fire, a pet to cuddle, some human warmth and charity.

In a world where even Santas have to have police checks, 2005 no doubt has some fairly dismal things in store for us and ours. Things that will test us, and our beliefs, situations we'd rather not be in, places where it would be oh so easy to cross by on the other side. We can retaliate though. Every time in 2005 somebody does something mean spirited or bad within your sight and hearing - say to them "shame on you, it's Christmas". Even if it's July 29th. Every time in 2005 you see someone needing a hand up, or a good feed, say to them "I can help you, - it's Christmas." Even if it's April 6th. Every time you are asked to turn your back on all the things that make each one of us the incalculable and never to be repeated beings that make up this crazy old world, say "No, I can't - it's Christmas, and I will give, give, and give again, until the need for giving, and for forgiving, is removed from the face of the Earth." Even if it's May 15th. Or December 2nd, or January 6th. Then it really will be Christmas every day, and we'll have gone a long way towards having something to really celebrate.

§

2nd January 2005

It has been a busy week in the Holme Valley. With Christmas finally out of the way, I've been able to begin the much needed re-organisation of the office. So far I have re-organised two bin bags of filing into the recycling, so I am going well.

Tig has been troubled with a problem with one of her claws, which I think I finally solved by pulling the offending bit of old claw off the new one underneath. Ouch! Anyway, she's now moving at normal pace again. That's the trouble with furry children, they can't tell you where it hurts. Russell has been taking his tablets like a good un, and eating like a house-end, so at least from his point of view, it's a positive start to the new year. Kitty remains welded to her "cat bed" in Colin's house, especially when the central heating is on and it's snowing or hailing outside.

The surprise development over the holidays though has been the growth of Dusty into the bad ass momma cat that rules the streets, now she has taken over possession of our bed. It's been quite amusing to see Russell's eyes grow as big as saucers as he sees her emerge from under the very duvet where he was sitting not a moment before, and the other morning Dusty was under the duvet and Nigel was on top of it; he then got off and I watched him pad very warily through the office, watching out for Dusty at every step, little knowing he'd just been rolling on top of her. Not the sharpest pencil in the box. This morning I left Dusty and Nigel in a state of armed neutrality on top of our bed. Like two muggers in a late-night railway carriage, neither wanted to be the first to fall asleep, for fear of what the other might do. They'll learn.

Of course, this week, the whole holiday has been overwhelmed, by a tidal wave.

We watched the news with dropping jaws, as each day brought further statistical carnage. Unlike other previous disasters, this is also one which has been played out on the internet. So much so that I found myself locked in a bitter controversy, on a message board, with someone who asked where God's compassion was in all of this. The problem is that God's compassion isn't newsworthy, so it never gets reported. All those acts of selfless kindness, the cancer patients who go into remission, and the people who are miraculously saved from some disaster of their own making, are hardly a blip on the newsometer. Whereas disaster footage ...well, good news is no news and bad news sells news.

Also, by definition, the mind of God is unknowable to mankind. That assumes you believe God to be eternal, omniscient and omnipresent, by definition, we cannot know what God knows. Therefore, theologically, it is entirely possible that God had a reason for this act which is unknown and unknowable to us. In the same way as we cannot imagine a being that could take upon itself the guilt and sorrow of 60,000 deaths, when we know from our own experience how terrible having just one death on our conscience would be. Of course, to God, life and death presumably do not have the same meaning as to us.

But then people ask "why did his creation (man) turn out to be so imperfect". This is a question I have often asked, and the only answer I can come up with is that it is to do with free will. Although God knows that man may go astray, mankind has to be allowed the free will to make his own mistakes (such as not having a Tsunami early warning system, which I understand will probably now be one outcome of this disaster) even though God knows how it will turn out, he/she/it has allowed mankind the freedom to learn by making mistakes.

You will never "prove" God's intentions one way or another - that is why religion comes down to faith in the end. Who is to say for instance that the Tsunami warning system which will be evolved as a result of this cataclysm would not save twice as many or a hundred times as many lives in a potential future disaster? Or that God didn't intervene, in the many miracles of personal survival now coming to light?

Incidentally, all this is no comfort at all to anyone who has suffered a loss in this disaster and I am sorry for my tone if you have, and you are reading this, but I was trying to respond specifically to the theological points.

I have just spent some considerable time logging on to the various blogs available which carry news of the Tsunami relief efforts and the impression I have gained is that people in the aid agencies are faced with the biggest thing that has ever hit them, are doing absolute wonders, but that thousands - maybe hundreds of thousands - of people who managed to survive the Tsunami are still going to die because of the limited resources available to the aid agencies and the lack of any overall co-ordinating forces on the ground which can use modern, up to date telecomms and monitoring to make sure that things get to where they are needed. Already on the blogs we are seeing people in one location posting things like "don't send any more blankets here, it is a waste of time, what we need is rice" etc., while another location is crying out for blankets, and by the time everything gets to where it should be, it may be too late. The aid agencies are doing heroically, as usual, but it needs something bigger than what we can provide by holding jumble sales and telethons.

People in the UK have been brilliant as usual, raising millions in three days for the appeal, but by the time this money is processed and turned into practical help, again, time will have ticked by. There are organisations in the world that already exist that have the materials and the manpower and the technological know how to take over the aid operation and make it work in time. Primarily of course, the US armed forces. Like it or not, the USA has the wherewithal to do this, but not the political will. Obviously there are some things where the UN can safely be left alone! Sorting out

WMD in Iraq, no, that's Bush's baby, but rescuing survivors of third world people, nope, that's one for the UN. Our own government is just as bad. Not a word out of Blair, no commitment to send troops to help.

I have long argued that apart from the essential forces needed for our own defences, the weapons industry and the world's armies should be transmuted to a world wide disaster relief civil defence organisation under the control of the UN. The same technology used to guide a missile can also be used to locate survivors and guide supplies to them. Maybe now is the time to start on this process.

If Bush and Blair want to be seen as the world's policemen and taken seriously, if they want people like me who they have turned into cynical non-believers by their cherry-picking actions to start believing in them again, get some boots on the ground in South East Asia, NOW and set up a telecomms network for the aid agencies to coordinate their efforts before yet more people die, this time of a surfeit of blankets. If ever there WAS a time for unilateral UKUS intervention, this is it.

So, it's been a pretty serious week, and by the time it got to New Year's Eve, I was feeling decidedly muted. We thought we would go out for a meal, but there were no meals to be had. One pub we phoned very helpfully said "as it's New Year's Eve, we have stopped doing meals in favour of a karaoke!". Well, thanks a whole bundle there. In the end, we ordered a takeaway from The Balooshai, the best curry house in Huddersfield by a country mile. Only trouble is, you have to go and collect it, they don't deliver. Town was deserted. Rainy, empty streets, and the only vehicles around were taxis and police cars. Happy New Year.

We ended up going to a traditional pub, at Linthwaite, where they brew their own beer and weave their own curtains. Or vice versa, having tasted the product. Despite a notice that claimed to welcome dogs, they made us leave Tiglet in the car, so we didn't stay long. Then we came back, to celebrate the bongs at home, me with Talisker, Deb with Amaretto. I swept the old year out, in the way Granny Wellgate had taught me, and came back in with a piece of coal. No sign of life from the neighbours, and apart from the fireworks, you wouldn't have noticed anything going on.

Un-noticed by anyone, then, a New Year slipped in. The sheep have started lambing (at least on The Archers) in the New Year snow. This reminds me of the stories about the genesis of the Council for the Protection of Rural England, when Gerald Haythornthwaite of the Sheffield and Peak District branch back in the 1940s, used to go and organise volunteers to look for lost lambs in the snow. This in the worst post-war winter we have ever had - 1948. I have a photo of Granny Welgate and her neighbour digging themselves out of their back gardens at Elloughton Dale. The snow drifts are higher than their heads.

The idea of the lost sheep in the snow always makes me think of the Bible, and the parable of the lost sheep from Luke 15: 3-7:

"Which of you men, if you had one hundred sheep, and lost one of them, wouldn't leave the ninety-nine in the wilderness, and go after the one that was lost, until he found it? When he has found it, he carries it on his shoulders, rejoicing. When he comes home, he calls together his friends and his neighbours, saying to them, 'Rejoice with me, for I have found my sheep which was lost!' I tell you that even so there will be more joy in heaven over one sinner who repents, than over ninety-nine righteous people who need no repentance."

The discovery of the lost sheep, for the shepherd, is, perhaps, routine. What would be a miracle to a shepherd? Three strange, rich, wise, foreigners, turning up at a stable where a child had been born because of a lack of Christmas accommodation? And their claiming that they had been led there by a star?

Next week, as well as Epiphany, marks the traditional anniversary of Plough Monday. The farmers' traditional prayer is "God Speed the Plough". This day (January 7th) is traditionally the first Monday after the Twelve Days of Christmas is over and represents getting back to work after the holidays. On the Sunday before Plough Monday, ploughs are taken to church for a special blessing. On Plough Monday, however, you are supposed to decorate your plough and have your plough-boy (called a Plough Bullock or Plough Stot) drag your plough all over the neighbourhood asking for "plough-money" ("a penny for the ploughboy") which is supposed to be spent in "a frolic," and food and drink. At the frolic, or banquet, later that day, the whole village joins in Mummers' plays, enacting ritual combat and symbolic death and revival, and Molly dancing. A queen, known as Bessy, is then crowned and farm workers do sword dances around the ploughs.

So: next week contains both redemption - for the lost sheep who comes back to the fold - and hard work, for the ploughboys starting the year to come. Well, I have always welcomed both, so keep 'em coming. As Paul Simon said: I need a shot of redemption

And to all you lost sheep out there - the aid is on its way, just hold on. Hold on. You may feel the shepherd has let you down, and I don't blame you. But maybe you don't know the whole story. Maybe you can't know the whole story. Come back to the fold, and come back to us.

9th January 2005

It has been a busy week in the Holme Valley. And a wild, woolly, and windy one too. On Friday night it was like that Ted Hughes poem

> This house has been far out at sea all night
> The woods crashing through darkness, the booming hills ...

On Saturday morning we awoke to some minor damage in the garden (a very heavy shrub in an equally heavy pot had been tipped over, and all the plastic chairs on the decking were all piled in a heap at one end, as if cuffed there by the angry sweep of a giant hand. There are a couple of tiles off Colin's roof) but all in all we got off lightly, compared to Carlisle, where they are probably still reading this by candlelight, and of course, compared to the Tsunami.

Bizarrely, the council chose Saturday morning to remove (at 9.15AM, using angle grinders) to metal and glass bus shelter just up the road from us. Deb slept through this and when she got up, an hour or so later, I was able to kid her on for some considerable time that it had actually blown away in the storm.

The animals dislike this weather even more than we do, if that is possible. This week, all four cats have subtly realigned their territories in response to Dusty having claimed ownership of our bed. Nigel has swopped sides completely, and now sleeps in the spare room in Colin's side, or, in extremis, under the heated towel rail in Colin's bathroom. Russell remains firmly lodged in the armchair nearest the stove, rejecting all attempts to evict him. Kitty is on her designer cat bed in the music room (not that we've had time for music). Kitty and I now have a new routine when it's time to feed her.

>   Me: "What do we want? Whiskas. When do we want it?"
>   Kitty "Naow"

Earlier in the week, before the stormy weather struck, we had a couple of spring-like days, when I found myself inexplicable singing Dowland's "Fine Knacks for Ladies" as I drove to the warehouse to do the stock-take. This led on to thoughts of another itinerant pedlar, Autolycus, and I found myself reciting

>   When daffodils begin to peer
>   With hey, the doxy, o'er the dale…

I haven't seen any daffodils yet, though the three pots of daffodil bulbs that Maisie gave us last year seem to have thrived on frost, snow, rain, and neglect, and are showing green shoots on the decking. Fair daffodils, that come before the swallow dares, and take the winds of March with beauty: I haven't seen any crocuses, yet though, my own personal harbinger of spring. According to Autolycus, the red blood reigns in the winter's pale. No, I have no idea what it means either, but it may be worth bearing in mind.

Last week, Russ the Puss went back to the vet and it was good news, he has again put on weight and now tops off the 3KG mark. All we have to do is keep stuffing him with food and with kidney tablets.

Tig also accompanied us to the vet, having gained an infection of the nether regions, dogs being so much more disgusting than cats. So she now has tablets too, four a day, which takes to five the number of pills we are currently pushing down various furry gullets. Kitty soon will need her 6 monthly rodent ulcer shot, and the vets have just put down a deposit on a place in the country. It's called Shropshire.

On Friday, Maisie gave us a large, leather-bound Bible dated 1885, as a thank you for some help on a problem with Windows 95 (don't even ask, don't even go there). It's a substantial tome, beautiful to handle, and, handling it, I recalled a notice I once saw outside of a church in a town I drove through, way back when. "If Jesus is the answer, what is the question?" Probably, in this case, "What would you say if you accidentally dropped this Bible on your foot?" would fit the bill.

The fact that this Bible somehow found its way on to the secondhand books market is a bit of a sad reflection on how we treat our religious heirlooms, though. In the same week, I happened to see a programme on TV about Salisbury Cathedral in which one Jonathan Meade referred to it as a monument to the credulous. And I had another concrete illustration of the state of decay of general "religious knowledge" when speaking to one of the young girls at the warehouse. We were talking about the calendar and anniversaries, etc, and she said she was looking forward to Pancake Tuesday. I said, yes, but after that comes Ash Wednesday, and she said that that was pretty tasty too. Puzzled, I tried to tease out what she meant. Apparently her and her family have always had corned beef hash on "Hash Wednesday" as they knew it. I suppose it makes a kind of sense. Pancake Tuesday, Hash Wednesday. At least they didn't smoke Hash, merely ate it.

It just goes to show though, what we've lost in the last twenty or thirty years. Only a million people go to church now, and I'm not one of them. Things like the Tsunami don't help, challenging people's faith and bringing to the fore the question that always troubles me, too: why doesn't a compassionate God intervene in the world to stop suffering?

As I said last week, I have been having arguments about this all across the internet. One of the most powerful arguments for the existence of God in this respect was on a message board where someone had posted the message "why didn't God intervene in the Tsunami?" and someone had put underneath - "How do you know he didn't?" While we don't like to think that it could have been even worse, nevertheless, when we wake up to the damage that just a minor storm in the middle of England can do, when we think about the awesome power of grinding tectonic plates that can knock the whole Earth an inch off its axis, it makes you realise that we are up against some pretty serious forces here.

And that's before you add in the human element. What if giving aid to the Tsunami victims prevents Blair and Bush from invading Iran and starting a third world war. In that scenario, God has taken upon itself the guilt and responsibility for 150,000 deaths to save the lives of millions. The bottom line is, no one can know, and it comes down to a leap of faith. Waves can be a force for good, for renewable energy. They can even be an expression of love, as Florizel says to Perdita in "A Winter's Tale":

> When you do dance, I wish you
> A wave o' the sea, that you might ever do
> Nothing but that.

Or Yeats's fiddler, who, when he plays on his fiddle in Dooney, folk dance like the wave o' the sea. Everything goes in waves, like Nigel Mazlyn Jones says in "Wave on Wave":

> And then a wave comes ...

So I handled this Bible, two years older than my Grandmother, and unlike her, still with us, and opened it at random, like you do: this is what I found - I kid you not.

> God *is* our refuge and strength, a very present help in trouble. Therefore will we not fear, though the earth be removed, and though the mountains be carried into the midst of the sea; though the waters thereof roar and be troubled; though the mountains shake with the swelling thereof.

Now that is decidedly spooky. Almost as spooky as now, when I am sitting at the top of the house listening to the wind groan and rumble through the trees outside and the doors clattering each time it gusts, because they won't shut properly and every time the wind moves in, the house breathes like a living being, slumbering in its sleep and muttering in a dream.

I don't mind Big G giving me signs when I have asked for them, but that was definitely taking liberties with our relationship.

I suppose I am being told to ride the wave, that every situation, no matter how apparently hopeless, also carries with it the seeds of its opposite. No matter how bad it seems at the moment, if you are stuck under some plastic sheeting in Sumatra or miserable in a flooded house in Carlisle, if you are remembering a lost and well-loved pet, as I know Sean is tonight, or staring for the umpteenth time at a duplicated letter of rejection, things **will** get better, and then another-nother wave comes. Or, as the Zen masters put it:

> Sitting quietly, doing nothing, Spring comes and the grass grows by itself

16th January 2005

It has been a busy week in the Holme Valley. I know I always tend to start that way, these days, but it really has been a busy week this week, with long term planning and only 50 weeks to go until Christmas! (now there is a cheery thought). It's also been a week of storms and problems. The "storms" bit is self-explanatory really.

We have lain abed listening to the wind crashing about in the trees outside, woken to find discarded branches in the driveway, driven through rain so hard that the windscreen wipers could barely cope, even on double click, and in the midst of all this, the engine on the faithful old car has decided to develop a serious head gasket problem, and is going off to the garage at Crosland Moor to be fixed tomorrow. I will be without it for three whole days and will no doubt feel like my legs have been cut off, even though Phil has boldly stepped into the breach and offered to chauffeur me to the warehouse and back. Just as well really, as stocktaking's still not finished, and the VAT return is once more overdue.

Tig, Freddie and Lucy have been as eager to venture forth for their daily "constitutionals" as ever. Deb and her mother, less so, especially when the wind is pelting horizontal sleet across the valley. The cats have been reluctant to leave the house except where absolutely necessary, but mainly spend their time drowsing and dreaming in various chairs and other warm places scattered throughout the house, whiskers twitching and paws trembling as they stalk the mouse of their dreams. Dusty has now firmly taken over our bed, Nigel has retaliated by seizing control of the armchair in the spare room,

Russell remains as near to the fire as he can get without singeing, and Kitty, well Kitty has a variety of places where she may be found, but not when she has to go to the vet. Twice this week, at the sight of Debbie approaching bearing the cat-carrier to get her inside to take her to Donaldsons for her quarterly "rodent ulcer" jab, Kitty has legged it through the cat flap. Of course, today, when Debbie was collecting the ironing from Colin's side of the house, where should Kitty be, safe in the knowledge that vets don't open on a Sunday, but curled up inside the open abandoned cat carrier, fast asleep and purring.

I've been working on the S. P. B. Mais book, the web site, the accounts, and doing some marketing, turn and turn about, so I have been shamefully neglectful of things like emails and message boards. I know for instance, that one of the founding members of my I-church group has recently suffered a sad loss, of her mother, and coincidentally, Jonty from the Archers' web site has just lost his mother as well. I hope both of them realise that they can email me if they need anything, although I have done precious little to offer any condolences. In my experience of these things, when my Mum died in 1986 and my Dad in 1992, it's not so much at the time that it hits you. For me, in both cases, making the arrangements and sorting out the funeral etc was something which carried me along, it was only afterwards that I sat down and tried to come to terms with the loss. I went through many mornings of waking up not having remembered my dad had died, and then it suddenly hitting me. Sometimes I had dreams where I had long conversations with him, and occasionally I still do, sometimes he is bizarrely present in modern circumstances, chatting to people he never even knew.

You can also be angry with them for dying. My sister and I ransacked my dad's house, convinced he would have left us a note at least to say goodbye, but we never found one. In the end, we came to assume that maybe he thought he had more time than he did. It's a completely illogical reaction, it's the mind saying "now you've really landed me in it, what am I going to do". The important thing is to deal with it without feeling guilty. The other thing that happens is you blame yourself. If only you had done this or that, but in fact, it's usually not your fault, believe me. They would not want you to beat yourself up, if they could tell you this, they would want you to get on with your life and remember their love and their life in the best way you can.

The only consolation I can offer is that - again, in my own experience - the hurt does fade after a while and is replaced with regret, yes, but also affection, and remembrance. Especially remembrance. I constantly think how my mother and father would have reacted to situations I now find myself in, and in that way, they live on, through my definition of them. Strange as it may seem, I find myself laughing about what I know they would have said or done, if they had been in the situation I was at the time. My mother, for instance, was a big fan of country and western music. At the time she was alive, my sister and I both thought this was a bit naff, and used to pour scorn on people like Jim Reeves and Slim Whitman.

Yet, here I am, nineteen years later, driving to work this week with Martin Simpson on the cassette deck singing about Patsy Kline and "Hawkshaw" and the boys, in the wonderful "Love Never Dies". In one of the verses, the singer describes how the guitar he has given Hawkshaw survives the plane wreck that killed Patsy Kline (it must have been absolute murder driving across America in the 1950's dodging all these plummeting country and western stars falling out of the sky in their malfunctioning planes - look out! It's the Big Bopper! Over there! Buddy Holly! Behind you! Jim Reeves etc etc. Think of the insurance premiums.)

> Love never dies, lust loses its shine for sure
> Friendship can fade or be forced to a close
> Frost follows clear skies in the flatlands I come from, but
> At that Arkansas truck-stop, love never dies.

Late last year, when the father of one of my ex's died, I sent her an email which said what a good bloke I thought he was (he was, he offered to set me up in business with a small shop, back in the 1980s, foolishly at the time, I said I would rather plough my own furrow) and I ended by saying that love never dies, and if you believe that, then you have to believe that the love that we felt for these people who have gone on before, and the love they felt for us, is still in the world somewhere, and we can still tap into it and use it.

When I lived with the girl in question, our house had six coal seams running underneath it, from the old Wharncliffe Woodmoor colliery, which had closed long before we moved to Carlton. It was only later that I found out the rough poetry of their names: Barnsley Main, Top Haigh Moor Seam, Lidgett Seam, Beamshaw Seam, Winter Seam, and Kent Seam. We knew at the time though, from local records and what old people in the area told us, that there were still bodies under the ground in these seams, unrecoverable from the great disaster in 1936 which claimed 57 lives and was the second-worst pre-war mining disaster in Britain, beaten only be Gresford in 1934.

People used to ask me if the thought bothered me, and I have to say that it didn't. The dead have gone from us in body, and have made their final statements, their lives are sealed off from us, just in the same way as those shafts were sealed when the colliery was finally closed in 1966. But to the people who knew them, who called them husband, dad or grandad, they never left completely, they never really went away, they were always at the edge of their thoughts, just as my mum and dad are to me, now.

I am not about to say that they are just in the next room, and "death means nothing at all". It isn't that simple for me, partially because I don't have Canon Henry Scott Holland's faith. But as I have written before, the exciting discoveries of modern physics are telling us more and more that there are other places, other dimensions, where lives which have ended in this dimension may be continuing and flourishing. Maybe we can come up with a word for this. We could call it "heaven". I find this of comfort, I hope others might. And if Philip Larkin and Martin Simpson (the unlikeliest of bedfellows) both say it, then it must be true: Love never dies.

23rd January 2005

It has been a busy week in the Holme Valley. And a frustrating one. I don't know about careless rapture, but I could tell you a lot about car-less rapture, after the garage took a week to replace the cracked cylinder head and rebuild the engine from the bottom up, fixing two oil leaks along the way. During that time the long-suffering Phillip very kindly got up very early and came and fetched me so I could get to the warehouse and my other office, every day. And delivered me home again in the evening. We've added another 250 miles to the van's odometer doing it though, and despite his kindness, by the end of the week I felt a bit like a parcel. All I needed was a label saying "not wanted on voyage".

Travelling with Phil has led to some strange journeys. I am used to having that hour-to-ninety-minutes journey alone, and ruminating during the enforced silence. With Phil, we had conversations. This showed up just how dull my wits are in the morning. We were listening to the news item about the scientists who have decided that only certain people are susceptible to mosquito bites and how it's a question of body odour. I was telling Phil that if that was the case, then I was safe, because any midges that came near me would certainly shrivel and die, when it occurred to me that I could not for the life of me remember what that stuff was we burnt in the garden, during our summer barbecues, to keep mozzies at bay. Eventually, it was bugging me so much I had to get the mobile out and call Deb.

Me: What do they call that stuff we burn when we're having a barbecue so we don't get bitten by mosquitos
Deb: Citronella. [Long pause] Has Phil's van got midges then?

Actually this isn't the first strange conversation we have had involving mozzies: once, when we were having a barbecue, our (Polish) neighbour leaned over the fence and asked us if we were "troubled by midgets [sic]" Several answers suggested themselves ("Who do you think I am, Snow White?") but in the end, we smiled and nodded.

Another morning, the conversation turned to the fact that Will Allsop - a visionary architect and town planner, wants to build a mega-opolis of the future along the M62 corridor, linking Liverpool and Hull. He is also the architect who wants to turn Barnsley into a Tuscan hill-town, complete with city wall, which is fine by me, as long as they lock them in at evenings and weekends.

Thinking of Hull took my mind back to the phone conversation I had had with someone when I told them I had been born in a Prefab, and for some reason they thought that was funny. I doubt Granny Rudd laughed very much when Bean Street came up in the cross-hairs of the Luftwaffe bomb-sight and vanished in a cloud of dust and flying bricks, in common with almost 90% of Hull's housing stock, 1939-45. Still, at least she got a new prefab out of it.

The weather continues to bite. As I type this, the central heating is on in both houses, the convector heater is going full blast as well (with Russell in attendance) in the middle of the office floor, I am wearing a Berghaus fleece (none of your cheap rubbish) and STILL my hands are blue with cold. And there is no sign of spring.

Actually, I say that but there are snowdrops in the garden. I know my official harbinger of spring is the first crocus, but I suppose I could say that the snowdrops herald the potentiality of spring, the inevitability of spring. Snowdrops always make me think of that song by Barry Dransfield, "Fair Maids of February" where he sings about the snowdrops that flowered too early

> But with no-one to court us, our courage it failed us
> And now we're lying beneath the snow

There have been times this week when I have felt as irrelevant as the snowdrops. The animals all hate this weather as much as I do. Dusty has permanently set up her winter HQ under the duvet of our bed, while Kitty is snuggled in the free cat-tent which we got with Felix tokens. Nigel has been under the heated towel rail in Colin's bathroom, and Russell can be found stationed squarely "front and centre" in relation to any heat source, fire or stove.

Tig has been suffering from what the vet describes as "arthritic twinges" of late, and suddenly yelping in pain. On Thursday night, I let her out at 11pm to do her necessary activities in the garden, while I tended the stove. Normally at that time of night, she is quickly back in again, especially when it is cold, windy and rainy, like it was on Thursday night, with the trees thrashing about in the wind down the valley and the plastic furniture blowing about on the decking.

So, I was quite surprised when she didn't come back in by the time I had finished my duties with the coal bucket, and even more so when shouting her and blowing the dog-whistle out of the conservatory door produced no response. The night was both wild and woolly, and there was no point in me going down into the valley to look for her. I cursed the lack of the torch, currently in the back of the dismantled car in the garage miles away at Crosland Moor. So I reluctantly shrugged on my coat and tramped up and down the road, shouting and blowing the dog whistle, to no avail.

I phoned Deb at work to tell her the bad news, and I phoned her mother, who was out at her friend Hazel's having a "biddy's night out". I scoured every inch of the house, upstairs and down, both sides, I even checked the garage in case somehow she had managed to slip past me while I'd been busy with the stove. Nothing. By ten past one, I was resigned to the fact that we'd lost her. I rang Debbie's mother to say I was going to sit up in the conservatory all night in case she came back, only to be told that she'd turned up on their doorstep, wet, muddy and bedraggled (the dog, that is, I can't speak for Debbie's mum).

Whatever spooked her must've been one hell of a twinge, to send her off down through the trees to the factory perimeter, along the path to the Police sports ground, over the cricket field at

Armitage Bridge, past the stables, and up the path past where Debbie used to live, and along the A616 for several hundred yards, dodging the late night drivers.

On Friday, I was cooking tea to the background of Kathleen Ferrier singing "What is life to me without thee" and it suddenly hit me how terrible it would have been if she hadn't turned up. In fact, how much everyone I know means to me, whether they be furry or non-furry, and what it would mean to lose any one of them. And I stood there thinking about this, and the immensity of it struck me as I thought what it must be like to be God, and to have to account for every sparrow. Then Debbie started up the planer in the garage (she was re-hanging an internal door and taking some off the bottom as it had been sticking in the wet weather) and Kathleen Ferrier's contralto was underscored by the keening whine of industrial power tools in a way in which she never intended.

So, it's been a week of winning and losing, of unexpected consequences. But then so much of life is. The snowdrops gain ground, but peak too early and are buried by drifts. Granny Rudd lost her house but gained a prefab. We lost

the dog, but we found her again. I lost some money from the bank account but in return I got my car back. Sometimes the winners are not always the favourites.

> The race is not always to the swift, nor the battle to the strong, neither yet bread to the wise, nor yet riches to men of understanding, nor yet favour to men of skill; but time and chance happeneth to them all.

What this means, of course, is that you might as well have a go. That job application you thought you weren't qualified for. That unresolvable situation, might just be able to be turned around. If time and chance happeneth to us all, so we're in with a chance, at least, to make things better. So you might as well go for it. You can win by losing just as much as others can lose by winning. And just at the point of hopelessness, the tipping point, is where the inevitability of spring comes crashing in, bringing goodness and, with it, sunnier days.

30th January 2005

It has been another busy week in the Holme Valley, desperately trying to catch up with a year that is already sprinting away out of our grasp.

Well, I would like to say that the cats and dogs have been frolicking in the spring sunshine this week, but if I did, I would be telling a big fat porky. Like me they have been cuddling up to each other and sharing their body-warmth, their mutual dislike of cold, dank weather overcoming their feeble grasp on any remaining "territories" as Dusty continues to be welded to our duvet and Nigel continues to sleep in Colin's/the ladycats' house. It's such a shame that, come the warmer weather, Kitty and Dusty will leg it to their summer home on top of Mrs Rocky's shed, and all this temperature-enforced integration will be forgotten! Baggis has suddenly started eating his KD Laing food again, just in time, as he's due back at the vet's next week.

Also this week, Freddie has been staying, for reasons which will become clear later, and Tia has also been spending a few hours each day in the "relative" warmth of our kitchen, where I have taught her to a) sit and b) give paw, with the aid of a jar of dog treats and continually saying "high fives" over and over again in a silly "bluebottle" voice. If only we could persuade Tiggy, Freddie, Tia, Dusty, Nigel, Russell and Kitty to all invade the duvet at once, we would never need to buy hot water bottles, and the central heating bill would be zero. Sadly, however, they prefer to do it in shifts, which hardly ever overlap.

Elections have been on my mind this week, both those in Iraq and our own forthcoming ones. I have this vision of Langland's "field full of folk", viewed from above, on the Malvern Hills, milling about, with the soon-to-be-spring sunshine dappling them, as they go about the ancient English traditions of Witan and Moot, settling disputes in the courts by means of a jury of their peers, as they have done for centuries past.

We have to be wary, of course, when we speak like this, of the "merrying of England" - the sentimentalisation of the past that has given us such horrors as "travellers' fayre" and the fiction that is the "ploughman's lunch". The only "real" ploughman I know,

James Hewison, always had ham sandwiches. Never a pickled onion in sight. So be warned.

Last week I wrote about "winning by losing" - about how just at the point where it seems that Spring will never come, when the snowdrops themselves are buried by new drifts, that is the point where "the snows they melt the soonest, when the wind begins to sing." About how the willow is the strongest tree because it can bend.

The opposite to winning by losing is of course, losing by winning, which we have seen a classic example of this week, in the attempt by the government to lock us all up if we disagree with anything they are doing.

They would never get it past Judge John Deed, if he were but real. Deb and I found ourselves watching this tosh on Thursday, and Martin Shaw was hamming it up perfectly, as the scarlet-clad judge, complete with sub-plot love interest. Debbie suddenly turned to me and asked what had happened to his other girlfriend, the one who was a lecturer at Cambridge?

Me: "Same actor, different programme. That was when he was being Adam Dalgliesh in P. D. James."

Somehow, she had conflated the two without wondering how Martin Shaw became ennobled to the bench one week on from being a mere Metropolitan Police commander the week before. Oh well. There are those who think Inspector Morse was set in Cambridge. Deb also suffers from "wrong trolley syndrome" in Sainsburys, and has been known to return from a foray, glance down into the nearest trolley (not ours) and say "What have you bought all that crap for?"

Me: "That's not our crap darling - it is crap which belongs to this gentleman" <points>

But her confusion is as nothing compared to that of those set above us: Charles Clarke is worried, to the extent of suggesting "house arrest for all" at the whim of the government, that, if he lets the Belmarsh detainees out into the world at large, unmonitored and unsupervised, they might start trying to subvert the very fabric of our society and civilization. But why would they bother? Our own leaders are already doing the job for them, so much more effectively, and with such gusto, that if I were a member of Al-Qaida, I might consider applying for an allotment, or taking up a hobby.

Clearly, from the government's actions in deciding to turn Britain into a society of fear, demonising imaginary threats to bulldoze through profoundly anti-libertarian legislation, abandoning the basic principles of English Law that have stood since *Magna Carta*, in favour of clandestine denunciation by the security services and evidence that cannot be admitted in court, they have shown their true colours, and not for the first time. Ugly colours, at that, but I suppose to be expected in an election year with opponents already playing the race card.

Clarke argues that these people are terrorists, or at least potential terrorists. Fine, if they are, arrest them, put them on trial, and if they are found guilty, bang them up and throw away the key. It's not me who has the problem with the due process of justice, it's the government!

He says that he has a responsibility to the British people to safeguard life and limb, and this is true: but it has been done effectively with the existing powers (themselves draconian in nature) since September 11, without the need to turn Britain into an armed camp, a sort of floating version of the "Green Zone". You might as well put barbed wire all round the coast and machine gun towers and CCTV cameras every thirty yards and have done with it. Only then will the freedom for which our fathers fought in 1940 be safe.

Just for once, I would like to see a politician with the courage to stand up, if the worst happened, and a terrorist outrage caused loss of life in this country, and say "Look, we regret what happened, we tried everything we could to stop these people within the law. The only way we could have done more would have been to abandon the rule of law and turn the whole country into a dictatorship. We are very sorry for the loss of life but these people died upholding the principles of law and justice, without which we are just as bad as the terrorists."

The arguments usually advanced in favour of this type of legislation are similar to those propounded by advocates of identity cards. If you have nothing to hide, you have nothing to fear. It's only the radical Muslims who will be targeted like this, at least until they get round to those who are friends of radical Muslims, then those who just know the friends of radical Muslims, of and while we're at it, animal rights protestors, and what about train spotters, Christians, and anyone who looks at Tony Blair a bit funny ...

This rather rose-tinted view of how governments and totalitarian regimes operate, encroaching little by little on the liberties of their citizens based on a set of values defined purely by the will of autocrats to stay in power, was probably also being aired in Germany in the early 1930s, when people stood by and let Hitler ride to power on a broad highway of paranoia and hatred. This week especially, we should remember where that particular road ended, in the railway sidings at Auschwitz.

I feel pretty strongly about this, because this week, my little nephew Adam was born, and for the second time in seven months, I am an uncle. There is nothing more calculated to make you feel old. Little Adam has spent most of his first week of existence sleeping and trying to gain strength, having been born a bit weedy and premature (when I rang Deb up on her mobile for more news she said "I dunno, it weighed five ounces or something - look, is this important? I am just paying for something in Homebase!")

It was actually 5lb 14 oz, but even so, he's a pathetic little scrap at the moment. As with Katie Elizabeth before him, I can't help but wonder what sort of world he will grow to see. If it's a world where we all have to live in a self imposed prison camp just to be "free" then perhaps we have got it inside out, and we need to think again. And quickly, before it's too late.

On the morning that Adam was born, for some reason, I changed the radio station in the car to Radio 2, because I was feeling beaten in by the constant concentration on heavy world issues on Radio 4, my preferred early morning listening on the drive across to the warehouse. I dropped into the middle of Gilbert O Sullivan (remember him?) singing "Nothing Rhymed"

> When I'm drinking my Bonaparte Shandy
> Eating more than enough apple pies
> Will I glance at my screen and see real human beings
> Starve to death - right in front of my eyes.

As I said for Katie, so I will say for Adam, I really hope that we create a world for these kids where they will never have to see that. This week at Davos, the Swiss ski resort rather scarily named after the leader of the Daleks, the people who can prevent it or actually make it happen, have all been gathered together in one room. We know who they are, and we should "fight and fight and fight again", to quote Hugh Gaitskill, to make sure our voice is heard, and poverty is driven from the earth.

> Woe unto you Pharisees, for you tithe mint and rue and every herb

I guess Jesus may just have been in favour of cancelling their debt and lifting the trade barriers.

Of course the Nazi's solution to this type of problem is well known. Had I been unfortunate enough to live at the wrong time, in the wrong place, I might have ended up wearing the correct-coloured star, just for having a bad leg. For Adam, and for all the kids born this week, I can really do no better than re-iterate the words of Si Kahn

> It's not just what you're born with
> It's what you choose to bear
> It's not how big your share is
> It's how much you can share
> And it's not the fights you dreamed of
> But those you really fought
> It's not just what you're given,
> It's what you do with what you've got."

What's the use of two strong legs, Adam, if you only run away. You have to ask yourself, what would Jesus do? He'd be leading the anti-internment marches, tending to the asylum-seekers, and turning the money-lenders out of the temple. That's my view, anyway. I look forward to teaching you more about this Adam, as well as the fielding positions at cricket, and how to bowl a googly.

A wise man once said - these are the days of miracles and wonders, Adam, this is a long distance call. The way the camera follows us in slow mo, the way we look to us all. The way we look to a distant constellation, that's dying in the corner of the sky: these are the days of miracles and wonders and don't cry, Adam, don't cry …

§

6th February 2005

It has been a wobbly old week in the Holme Valley. Particularly on wobbly Wednesday, which was followed by terrible Thursday. The weather has been cold but non-committal, snowdrops a-plenty in the garden, but no crocuses. The three tubs of daffodils which Maisie gave us last year appear to be sprouting through again, so they obviously thrive on neglect and bad weather, both of which they have had lashings of, this winter.

The animals have been quiet, going about their normal ways, sleeping in the warmest places they can find. Tig, Freddy and Lucy have had their regular walks in the woods. In some respects, it has been just a very normal week.

But this week has also seen Russell return to the vets on Wednesday for his monthly jab and checkup, and sadly, this time, it was anything but normal. I could see Mick the vet was concerned when he brought him back in, and said they had weighed him, and his weight had dropped to 2.5KG. The upshot was that he thought there was something else going on inside Russ the Puss, and it was either inflamed bowel disease, or "some form of low-grade cancer". My first thought was "I didn't know cancer came in grades", but by the time I had taken it in, Mick was already outlining the options, one of which was to inject Russbags with a new injection which would de-inflame him, if it was the former and not the latter. And thereby give his food a chance of staying inside him long enough to do some good. Which was what we agreed, and I took him home, having made another appointment.

All through Wednesday night and the early hours of Thursday morning, I failed to get to sleep, churning thoughts over and over in my mind. On Thursday I finally dragged myself up as the ragged streaks of dawn were glimmering in the eastern sky, and went through into the office. I could see that Russ was stretched out on Freddie's dog bed, in here, and that his head was down and he looked ominously still. I stopped dead in my tracks, but Tig, bless her, squeezed past me and went and licked him, at which point he woke up, and looked at me wearily.

Relieved, I went downstairs, but he didn't follow. I didn't want to get Deb out of bed to pick him up and bring him downstairs if he was feeling yucky, especially as I found he'd been sick during the night and I had to clear that up as well. It seemed best to leave him where he was reasonably comfy. As back luck would have it, Deb had to go out all day for a meeting, and therefore I arranged for Deb's mum (the Neigbourhood Witch herself!) to look in on him during the morning. She phoned me to say he'd obviously got himself downstairs and was curled up in his favourite chair, sleeping.

I felt helpless and a long way away. True, in one sense, people would say, well, he's just a cat. And others would say, well, they have to go some time, but to me he's been a companion for the last twelve years, especially at the start when I was alone, and bereft, and it was only the thought that he was relying on me for food that got me out of bed and to my desk, some mornings; I owe him at least, enough to put up a fight for his life. And so I found myself praying hard to St Padre Pio at various times in the day, though with the Pope at that time rapidly deflating in a Rome hospital, St P-P may have had other things on his mind, and may have had to refer my request on to Big G himself, with the equivalent of a celestial post-it note asking for help...

If I was an ancient Egyptian, of course, I could have offered up a prayer to the goddess Bast, goddess of domestic cats (and lesbians, surprisingly enough). I have often wondered about that. How do you get to be goddess of domestic cats and lesbians? Did she sleep through the alarm clock, the day they were sorting out who was going to be god and goddess of what? I can just imagine her arriving half an hour late, flushed and breathless, and the Pharaoh's Caliph holding a clip board (or Caliph board) and saying "Look, love, if you can't get here on time, it's nothing to do with me, The Nile, The Sun, Fertility, and the Sky-Boat to the Underworld have all gone. It's either the domestic cats and lesbians, or goddess of wheelie-bins, that's all that's left: take your pick!"

Of course, I am not meaning to mock the ancient Egyptians, who made such a wonderful job of communicating throughout the ancient world, with their wonderful language of hieroglyphics, which is especially useful, of course, if you want to write about people with funny heads walking sideways.

But I digress. By the time I got home on Thursday night, I had spent a lot of time reading up about Cat Inflamed Bowel Disease on the internet, and knew more than it was healthy to know about cat poo and how to tell, from scrutiny of it, whether it was more likely to be IBD or cancer. Which, I suppose, isn't a lot different from what the Egyptians did. So I shouldn't scoff. (In any sense of the word "scoff," having looked at the pictures!)

Russell, however, seemed much more inclined to scoff. In fact he scoffed half a tin of pilchards and some processed chicken slices. And kept them down, and in. By that time I had already been emailing the various friends who've been helping me pray for him, of all types and denominations, so their influence might have helped. These are people who have emailed me since I started this online diary/chronicle/epilogue last March.

On Saturday, things looked a little better still. (Despite the fact that, in the driveway, transferring stuff to the back of the car, I dropped a box of print which was the equivalent of five reams of paper onto my bad ankle, fortunately only from about knee-height.) Baggis was taking strips of shredded chicken roll from my hand, and seeming generally perkier, once we had managed to get some

Kao-gel down him. He has also taken to sitting actually in the hearth, directly in front of the stove, toasting his whiskers ("My Lords, Ladies and Gentlemen, I give you... Russell's whiskers!") It was with this in mind that Debbie decided to try and get a huge lump of clinker out of the stove, and ended up dislodging the riddling-plate with the poker, so that most of the red hot coals fell through into the ash-pan beneath.

There were only two choices: let the fire go out til the stove was cold enough to sort it all out, or try and fix it with fiery coals raining all about. With Russ in his current state, I didn't want the former. So, like some latter-day Shadrach, I managed to pull the ash-pan out, using the metal tool supplied for the purpose, although the manufacturers don't expect you to do this when it is glowing red-hot itself and full of red-hot coals. Gingerly, I lowered it down to the stone hearth and got on with trying to whack the riddling plate back into place, now that most of what had been stopping it going down had been removed. It was then that I noticed my right shoe (which had shifted to rest against the side of the ash pan during my efforts, and which did, yes, contain my right foot) was on fire, but fortunately I managed to stamp it out.

So we have reached today. Steeling ourselves for the worst, and hoping for the best. And we go on into next week in the same way, in the best traditions of those Fenwick ancestors of mine who charged into battle crying "A Fenwick! A Fenwick!" in both the '15 and the '45. As one of my dearest friends said, with more truth than she knew she had mustered, "Perhaps Russell is a Fenwick too". Well, me, and Russell, and the Fenwicks, we all stand together and we say "bring it on!".

It's been such a fraught week, I haven't had a lot of time for spiritual contemplation. The dreaded syllables of "cancer" knocked the equilibrium of the gyroscope of my thoughts and sent it spinning, haywire. But today, one thought has struck me (half baked, half digested - no change there then!) and it is this. Of all the people who pray for Russell, there must be a lot of different faiths involved. Anglicans, obviously, since he's the virtual cat of I-church, appointed by Alyson, no less. Catholics. Agnostics like my sister (she makes up for it by being a nurse, maybe that's where she finds religion, in the healing process, though she'd never call it that) People who practice various spiritual beliefs of their own, involving candles and incense, Quakers, Methodists, and it just occurred to me, and I offer it as a thought, no more than that, that all of these people are like leaves on a massive tree of spirituality, all ultimately drawing nourishment from the great tap root itself (Himself?).

It makes a nonsense of the way in which religion has been used to fight wars. Just for a fleeting moment I had a vision of a new church. A new church for a new era, where all the leaves recognised they were leaves like all the other leaves, and that they had all sprung from the same route. Imagine a church with the intellectual rigour and the anthems and the cathedrals of Anglicanism, the pomp and majesty and symbolism of the Catholics, the contemplative and peaceful life of the Quakers, the reforming zeal of the Methodists, assembling hand-loom weavers on the windy moorlands of Northern England to sing ragged hymns and tell them there can be a better world in this life AND the next; the innovation of the people who are willing to believe in things like spiritual healing - and who is to say they are wrong, it could just be science that we don't understand yet.

Imagine if we all rose up together one day and went to one place and let out a resounding shout that war shall cease and poverty shall cease and everybody shall have enough food and water.

If my tiny little email list of prayerful people can (seemingly) save Russell's life for a little longer, by holding him in their affectionate thoughts, what could thousands of us achieve? What could millions? Bring it on!

13th February 2005

It has been a busy week in the Holme Valley, and almost a tragic one. Almost, but not quite, yet. Normally at this point I'd describe the weather, but to be honest, last week, I haven't noticed.

The week started out in the normal way, with the cooker still disconnected and no prospect of the plumber coming to fix it, and me trying to cook pancakes for Shrove Tuesday on a camping gaz stove with an omelette pan. All went well until the time came to flip them. I'd forgotten to allow for the fact that the heat from a camping gaz stove is minimal, and the batter takes a long time to heat up. Consequently, what I tried to flip was mostly still liquid, and landed partly back in the pan and partly across the sink, in a splattery mess. Deb commented acidly that she'd "always known I was a useless tosser" and made herself a sandwich instead.

On Ash Wednesday, while Gemma and her family were no doubt settling down to Corned Beef Hash, we were busy taking Russell back to the vet. Mick's manner was grave as he outlined what he thought was happening. Russell's problem in the digestive region had lessened, but they think he's not producing any red blood cells and he was very tired and very anaemic. And he still has massive kidney and heart problems.

Mick's diagnosis was that it would be better to end it there and then, but I could not bring myself to do that without giving it one last go, so we brought him home again and he goes back on Monday. Mick did give him a cocktail of steroids and vitamins which perked him up a bit and when we got back, we made up a warm bed, inside the hearth, for Russ, and a litter tray so he didn't have to go out into the cold night to do his necessaries.

He spent some time on Wednesday night eating cooked chicken and grated cheese, with Deb hand-feeding him.

Thursday and Friday passed in a blur. The plumber came, and went, leaving a bill for £45. I noticed that the Goddess of Wheeliebins had carelessly allowed the dustmen to leave ours all over the drive. Other than that, I immersed myself in the world of what E. M. Forster called "telegrams and anger".

When I did come up for air, it was then that I found myself blubbing. On Friday night, I got back, and sat in the chair by the stove. Russ roused himself from his cat bed in the hearth, and jumped on me, settling down on my chest, and purring feebly. I shut my eyes and found myself praying, to Big G, St Padre Pio, or whoever:

"Look, if he has to go, God, let him go now. I offer him up to you. Just take him now, while he's happy and he can feel my heartbeat under him, and he's warm and he's purring and being held, just let him slip away."

But he didn't, so after a decent interval I fed him some more chicken instead, then he settled back down. Since then, he's been eating Beef and Liver Dog Food, he's been outside a couple of times, and he's been snoozing in his warm cat bed in the hearth and using his tray when he has to. We know that, if he starts to exhibit signs of pain and distress, that will be the cue for ringing the vets' emergency number and getting him out here to do the necessary. But at the moment, we just take things one day at a time.

So certain was I on Thursday that he wouldn't make it, that I had even worked out what I was going to say in this column today about him, and that it would do for his epitaph. Since I have already published my *own* epitaph a few Epilogues ago, I might as well do the same for Russell now, then he too can be one of those lucky people who get to read their own obituary because the papers got their death wrong:

"In November 1992, when I had lost my partner, and my dad, plus Silvester, and Halibut, the two previous cats, all in the space of six months, the Cats' Protection League asked me to look after Russell for a few weeks 'til they could find something more suitable. On his way round to my house, he'd already escaped from the cat carrier in Dean (CPL volunteer)'s car, so he was handed to me through the door, alive and squirming, a kitten, the size of one of my palms.

He named himself, from his onomatopoeic habit of getting into open boxes of books waiting to be packed, and rustling constantly in the brown kraft paper we used for sending orders out to bookshops at the time. After saying "what is that rustle?" a few times, the emphasis changed and the comma got shifted.

He celebrated the passing of the first month in my possession by eating a GPO parcel band off the desk and having to have an operation which cost £127 to remove it from his innards. After that, he led a fairly blameless life, scaling the net curtains, bringing in earthworms as presents, doing all the things cats do. He celebrated his next major injury, breaking his leg, by lying in the sun in the window, giving himself dehydration, so he had to be revived by being wrapped in a damp towel. On his return from the vets with his leg strapped up, he promptly climbed on top of the wardrobe.

I can't say he was the best cat in the world, because there were times when he was the worst cat in the world. He was an accomplished food thief and beggar from plates. A snapper-up of unconsidered food generally, and not just trifles. In his prime, no worktop was impregnable, no dish too heavy to tip over and lap up the contents.

His other endearing trick was to invade the duvet in the middle of the night, often when wet as well as cold, then lie across your throat like a giant furry purry scarf, until you woke up unable to breathe and thinking you were having a cardiac, only to realise that this particular cardiac arrest had decided to purr.

It is always dangerous to start imbuing animals, which are essentially instinctive, with human characteristics, but I can honestly say that it was only the thought that he was relying on me that got me out of bed and to the office during those dark days of the winter of 1992/93. Without him, I would probably have given up. Without him, I would have been utterly alone instead of merely bereft, and for that I do owe him. To quote the Auden poem, he was my working week, and certainly for the last year or so, writing about him, he's been my "Sunday best".

He was a good little cat. He eventually became famous, as the virtual cat of I-church, but he never let it go to his head. He still hid from visitors in the cupboard under the sink, only emerging at the sound of food preparation.

That, at least, is true, and, with his small cat spirit going out into the vast dark that lies beyond, I have no doubt that all the trumpets in cat heaven will sound at his passing over, with lashings of sardines and cream all round.

Night night, Baggis. Go sleepies."

Like I said, **I thought** I'd be writing that epitaph this weekend, but for the second time in these columns, he's proved me wrong. Even so, I've been thinking a lot this week of giving up doing this writing every Sunday, or maybe only doing it occasionally for a while, so I can concentrate on what I once called "the things that matter." It's OK me sitting up here thinking I am some sort of big shot writer, justifying the ways of God to men and then sterilising it with Milton, but there are four other furry beings apart from Russ the puss that rely on me to get things right and earn some money, and some humans too that rely on me for help, companionship and inspiration, which shows you what a fix THEY are in right now! And like the song says

> What's the use of two good ears, if you can't hear those you love.

I have to concentrate on turning things round now, and making sure they are all OK in the difficult weeks ahead, starting with Baggis. But at the end of it, I will still be me. And don't think for one minute that I am not eternally and endlessly grateful for the messages of support for Russ that have come winging in from places like Korea, Park Forest Illinois, Brighton, and other exotic spots on the globe, as readers of these weekly updates heard the news and responded, on the Archers Web Site and on I-church.

So, thank God I have still got Tiggy, Nigel, Dusty, Kitty, and Russ, for a little while longer, who knows. And thank God for my friends. Life is lent, as the Anglo-Saxon Bard puts it, but for the moment, it's Sunday night and once more I am here at my desk in the office at the top of the house, frozen stiff, with the hood of my fleece up, listening, indeed, even as I type this, to the sound of Dusty making a nest in the accounts filing. (If only she could hold a pen or use a spreadsheet, she might be some use, but, as a cat, her idea of "trial balance" is to jump up onto something rickety to see if it will hold her (considerable) weight.

I've been doing these Epilogues for a year now. 52 weeks out of my life, and a twelfth of Russell's so far. There is about 70,000 words of the stuff: mostly, if the parodists are to be believed, consisting of, "sick cat/the light on the Humber". On the other hand, you could read it as possibly the longest feline love letter in history, yet Russell's not even a lady-cat, and I'm not gay, (nor, indeed, a cat) so where does that take us? The plain fact is, though, even if I sat and wrote another gazillion words about him, it won't bring him back when the time comes.

Whatever happens with Russell, I will write a postscript, an Epi-epi-logue, if you like. But just in case I am not minded to write next week, for whatever reason, and because I don't want to end on a cliffhanger, I just want to reiterate what I believe this last year's taught me -

The indomitable nature of the human spirit
The holiness of the heart's affections
The value of friends
No retreat, Baby, no surrender,

and - probably most of all - in the words of Philip Larkin

> What will survive of us, is Love.

So we go into tomorrow, into a new week of new challenges and new problems. We shall not cease our exploring, and the end result, as Eliot says, is to end up where we started from, but to know it for the first time.

Night night, everyone. Go sleepies.

20th February 2005

It has been a busy week in the Holme Valley: and a draining one. Actually, it was last week that did the draining, this week we're just drained. Cause and effect. The weather remains stubbornly cold, what I recall of it. And when it hasn't been cold, it's been very cold. Even the sunshine has been what Bob Copper called the pale, counterfeit gold of February. "February fill-dyke" was what my old gran always used to say, and with snow forecast next week, who's to say she was wrong.

With five degrees of frost on the morning that the Kyoto agreement on global warming came into force, the irony has not been lost on me. Our central heating has been struggling manfully with the temperatures (and usually failing) The animals have been making their own arrangements to cope. Nigel has taken over the spare bedroom, taking advantage of the fact that this is the first place which the rays of the sun strike and warm each morning as it rises over Berry Brow. Kitty has devised a new Kitty-hole, shunning the warm fur fabric cat bed and the Felix play tent, and creating a nest for herself amongst the decorating tarpaulins in Colin's kitchen, where she nestles and rustles away unseen, to her catty little heart's content, harvesting her own cat-warmth through the night, only emerging when I come in to feed her and catechise her about Chinese communist leaders of the 1970s (Mao!)

Dusty has taken to nesting in the filing in the office (I knew there was a reason not to do it) alternating this with stints of laser printer watching, having temporarily usurped Russell as chief "printer's devil", checking each sheet of A4 paper as it goes in at one end and miraculously emerges out the other, as the big Epson C900 churns out page proofs of SPB Mais. Given the preponderance of this wonderful machine to jam, stop, or otherwise have a fit of the vapours at the slightest provocation, I share her wonderment at the way it's run today.

Russell's incredible convalescence continues for the moment, thanks in no small part to you people who prayed for him. You will never know how grateful I am. Mick the Vet said that a) he was delighted to have been wrong and b) it was like looking at a different cat. Russ has been fortifying himself and fighting his anaemia by wolfing down plate after plate of Liver and Beef dog food. Not exactly the ideal fare, but at least for the moment he seems to be thriving on it, and as I type this is curled up in his favourite chair in front of the stove, which is chucking out max heat, Debbie having bombed it up with coal about an hour ago.

We're not out of the woods yet, he still spends a lot of time sleeping in his bed in the hearth, and he's only been outside a couple of times since he came back, but on the other hand every day at the moment he does seem to be growing a little stronger and every day is a small miracle. This morning he jumped on the bed, meowing for food, and invaded the duvet, purring with all the strength he could muster. I just pulled the duvet over him and beamed a silent prayer of thanks.

Freddie has been staying with us, another furry hot-water bottle come bedtime. Granny is spending a week with Becky and Adrian and the vastly-growing Katie. At first, Freddie behaved like a spoilt little mummy's boy dog, sulking on the chair in full-on "I'm an abandoned orphan doggy" mode. As he's got more used to being here, however, in the last couple of days he's managed to have a disagreement with both Nigel and Dusty. Unfortunately, as has been observed before, Freddie is the only one who doesn't know he's only nine inches high, and he's completely oblivious to his chances of losing a large chunk of his snout if he keeps on annoying bad-ass momma cat Dusty, whose evil Medusa glare alone petrifies Nigel, every time she fixes it on him.

I've had little energy, and less motivation this week. The crisis over Russell really sapped my strength and I'm also conscious of the need to keep up the effort on that front, and not take my eye off the ball. That's one reason why I was wandering around last week singing "Take this badge offa me" and considering giving up writing these Sunday summaries. After all, if I feel too drained to find any spiritual sustenance, what am I going to write about? The holes in my socks?

I had another blow on Friday night when the clutch went on the car, leaving me stranded in Midgeley for an hour, while Green Flag turned up and towed me to Pennington's garage at Crosland Moor. By the time Debbie made it up there in the camper van to pick me up, I was cold, tired, hungry, and dispirited. It was 10 past nine and I had been awake for seventeen hours.

Since I wrote about giving up, I have had quite a few emails urging me not to. There is a pleasing symmetry to stopping after almost exactly a year, and in the next two weeks we've got to get S. P. B. Mais off to press, we've got a crunch meeting with Waterstones on Wednesday in Brentford (home of nylons) and the annual bank review coming up. At the same time, though, I have been taken to task over the parable of the talents. "On a huge hill, cragged and steep, truth stands, and he that will seek it, about must, and about must go".

Perhaps I have been looking at this the wrong way, from the inside out. If people really do find this stuff useful, then maybe what I am meant to do is to create some good out of the situation. If it works, a book creates revenue. That revenue could be given to the PDSA or the CPL, or perhaps a more struggling cause like Mossburn Animal Centre, in gratitude for Russell's continued health. Well, it's one way of looking at it, and would of course mean a fair bit of extra work.

I don't know what I should do, to be honest. I feel I am groping my way forward, a step at a time, and time itself will make things clearer. When I wrote a couple of weeks ago about different religions being like leaves on one tree, a friend sent me her version of this idea. That God was like an elephant, but that we were all so close to it, that we could only see our own particular bit of the elephant, so those of us next to the legs, saw God as a tree trunk, and so on. We can't step back and see the wonder of the whole elephant. Or something.

Well, in the words of Michael Stipe, this weekend has been a bit like pushing an elephant up the stairs, waiting for a message from the great beyond ... and all I have got to say at the moment, is "never give up". Even when the odds are so stacked against you, you may as well have a go. In fact, what have you got to lose? It is better to live one day as a tiger than a thousand years as a sheep, or so the Chinese proverb says. This is all getting very zoological.

Interestingly enough, if you mouth the words "Elephant Juice" silently, it makes exactly the same mouth-shape as "I love you". So, in the words of Jesus, elephant juice each other as you would be elephant juiced, and all you need is juice (and an elephant, of course)

So, time to sleep, perchance to dream. The words of Mercury are harsh after the songs of Apollo. Tomorrow is another day, Monday, in fact, and Phillip will be here at 7.40am to give me a lift in the van. I think I might have got my elephant as far as the landing, at any rate. He'll be fine there til tomorrow. Sleep well and consider yourselves Elephant Juiced, by a grateful cat and its more grateful owner.

27th February 2005

It has been a busy week in the Holme Valley, and a wintry one. Still no signs of spring, and as I sit here typing this, the cold is so biting that here in the office, despite Colin's central heating going full blast AND the halogen heater next to my chair, I can still see my breath every time I breathe out. I am wearing a poncho with a hood, and I look, and feel, like Clint Eastwood's grandad today. The animals are all seeking the warmest places: Russell, whose miraculous recovery continues, thank God, is curled up in the chair next to the stove, having demolished yet another plate of "Beef and Liver" dog food. Tig's on her settee, with her nose in her tail. Kitty on the settee in the corner of the music room, curled round so tight that you can't really tell which end is which. Dusty is burrowing into the duvet on our bed and until very recently, Nigel was perched on the desk next to the nice warm laser printer.

Freddie returned home on Friday night, when Granny came back from baby-viewing in Southampton. I was deputed to turn out and pick her up from Wakefield westgate station on Friday night. Freddie barked his head off when he saw her, and then fastened himself, limpet-like, to her bosom, all the way home, except for a brief interlude where we met up with one of Becky's ebay purchases, in the form of a baby toy mobile thing, in the Co-op car park at Ossett on the way back. The scene was redolent of some underhand, criminal activity, meeting up in a deserted car park, but persuading the guy to turn out and hand it over in person to her mum saved Becky eight pounds in postage, and probably cost as much in diesel. And it was an experience, I thought, as I threaded my way back through Horbury, with a silent nod towards whoever it was who said you should try and experience everything in life except incest and Morris-dancing.

Debbie is downstairs shifting things in preparation for the descent of the plumber who is arriving next week like a *deus ex machina* to fix the shower and install a downstairs loo in what used to be Colin's pantry, including stud wall and all necessary plastering, according to his estimate. Let's hope he's used to working in sub-zero temperatures.

For this week has been the week of the snow, and it looks like next week will be as well, the way things are going. I have a special antipathy towards snow. And it doesn't like me much either. I don't even think it's particularly beautiful. It's just cold, obstructive, disruptive and slippery. So my heart sank on Thursday when I saw the state of the driveway. Kettles of hot water, some rock salt, and a brisk session with the yardbrush were enough to make a sort of pathway from the door to the car. The road outside our drive was clear, deceptively so, as I was to discover. By the time I got to Brockholes, the road, which is the main A616, was white over, and I was beginning to question the wisdom of having set out. The snow warning signs at the side of the road were telling me helpfully that Buckstones and the Snake Pass were both closed, not that I was planning to go there anyway, but clearly things were much worse than I had thought.

Out of New Mill, there are two choices, either up Sally Wood or over Stocksbridge, which involves tacking the Stocksbridge bypass, one of the most dangerous roads in England at the best of times, and this definitely wasn't the best of times. Fortunately, just as I was dithering, a huge tipper truck started lumbering up Sally Wood, scattering snow as it went, so I gratefully dropped into his wheel tracks and followed him all the way to the top. It was almost like having my own private snow-plough. And so I made it, eventually, to my other desk, an hour late.

By the time I set off to come back, that evening, a lot of the snow had turned to slush. I was feeling pretty confident that I would get back OK, and had got as far as Darfield on the A635 when a Ford Focus pulled out straight in front of me, from Nanny Marr Road, a side-street whose chief claim to fame up to that point had been having a mildly amusing name. I hit the horn and the brakes simultaneously. He accelerated out of the way, my front wheels locked, there was a dizzying moment of screeching and I spun through 180 degrees, ending up wedged across the mouth of Nanny Marr Lane, facing back the way I had been coming from. Mercifully, there was no other traffic about.

A friend of mine told me recently that she had had a nightmare where she felt like a helpless little child, and all she could do was repeat that she was frightened over and over again, in French for some reason (such is the logic of dreams: I once dreamt that I had invented a triangular web site that could be projected onto the back of doors - why?) J'ai peur. And it was with a very similar feeling that I drove gingerly the remainder of the way home. J'ai peur. Or, as Leo Kottke sang:

> Sometimes I feel like a tiny island
> Floating in the sea

What lesson was I supposed to derive from the experience? Like Eliot, I had the experience, but missed the meaning. On the one hand, it was a demonstration of how, even in the 21st century, our sophisticated transport is still at the mercy of natural conditions. On the other, it was a further graphic illustration of the idea of what might have been. In another dimension, perhaps, I ended up as kebab meat, and my car a shattered wreck. Or was the crucial point that I had been saved - someone watching over me to ensure that there wouldn't be another vehicle in the wrong place at the wrong time? But then why give me the experience anyway, if Big G knew I would get through it OK? Unless it was to set me thinking, which it certainly did.

I could say that the true nature of courage in the face of adversity is to go out there and do it again, whatever "it" is, even though you are afraid. Even though inwardly, you are saying "J'ai peur". Well, I certainly was. But
I don't think I am particularly courageous. More so on some things than otrhers, perhaps. Maybe another, worse skid is coming, where I can put into practice what I learned in that first skid, and save someone's life.

Everything comes down to whether you think life has a purpose, a meaning, or whether you think things just happen at random, with no pattern, no design. As I have said before, there is no absolute proof to be had. Ultimately, everything is a matter of faith.

So I go into next week having faith that things will get better. Faith that the snow will melt, and the crocuses finally show through in the garden. I have been putting the S. P. B. Mais book to bed this week, and reading about how his writings helped popularise the countryside and encouraged people in the 1930s to go out on countryside rambles, a movement that eventually led to the mass trespass on Kinder Scout and the establishment of the Peak District National Park. To get myself in the mood, I have been playing "The Manchester Rambler", by Ewan MacColl:

> The moorland has oft been my pillow
> The heather has oft been my bed
> And sooner than part from the mountains
> I think I would rather be dead

And I found myself getting Lake District withdrawal symptoms. Maybe a trip in the near future to see my good friend Dr Keswick will set me right again, and give me a bit of direction and certainty, two remedies for life's little buffets which I am definitely lacking at the moment. There is much to be done, and people are relying on me to do it, so it's time to snap out of it and set to work with a will, even though "J'ai peur" sometimes. I may be a wage-slave on Mondays, but I am a free man on Sundays, like the song says.

So another week passes, another month passes, and this week, like last week, I have more questions than answers. Teach us to care and not to care: teach us to sit still. Teach us to think about what might have been but not to be paralysed by it. Help us to go out there again and face our dragons, especially when nous avons peur. In the words of Karine Polwart's song

> Oh, oh, the night is long
> But life is longer still ...
> Oh, oh, the night is long,
> But the sun's comin' over the hill

Hang on in there folks, spring is coming ...

§

March 6th 2005

It has been a busy week in the Holme Valley. Not much in the way of springtime in a week which has been an endless succession of bitingly cold monochrome days where the roads are black and the fields are white and the wind sings over the snowdrifts. It is exactly a year this week since I posted my first "real" Epilogue on the Archers Web Site, and a lot has happened since then. 365 days.

Who would have thought, last year, when I typed those words about having sat on the roof of England, and about March coming in like a lion and going out like a lamb, that the government we elected with such high hopes for a better future in 1997 would, in a year from then, be conspiring to pass shoddy legislation to lock us all up without the benefit of a trial, on the say-so of a politician.

Still, what would Jesus do? Well, I guess he would carry on towards his inevitable conclusion. Winning by losing. Personally, I don't think Jesus is that bothered about Tony Blair, or any of the others for that matter. Render unto Caesar and all that.

Anyway, apart from the snow, which has, now, mercifully, all but gone, there hasn't been a lot to write about this week. Snow and adversity just about sums it up. There have been some good bits though. Russell continues his marvellous recovery. I keep trying to remember to thank Big G from time to time but as this week has been a succession of days when the prayer of the roundhead soldier in the English Civil War would not have seemed out of place, it's hard to remain as constantly thankful as I should be.

Oh Lord, thou knowest how busy I must be this day: If I forget thee, forget thou not me.

As one of my more blasphemous associates once put it, "sudden prayers only startle God". I prefer to think that he/she/it knows how grateful I am, and that I have promised to mend my ways, and go to Santiago de Compostella and San Giovanni Rontondo, and to give any money from the book, if there ever is a book, to a good cause to do with relieving the suffering of animals, preferably one that actually needs the income. If God really does know all the innermost secrets of our hearts then he knows this too. In fact he knew before I did, which is a freaky thought.

The rest of the cats have been restive, like they can sense that Spring is coming and like me, they are frustrated by its slowness. Likewise Tig, who views the snow with the same degree of world weariness that I feel. Freddie, who was staying with us til Thursday, has a different attitude, running round in small circles and yapping at the snowflakes as they fall. It must be nice to have that much energy.

Otherwise, the week has been marked by normality. On Monday, the plumber didn't come On Tuesday, he phoned to say that he was just finishing off a little job in Mexborough. On Wednesday, he phoned to say he was snowed in. We never heard from him on Thursday or Friday. So everything in the kitchen sits in a state of suspended animation. Actually that is a kind way of putting it. Other descriptions include "thieves broke in and hoovered".

I got home on Wednesday to find that Deb had already started moving the kitchen units that are to go next door when Colin's plumbing is finally connected. One of them was upside down, minus its legs and with the doors facing the wall, not outwards into the kitchen as you might have expected. In response to my slightly raised eyebrows, she simply said "Yes, it's upside down. Deal with it, and move on." Obviously a bad day. I took her advice. I said no more. When I asked where the frying pan was she said "In the garage" - like I should have known.

Despite her struggles with Ikea MDF, I think actually Deb has been the happiest of all among us this week, mainly because she has now got her wireless connection set up for her laptop, and can sit downstairs by the fire, still surfing the internet. As she gleefully announced, I have now become a virtual husband and the only time she needs to see me in person or be in the same room, is when I cook her tea! I was struck by the irony of this. This was the woman who, when we first connected to the internet in 1997, denounced it as a "giant electronic anorak" and this week I found her wirelessly surfing for sites that allow you to buy ponchos online. If I cared to, I could work in some delicious irony at this point. Especially about the similarity of ponchos to anoraks.

Looking back over the week, at first, I was struck by how boring it was. A combination of work, snow, struggle, more work, and trivial domesticity. Yet this is life. Such things actually make up the days of our lives. "Some days are diamonds, and some days are stone", as Raymond Froggatt sings. Thing is, without the stones, you would never know that you had a diamond. And God knows before we do, which is which.

Tomorrow I have to go to Oxford for a meeting which I do annually, at about this time of year. Thursday is the annual bank meeting. Two days I can be pretty sure will be stone. But who knows? Days are where we live, and to answer the question of what days are, as Larkin says, brings the doctor and the priest running across the fields.

So folks, days are all we have, and some days the plumber won't turn up, and some days the kitchen cabinets will be upside down and legless, and some days, yea, even I will be upside down and legless, especially if Sainsbury's keep having special offers on Apprentice Sheep and Fuller's Winter Warmer. I will be lying under the table with the empty can of Special Brew, which in itself is a form of prayer, provided Big G looks down and shakes his head and says "I don't know" with an affectionate laugh about the fantastical tricks I get up to before high heaven.

And some days will go better than others. And some days will be difficult, with phone calls to make and favours to ask.

I had a conversation during the week with someone who said "why do bad things always happen to me" and I said at the time, I think you will find that good and bad thinks happen to all sorts of people, seemingly at random. If there is a pattern, maybe we are too near the weave to see it. But good things are just as likely as bad. The weaver has woven, but we can still alter the pattern as we go along. The tapestry is finished, but we still get to decide where the threads go. Or something like that.

We should make the best of our days, however stony. Summer's coming. The snows they melt the soonest, when the wind begins to sing. And so we, too, should sing, once more with feeling:

> I thank you for the days, those endless days you gave me.
> I'm thinking of the days, I won't forget a single day, believe me.

13th March 2005

It has been another busy week in the Holme Valley. At last we have begun to see some sunshine again. Over Stocksbridge way though, there are still signs of stubborn resistance on the part of the snow, where it lies in some higher fields, shrinking daily, but looking for all the world like the outline of an incredible South Sea island on a map, or an abstract version of an ancient white horse, carved from a chalk downland.

Russell continues food-and-attention-yowling, and has started going out more now that the snow's gone. It doesn't stop him scuttling back in and sitting actually IN the hearth, even though we've moved his cat bed out now that he's officially no longer convalescent. I noticed the other day that he'd got so near to the stove he'd actually singed his whiskers on one side while toasting them, and they were all curled up like a cartoon cat's. Stupid mog.

The rest of the animals have been doing their usual thing, and even Dusty and Nigel seem to be getting along, or perhaps their liking for warm windowsills and duvets has overcome their mutual antipathy, Maybe they have decided they are all part of the same cat-smell after all. Mmmm. Yummy.

It's been a busy week for Deb, too. The camper van scraped through its MOT, and the plumber didn't turn up, but we have had plenty to occupy us in the meantime, picking up on media interest about Maisie's book on SPB Mais, setting up web cams on the wireless network, and in my case going to Oxford on Monday and Sheffield on Thursday for the bank meeting.

Oxford was its usual self. No other city, with the possible exception of York, makes it so difficult to drive there. I can understand why of course, but the people who run Oxford give you the impression they would much rather you parked in Shropshire, if you must bring your car at all. By the time I got back on Tuesday night, I was really past eating anything, but we decided to have chip butties. Having chipped the spuds, I decided to parboil them first, so I filled the wok (the biggest pan we have) to within an inch of the brim with water and set about my task with a will. Suddenly I was aware of Deb at my elbow:

Her: You MUST be joking!
Me: What do you mean?
Her: The amount of oil you have got in that pan!

Whereupon I flicked some of it at her to show her it was water.

Her: I didn't know you could fry things in water
Me: We chefs refer to it as "boiling"

Sometimes I *still* worry about that girl.

The bank manager (our third in as many years) was suitably impressed by who we are and what we do, and the highlight of the meeting was when I gave him a copy of our (out of print) book about the Knights Templar and told him how they invented modern banking. Let's hope it put a spring in his step for the rest of the day as he no doubt imagined himself clanking along the corridors of their modern chrome, steel and plexiglass office in surcoat and chain mail.

This morning, I was having my usual quiet Sunday morning mooch, having let Tig and Freddie into the garden. The coffee was perking, Bach was on the Cd player, all was well with the world. Suddenly Deb erupted into the room like a small but deadly hurricane, making a beeline for the vacuum cleaner. The austere mathematical precision of the Goldberg Variations was undercut by the powerful industrial whine of the Dyson Cyclone. She has to get on with the housework, she says, because it is "green bin day" tomorrow.

Green bin day is the council's attempt at sustainability. We have to put certain things aside from the "normal" rubbish into a separate green wheelybin. I am convinced the council just takes it all away once a month and empties it all into a giant asbestos-lined landfill site, but you have got to have faith.

Faith is what keeps you going when everything else is hopeless, I suppose. In some respects this week, we've seen our faith rewarded, with good news on various fronts. With faith goes hope, of course, and we do indeed feel more hopeful - about some things, anyway. And of course, as this week included the ubiquitous "Red Nose Day", it's been difficult to avoid the charity!

While I always say "good luck" and wish the people who organise these events well - every little helps, after all - I do struggle a bit with the concept sometimes. It is a very big dilemma - there is obviously a crying need for some of their work, but on the other hand, if the charities step forward with their response, it takes the pressure off some of the governments that should be tackling the problems. On the other hand, if the charities do nothing, and the governments refuse to be bounced into action, then the weak, the poor, the innocent and the vulnerable suffer and die, because I have had a fit of "principles."

I also think that some big charities have almost become self-perpetuating, and I have reservations about giving to an event that pools the donations - I wouldn't like to think of any of my money going to a medical charity that does animal experiments, for instance. It is a very dodgy moral area. But mostly my reservations are because it lets the government off the hook.

I am finding it increasingly difficult to find anything good to say about politics as a whole, particularly in the current nasty, febrile, pre-election miasma. I know this is not a political forum, so I don't want to argue the rights and wrongs of any particular legislation, but I am finding it very hard to forgive politicians. I haven't been able to find it in my heart to forgive Blair about Foot and Mouth yet, let alone any of the more recent stuff. I don't suppose that my lack of forgiveness would cause Blair, or Mrs Thatcher, to lose any sleep, but it does worry me, because it is the thing I find hardest of all about Christianity.

I remember when I first read the story of the Crucifixion, with Jesus on trial in front of Pilate (this was before Pilate invented his famous set of exercises and went on to make videos). I sat and listened to the story in RE at school, and - because I had been raised on W E Johns and the Wolf of Kabul, and various other stories where with one bound the hero was free, I was waiting for the bit when Jesus managed to cut through his bonds while no one was looking, grab a surprised Legionary's sword, and fight his way out, preferably swinging from a chandelier, Errol-Flyn style. The only other thing I read while a child, which had a similar effect on me, was Enid Blyton's description of the death of Robin Hood, with similar results.

Maybe that was what set me off down my outlaw path, two people who said you should take from the rich and give to the poor. Governments holding the third world to ransom, please note.

No doubt one day, I will end up in the same position as Robin Hood, and my merry men will cluster round me as I will feebly request my longbow for the last time and tell them wherever my last arrow lands, there they should bury me. On top of the wardrobe, probably.

Anyway, I digress. Yes, the Crucifixion. I found it difficult to forgive the Romans, and I find it difficult to forgive the present Pilates (there's that exercise video again) set in power over us. Probably because they have a similar disregard for truth. Forgiveness is obviously something I need to work on, big-style. I think the key to it is the idea of winning by losing, which is probably what Big G had in mind when he arranged the whole Jesus thing. I am really crap at forgiveness, even when I try and divorce the person from their actions.

I am sorry. I have strayed once more into controversial territory. Perhaps I should stop writing this stuff. I am still out of sorts with the world, despite the small signs of hope, the natural gifts that Spring brings. I am not intending to slag off one party as against another. Part of my problem is that, morally, they all seem as bad. The whole area of Church and State, and where your allegiance lies, is a difficult one for me. I need faith that things will come right, hope that all will be for the best, and charity towards those who, it would seem, bear us malice. "I pity the poor immigrant" as Dylan sang. although perhaps a more apposite Dylan lyric is "George Jackson"

> Sometimes I think this whole world
> Is one big prison yard.
> Some of us are prisoners
> The rest of us are guards.

Oh well, if they put me under house arrest for sedition, no doubt I will have plenty of time to practice forgiveness. And I will be following in an honourable tradition (Blake). And my mortgage will be paid, presumably by the taxpayer, since I won't be able to get to the office. And my food will be delivered, since I have no intention of going on hunger-strike, and Deb will still have HER internet connection. Since she is innocent of anything, apart from marrying me. With a policeman at the end of the drive, we will be considerably safer from burglars than at present, and if I get fed up, perhaps one of you can email me a file with a cake in it.

20th March 2005

It has been a busy week in the Holme Valley. There are daffodils out in Colin's garden, which means there are presumably also daffodils out in flower on his grave, too, across the way in Lockwood cemetery, as Halina planted them there in 2000. Not that I have been able to get over to see them. There are probably daffodils in the Lake District, too, nodding and dancing in the breeze, not that I have been able to get to see them, either, yet, this year. And for all that, it's still not officially spring, unless the crocus phase was so fleeting that I missed them. Fair crocuses we weep to see, ye haste away so soon.

This week has been dominated, latterly at any rate, by computer problems, first the big Epson printer deciding to keep up its convincing impersonation of a white elephant by getting a self-adhesive - and allegedly laser-compatible - sticky label caught inside it and runing a transfer belt which cost £182.77. Then finally my computer, the server for the whole system, caught a bug from which it has still not fully recovered.

The animals, of course, are oblivious to all of this. Both Dusty and Russell view laser printers simply as another form of heated cat-bed. Dusty also managed to jump into an A4 box of receipts which I had collected together ready to write them all up for the VAT return, and scattered them to all points of the compass. So much for trial balance. Kitty has made a nest in the plumber's donkey jacket, which he very unwisely left in the building site that is Colin's kitchen over the weekend. Nigel is losing his winter coat, or to be more accurate, redistributing it to each according to his needs. Unfortunately his assessment of our continuing requirement for cat fur differs from ours, hence the whine of the Dyson has been once more echoing through the house several times a day.

Tig has been watching the misdeeds of her various "puppies" - which is how she seems to see them - with a world-weary sigh as she settles down on her sofa, soon transporting herself to the land of doggy dreams where her paws and nose twitch as she chases imaginary sheep and rabbits (both of which terrify her in real life).

This week also marked the resumption of Russel's monthly visits to the vet. Happily, the remarkable recovery continues and he's now back up to 2.7KG, only 200g off what he was when he had his last "do". A living testimony to the power of prayer. He came back on Wednesday and celebrated by demolishing yet another plate of his favourite dog/cat food.

I decided on more traditional fare. West Country Cheddar, fierce English mustard, a couple of hunks of fresh bread spread with real butter, not margarine, even though my cholesterol is 6.5, and a smattering of pickled shallots. Have you ever noticed, by the way, that "shallots" is almost an anagram of "halitosis". Are these facts connected? A ploughman's lunch, in fact, even though it was Wednesday teatime, and the only real ploughman that I know, James Hewison, always had ham sandwiches.

I mused on what S. P. B. Mais wrote about a character in one of his novels:

> When a publican unexpectedly asked if he 'could do with a bit of cheese and pickled onion' he was moved to tears and commented bitterly, 'this is coming near to being the most poignant question in the language'.

I wouldn't necessarily go that far, but for all its made-up-merrie-Englandness, the plangent taste of a tangy cheddar and a really *good* pickled onion is one of the more defining experiences of life. I accompanied my repast with two cans of Adnams' Southwold Special Bitter (on which they very helpfully print a picture of the Southwold Sole Bay lighthouse and give the frequency of its flashes, so that if you do ever find yourself becalmed off Southwold with a can of Adbams to hand, you know what to look for.) Even though you can taste the salty swoosh of the North sea and sniff the ozone in every mouthful of the beer, overall, I always feel there's something essentially "West Country" about bread and cheese - not just the Cheddar of course. It always brings to mind that wonderful line in the traditional song "Tavistock Goosey Fair" by the famous composer, Trad, Anon.

> Us smelt that sage and onion half a mile from Whitchurch Down

There is more English social history in that one line than in any ten pages of Trevelyan.

Mention of Southwold always reminds me, as well, of the time my father bought a copy of the 1972 edition of "Reid's Nautical Almanac" at a jumble sale. I still have it, somewhere, even though there isn't much call for maritime skills in Huddersfield, where you can usually see from one bank of the canal to the other, unless it's an exceptionally smoggy day. I don't know what prompted my Dad to buy it either. His chief connection with the sea was to sit on Brough Haven watching the tankers, barges, and yachts go by, along the Humber. His grandfather was another matter, having died at sea on his trawler and having been buried in a canvas shroud off the coast of Morocco. Full fathom five and all that: of his bones are corals made.

Anyway, I was browsing through "Reid's Nautical Almanac" one day and became fascinated by the section that breaks up the coastline of Britain into manageable navigable chunks, a bit like the Radio 4 Shipping Forecast. Especially amusing is the section marked "Bloody Point to Ipswich". I imagined generations of "Yotties", adrift in the fog in the Orwell Estuary, sailing in close to land, close enough to shout to a gnarled and wizened yokel on the shore: "Excuse me! Bloody Point to Ipswich?" At which, no doubt, said yokel, startled by so direct a request, would shoot out a bony finger and reply, "'Tes that way, Zur!"

But I digress. Oh yes, ploughman's lunches and Englishness. Something I have dealt with before. It's coming round to that time of the year when the Englishness in me asserts itself again. There is other English food of course. As Jeanette Winterson remarked, Oranges are not the only fruit. Fish and chips is one of the things I miss most about being vegetarian. When Maisie started teaching at Barnsley College, having moved up to Yorkshire from the exotic hinterland of Balham, she was cajoled into taking part in the lunchtime fish and chips run to Grimethorpe Chippy.

Thus it was that she found herself at the head of a queue of hungry Yorkshire folk on their dinner hour, and pronounced her order in those immaculate cut-glass, RP English vowels for which she is celebrated. " Oppen or Wrapped?" replied the fishmonger. Maisie, who had no idea at the time that you could specify whether you wanted your fish and chips left open to eat now, or wrapped to keep them warm until you could consume them later, couldn't understand a word that he was saying, and decided, on the face of it, that the best thing to do was to just smile sweetly, and repeat her order again." Aye. Oppen or wrapped?"

Eventually, someone from behind her in the queue interpreted, and there wasn't a riot.

There wasn't a riot. In common with many other times in our history. So where is all this leading, now it's got to Sunday and I am sitting here, waiting for the computer to finish its weekly virus scan and staring at a half-written poem on the back of an envelope that contained the bank statement when it arrived two days ago, but which now, inexplicably, no longer seems to do so (how symptomatic of my whole life that is!) It's Palm Sunday as well, and I haven't mentioned palms, or donkeys. Apart from those in jackets.

Well, if I did have a message for Palm Sunday I guess it would be about mob mentality. How the same mob that welcomed Jesus turned on him a few days later. And how the concept of Englishness - or at least my idea of it - of an outlook on life that sees value in bread and cheese for all, in the whiff of sage and onion from a country fair, in hapless maritime exploits and self-deprecation, above all, an innate reasonableness, tends against the coming of the mob here. That's not to say we haven't had our mobs. From Peterloo to the Countryside Alliance; from the miners at Tonypandy or Orgreave, to the Poll Tax Riots. We've also had millions marching peacefully, to demonstrate against war. We are currently entering a period when it seems to me here in England that politicians of all parties here are attempting to stir up mob mentality in a quite disgusting way to further their own ends in the forthcoming election, and it behoves us very well, in my opinion, to remember the more reasonable sides of our nature, and not be swayed by these shameful, scapegoating tactics. Their England is an England of twitching curtains, mean-spiritedness, turned backs, closed doors and "Shop-thy-neighbour". And some of them have the sheer brass neck to claim to speak for traditional British values.

It may be a grotesque image, and I am not wanting to negate the central event of many people's faith, but I would like to think that our response to meeting Christ (and all the poor, the marginalised, the spat-upon vagabonds he stands for) as he staggers along the Via Dolorosa, should be to take that heavy cross off him, sit him down, and offer him a cup of tea and a cat to stroke. And a hunk of bread and cheese, with perhaps a pickled shallot and a pint of Adnams' best. And some fish and chips. Oppen or wrapped.

27th March 2005

It has been a busy week in the Holme Valley, and one where I have been struck by the irony that the latest series of "Dr Who" coincides with the clocks going forward. The message (at least from the BBC) seems to be that (limited) time travel into the future is possible, even if you don't have a Tardis! Incidentally, the real Tardis (the one they used for the original 1960s cult series) is at the Avoncroft Museum of Buildings in Worcestershire, where we launched "Jordan's Guide to English Churches" in 2000. I have a picture somewhere of me standing next to it. Five years ago, at least in our universe.

Well, finally, Spring is beginning to show a few tentative signs. As I write this, the catkins and the buds on the tracery of what have been bare branches outside my office window all winter, are now bursting out in all directions with a green that is so bright and young it's almost yellow enough to hurt your eyes, especially in the sunshine. Still no crocuses though.

Tig and Fred are relishing the prospect of longer days ahead, and longer walkies - as indeed are we wall, though our plans to get away to the Lakes this Easter have been thwarted by the Invasion of the Plumbers (which in itself sounds like a Dr Who episode, like the ones where the Daleks brandish sink-plungers). Of which, more later.

Kitty has skedaddled each time John and Colin (the plumber) have arrived, only returning long after they have gone. It's rather odd that one Colin is doing up another Colin's house, even though one of them is currently deceased (not the plumber, obviously) and I suppose Colin is a fairly common name. Nigel is still spreading fur and happiness wherever he goes, in equal proportions, actually, if anything, with slightly more fur: Dusty has once more taken central place on the duvet, which makes it very difficult to turn over during the night. She also has a fascinating range of nocturnal purrs, some of which sound like trimphone ring-tones. Once or twice, in a sleep-befuddled state, being woken by her in the early hours, I have almost picked her up and tried to answer her, a la Victor Meldrew with the puppy.

Russell is OK, although I am not certain he's not getting fed up of his dog food diet and starting to look further afield, at least in culinary terms. He's also lost his cat ID barrel off his collar, which will be another £2.50 at least to replace. It's just as well he doesn't stray far from the fire. I am still grateful for every day he continues purring, though.

For me, the week's been dominated by computer problems (happily, now fixed, it would seem) and the launch of Maisie's new book on S. P. B. Mais, *An Unrepentant Englishman*, which is coming up next week. For Deb it's been dominated by kitchens and ballooning.

It turns out that Gez knows somebody who owns a hot-air balloon and they have offered to take Deb up for a flip, following her microlight exploits in Australia two years ago. Twice last week, Debbie got up at some ungodly hour ready to drive over to the field where they were planning to launch at dawn, and twice she has been phoned up at the last minute to say that the weather is too rainy to fly, so her great balloon dream is unfulfilled at the moment. It strikes me that any form of aerial transport which relies on fine weather for its success doesn't really belong in the English landscape, and I can see why they invented aeroplanes, probably for the same reasons that I switched from motorbike riding to driving a car many years ago. Other than that, it's been kitchens, kitchens all the way, apart from today, when Deb's quest to buy herself a new power-drill from Argos was thwarted by the Easter Sunday Trading Laws. She's been busy putting up cupboards and screwing together cabinets. The other day she rang me up at the warehouse:

"Have you seen the linseed oil?"

"No, I didn't know we had any, why do you want linseed

oil?"

"I want to treat the worktop"

"Can't you just take it to the zoo?"

Click. Brrrrrrr.

I am really looking forward to the kitchen being finished, so I can start cooking properly again. I did manage a half-decent pasta last week. Next day, there was a small amount of pasta left, but it wasn't really fit for human consumption. I hate wasting food, and, feeling at my most hippyish, I decided to distribute it for the birds and animals. I took it to the edge of the decking, outside the conservatory door. "I give this pasta back to the Earth which bore it, with thanks", I intoned solemnly, swinging the pasta drainer in an arc, casting the pasta out over the garden, expecting it to spread out over the lawn. Instead, glued together by the day-old starch, it flew in a solid lump like a cannonball, landing, with a thud redolent of a Christmas pudding, under the hedge, where Tia, next door's dog, proceeded first to sniff, then to eagerly devour it.

So, next week, while Deb continues ballooning and kitchen-building, I will be revisiting some of my past haunts in Chichester at the book launch at the West Sussex Record Office on Wednesday. (11am, come along, you'll be welcome) I am looking forward to renewing my acquaintance with the Cathedral and Bishop Storey's Cross (as we used to say at the time, in best Morecambe and Wise tradition: "Bishop Storey's Cross? - I'm not surprised, he's been dead since 1547!") To get myself in the mood I have been listening to a CD of Elizabethan madrigals today, including Wilbye's "Flora Gave Me Fairest Flowers", and "Hark All Ye Lovely Saints Above", by Thomas Weelkes, who was the Organist of Chichester Cathedral a mere half-century after Bishop Storey built the Market Cross. It says on the sleeve notes that little is known of Weelkes, and "his later years were overshadowed by drunkeness", something which might well appear on my sleeve notes, if I ever have any.

I will also look forward to seeing the Cathedral's Arundel Tomb again, the one which Larkin wrote his famous poem about, with that last line to which I keep returning so often it's become a touchstone for me, especially when I think about dying: "What will survive of us is love". I'd like to think that this is true.

I haven't been in a very loving or forgiving mood this week. The election "which dare not speak its name" is still annoying me, and I have also been composing snotty letters to the person who owns the web site that sent me the email with the virus that started all the computer chaos off. I also decided that I was going to go to a meeting of the fans of The Archers and hope to confront someone I had locked horns with about the subject of an earlier Epilogue. I was brought up short by an email from one of my friends asking if I really intended to do this, which made me realise how out-of-proportion this was all getting - almost like a vendetta. (I always think that "vendetta" sounds like a small Italian scooter - so instead of going off in a huff, one could perhaps embark on a vendetta - anyway, I digress)

It made me realise, getting that email, how potentially unpleasant I was becoming. This is a time of the year when I should be concentrating on forgiveness, but for the third week running here I am struggling with the very concept. If Jesus could forgive people for driving nails through his hands and feet, and subjecting him to a horrible death, how much easier should it be for me to forgive a computer virus, or a bad-tempered disagreement on a message board. Severe lack of perspective alert!

I have to remind myself that the reaction to Jesus dying on Good Friday was not the turmoil of a vengeful uprising with Roman blood staining the gutters of Jerusalem, but two women going quietly into a garden two days later, and seeing a massive stone cast aside from an empty tomb by an angel with a face like lightning, who quietly told them that there was nothing there for them to see. I need to realise, I think, that if I want what remains of me to be love, I need to cast aside some of these stones. Apart from anything else, I'd have more energy for things that matter.

It reminds me of a story from the Zen tradition. The Zen Master and one of his novice pupils were travelling for many days across rough country between monasteries. Eventually they came to a ford through a fast-flowing river, where a beautiful young girl stood at the water's edge. The Zen Master asked her what the matter was, and she replied that she was too frightened to attempt to ford the fast-flowing stream. Without further ado, the Zen Master hoisted her over his shoulder and waded across, followed by his pupil. He put her down at the other side of the river, and she thanked him profusely and went on her way. The Zen Master and his Pupil toiled on along the road, but the Master noticed a difference in the Pupil's demeanour. Whereas before they had been talking and arguing, now he was sullen and withdrawn. He asked him what the matter was.

"Well, it's not right, a respected man of your religious standing, picking up that young girl like that and manhandling her across the river, showing off her legs and all that!"

Whereupon the Master fixed the Pupil with a fierce glare, saying: "Why are you still carrying that girl? *I* put her down at the river!"

Teach us to care and not to care. Teach us to let it go, sometimes.

3rd April 2005

It has been a busy week in the Holme Valley. If not the start of spring, then at least the end of winter. Each day I have watched from the window outside this office as yet more catkin buds open on these branches. The cats have welcomed the warmer weather, especially Nigel, who is in mid-moult, and Kitty, whose rodent ulcer condition is always improved by the coming of summer. Dusty has tended to treat the warmer days and lighter evenings with indifference, and Russbags has been stuck in his chair by the stove, still very thin and still very much recuperating.

Tig has been playing football in the park: I have been grappling with the VAT return and the print queue. Debbie has been pruning trees in the garden in the dark, because she does not like the neighbours seeing her doing it. No, I can't understand that one either.

Wednesday was a pivotal day of the week for me. Up at 5.15am for the drive down to Chichester, for Maisie's book launch. For some reason, Wednesday slipped back momentarily to the weather of November, rather than March. I thought, as I went along, that the fog would lift when the sun came up. But no. First I had fog, then, rain, then foggy rain, then rainy fog, all the way down the M1.

The launch itself was great. People mingled, they listened to the speakers, the food was munched, the wine drunk, and I saw people I had not seen in too long a time, spending some precious hours with them. All too soon it was time to set off on the long drive home.

I had had a bad feeling about the day, for some time now. I should have trusted my instincts. On the homeward leg, I got as far as Pease Pottage, where I was queueing at the roundabout to go across into the services. It was the sort of roundabout where if you don't wait for a gap and then go for it, you sit there all day. I saw a gap, and went for it, unfortunately, the Toyota Yaris in front of me didn't, and the end result was the loss of my headlight on his rear bumper. The car in front is a Toyota. In this case, it certainly was.

After we'd swopped details and he'd driven off, I looked at the state of my bumper. Bent almost back into the tyre, and the headlight glass completely smashed. Two hundred miles from home, and getting dark.

There was nothing for it, but to set off and hope for the best. I brought to mind all of those people who won the VC for climbing out on the wing of burning Wellington bombers and thought well, if they can do that, I can do this, so I rejoined the motorway and pointed my wheels northward.

It was dark, and rainy, and I only had half my normal headlights. By the time I got to the M1, I was ready to give up. But I kept repeating a sort of prayer to myself, that if I got home OK, I would try and be a better person. It was dark, it was rainy, and for a lot of the time, I was sailing into the unknown and unseen at

70MPH with the bumper only half an inch away from the tyre, but somehow I made it home, at 11.15pm

Faith will get you through, I suppose. I was reminded of this by the death of the Pope. He was in a similar situation, entering a very dark time, sailing into the unknown, but praying that he would get there OK. I was fortunate enough to hear him preach once, at the Knavesmire (York Racecourse) in 1982. I can't remember the subject of his sermon, but I can remember that it was a brilliantly hot sunny day, and that Basil Hume waved at me (or so it seemed) from the back window of the Popemobile. I also remember being in a huge crowd of people chanting "Saints of God, come to our aid" and what a profound spiritual effect it had on me.

Whatever you think about him - and he certainly had his detractors - the Pope lived by what he believed in. Living by what you believe in isn't always a good thing - one has only to think of Adolf Hitler and Margaret Thatcher - but in the Pope's case, he genuinely thought he was trying to do God's will.

Just when I am still struggling to come to terms with the ideas of forgiveness, his death - or to be more accurate, his life - has opened up another vast moral chasm for me. I can't begin to agree with some of his views on women and on contraception, in particular as they affect the developing world, but I have to admire him for sticking to his beliefs. He told it how he WANTED it to be - or how he thought Big G wanted it to be, rather than how it was. And this refusal to compromise lies at the heart of his mission on earth. If everybody lived according to the natural law of God, then everything the Pope said would have made perfect sense. The fact that people didn't, as he saw it, was OUR problem, not his. Or our problem, not God's.

So in addition to not being able to crack the idea of forgiveness, I now have to grapple with whether the spiritual life should compromise with reality as it is lived, or ignore it. Don't expect any answers this week. And in addition to that, I will no longer be able to do my Pope impersonation, by putting a jiffy bag on my head, and intoning in a heavy Polish accent that it gives me great pleasure to open this bring-and-buy-sale. An impression which is only vaguely funny if everyone else who witnesses it has had at least as much to drink as I have. One area where I had to admire John Paul, much as I disagreed with him, was in the manner of his dying. We tend to sanitise death in our modern society, he embraced it full on, and was determined to make sure his grapple with the grim reaper was reported blow by blow, as a lesson to us all.

Next week, I hope (d.v) to attain the age of fifty. As Orwell said, by the time a man has reached fifty, he has the face he deserves. Naturally, my thoughts have been turning to the fact that in twenty years time (which seems but the twinkling of an eye) I will, if I am spared, be seventy, and have attained the Biblical span of three score years and ten. Contemplating your own bodily extinction is not pleasant. But John Paul has shown that at least it can be a triumphant experience as well as a profoundly sad one. If you have to go, what better way than on a Spring morning when the catkins are budding, your friends are all around you, and there are crowds of thousands of well wishers singing psalms outside your window.

Certainly, when the grim reaper cuts the legs from under me, I would like to have started something new that morning. If it goes on to annoy the government, even after I am gone, so much the better. One of the things I like about the Catholic church is its clearly defined promotion path for dead people, if they work hard enough, to eventually become saints. You settle into eternity, you get to know the ropes, you perform the odd intervention here and there, you save a life or two, you stop something going wrong, and before you know it, you are officially a "blessed". Next stop, sainthood. Saint Karol Wotiljya. You heard it here first.

10th April 2005

It has been a busy week in the Holme Valley. I became fifty. And we are down to our very last bag of coal, so I very much hope that Spring comes next week, or I will have to trouble the coalyard yet again. So far this winter, we have spent over £150 on coal. Who says the coal industry is dead! The weather turned colder again this week, so we've actually been burning more coal than would otherwise have been the case. So much so, that on Thursday night, just after I had "bombed up" the fire, we had a knock on the door from a concerned motorist who was just passing and noticed that "our chimney seemed to be on fire". I was able to reassure him that I was just me stoking up the stove and practising for when they elect the next Pope.

Well, what a week. The animals were the only beings to be unmoved by my reaching fifty. That is, unless you count being awakened at 3.45am on the morning of my birthday by Dusty and Nigel having a nocturnal altercation that ended up with one of them knocking over the propped-up door in the demolished bathroom, but by and large I think only I saw it as somehow significant. By the time a man reaches fifty, says Orwell, he has usually achieved the face he deserves. Something I bore in mind the next morning when the alarm went off at 6.30, and I staggered to the bathroom mirror in my sleep-deprived state.

Baggis has spent the week devouring Sainsburys Beef and Liver *cat* food, at least we have got him back on to food for the correct species now. Next stop, KD Laing. Kitty, who will eat anything, has been chomping her way steadily through a carton of "Whiskas Senior in Jelly" (sounds like the sort of fare more appropriate for 50-year olds than cats), and it's only us humans that seem to have anything like a degree of uncertainty in our diet. Hence my surprise at the sudden appearance of pizza for my birthday tea, followed by a garishly pink-iced spongecake in the shape of a pig, decorated with mini-champagne bottle candles. The effect is better imagined than seen.

Of course, for us, it's been another week overshadowed by the death of the Pope, and the general election (zzz zzzz zzz) with all the major parties once more claiming that the British way of like encompasses stoning strangers to death and stringing up felons from lamp-posts, or so it seems. What next, Trial by Ordeal? Although I am pleased to say the Royal Wedding seemed to pass me by with barely a mention. Mainly because I was too busy working on the final galley proofs of "Hampshire at War" to pay it any attention. At the start of the week, for some reason, I heard Jimmy Cliff singing "Many Rivers to Cross" on the radio, while I was driving to the warehouse, and somehow that seems to have become stuck on my own internal jukebox as my theme for the week as a fitting fiftieth birthday theme:

> Many rivers to cross
> But I can't seem to find my way over
> Wandering I am lost
> As I travel along the white cliffs of Dover
> Many rivers to cross
> and it's only my will that keeps me alive
> I've been licked, washed up for years
> And I merely survive because of my pride

This is only the second song I have ever heard that mentions the White Cliffs of Dover by the way. We'll draw a discreet veil over the other one! Of course, you can only survive because of your pride for so long. There's only so much "living off the love of the common people" as Prince Charles may eventually find out. On Thursday, we were watching the news, which mentioned that the Cardinals had finally read John Paul II's will. "I wonder who he left the Vatican to", opined Debbie in the background, Later, she claimed she had been joking, but I am not so sure.

On Friday, I found myself tuning in to JPII's funeral, again while driving, despite my earlier vow that neither Papal Demise nor Royal Nuptial should cross my aural threshold. Oh well, I suppose one out of two isn't that bad. Actually, I have to say that I found the event strangely moving. Once I had got over my disbelief that Big G hadn't stuck down Mr Mugabe with a well-aimed lightning bolt, I was carried along on the shifting planes of the chanting, as it rose and fell, like the tides of the sea, bearing me with it in spirit at least.

Bizarrely, just as they were singing "The Lord's my Shepherd" in Latin, I drove past a huge field of sheep, many of which were accompanied by their recently-born lambs. It always tears at my heart to see the lambs at this time of year, and to wonder what fate is to befall such innocent, trusting creatures.

While I would never personally don a balaclava or blow anybody up about it, it does seem to me to be time for a massive re-evaluation of what we are doing in terms of mechanised farming all over the world, and the welfare of such livestock. How anyone can look a lamb in the face and then order it to be sent to an abbatoir is beyond my comprehension. How anyone can then squander natural resources by freezing its chopped up remains and flying them half way round the world, beats me too. Many rivers to cross, and that's just one of them. I know that not all farmers are bad, but it's a job I could never do. And yet I have to feed my dearly-loved pets meat products because in a fallen universe, they ended up as carnivores. Many, many rivers.

Anyway, I digress. I was talking about the Pope. Or the "late Pope". I also have a problem with this concept. On the wall, in the pub I used to drink at, The Murrell Arms in Barnham, there used to be a glass case with a stuffed duck inside. This was the last remains of "Bibbler", a Khaki Campbell, who had formerly been the oldest duck in England, at the time of his demise. The problem was that the caption said that he WAS the oldest duck in England, which was clearly not the case, owing to his being, er, dead. "Oldest former duck in England" would have been nearer the answer. Despite my mentioning it to the landlord several times, it never got changed. It's probably there to this day.

So remember, JPII was only probably the oldest "former" Pope, and as such, we shouldn't put him the the glass case of Sainthood until he's earned it. However much that process now seems inevitable.

What I meant about the Pope (late Pope, sorry, there I go again) when I wrote about him last week is that you have to admire his refusal to compromise his vision, whether or not you agree with the consequences. As someone wrote about him, very acutely, I thought, he was concerned with souls rather than bodies.

I am not sure I *do* agree with the consequences, though. It's a very big problem for all religions. To what extent to you compromise on your original ideals to keep pace with the changing conditions in the world? To a certain degree all religions seem to have the same problem at the moment, in that they are seen to lack relevance to the needs, aims and aspirations of modern life, even the Church of England, which has been rather unkindly described in the past (not by me) as more of a hobby than a religion. Change has been forced by external pressures, as well, such as a society which now sees divorce as nothing special, even in its Royal Family. In some cases, this feeling of being threatened by change has led to a worrying hardening into fundamentalism, both in Christianity and Islam, though thankfully, not so much here in our little island backwater.

JPII's answer to change was to continue to re-state the fundamental beliefs of Christianity as he saw them... regardless of the consequences. Like the man said, he was concerned wit souls, not bodies, but it was not always fashionable (or desirable) to say so, there and then.

How much and where should religions compromise their ideals, is the central paradox of JPII's life - too much, and you lose the essence of what it is that made your religion what it is, too little, and you become irrelevant to the world as it exists. The former would be like the Quakers saying "OK, we accept that there are now wars everywhere, so we are now going to start enlisting in the army": the latter would be like a church saying well, people shouldn't have extra marital sex and children should only be conceived in marriage and er ... oh. That's what makes JPII such a paradoxical character - you have to admire him for sticking to his beliefs and for standing up against the state capitalism (often erroneously described as communism) of the Eastern Bloc, particularly in its oppressive attitude to personal and social freedom and freedom of speech and worship, but the effects of his stand for traditional Catholic values in places like Africa are sometimes pretty dire (in terms of social policy, though Catholic relief organisations do a lot of good on the ground). Having said that, there are other forces (such as the status of women) than just the Catholic attitude to contraception which conspire together to create the tragic situation over Aids.

After hearing all the hooh-hah on both sides of the debate about abortion, for instance I have also come to the conclusion that perhaps personal sexual/medical morailty and behaviour may be an area where the Church should not have absolute power to legislate, or rather, not have the power to legislate absolutely. simply because there are always going to be special features about individual cases that make a mockery one way or the other of any official ex cathedra pronouncements. Abortion may be right for some women, wrong for others, though in the case of abortion, because the woman invariably ends up being lumped with the job of child rearing, the woman should always perhaps have a greater say. Similarly with stem cell research. If you could save Hitler's life by using a "spare embryo" would you want to do this? Likewise, if you could save the life of a morally good person by using the same embryo, would you allow that embryo never to develop? The sort of absolutist, one-size fits all moral stance by the church totally fails to acknowledge the vast spectrum of individual human experience and need. I don't think you can say that abortion is ALWAYS wrong or that stem cell research is ALWAYS right. I am seriously confused by this. Many rivers to cross.

At the end of the day, maybe it's for each individual to reach their own accommodation with God as they see fit, and not for a Pope, Archbishop, or Imam to rule across the board in these matters - except of course that they would say that the job of the church is to give moral guidance based on the revealed truth of God as they see it, but if God really is all loving and all forgiving then God would welcome abortionist and pro-lifer alike into the fold at the end of all things, just as Jesus allowed Mary Magdalen to was his feet, as Big G knows they are all part of his/her/its great plan, which we cannot comprehend. I don't know. Sometimes I wonder why we are trying to live our lives by a book which was originally designed, in part, as a desert survival manual for the children of Israel.

Saying something is always against the will of God, or Allah for that matter, seems to me to be sort of reducing the ability of God to be subtle, if you ask me, and can also be used as an instrument of social oppression. This is where I think JPII was at his wrongest, but then at least he was willing to attempt this difficult terrain, whereas most modern leaders would have funked it.

So, this is what has been going through what passes for my mind this week, with not a lot of conclusion. I am sorry to anyone I have offended with these ramblings. It's my age. Like I said, many rivers to cross. Maybe Debbie's question isn't so dumb. Whoever he leaves the Vatican to, JPII will be a hard act to follow.

Whoever the next Pope is, I am glad it's not me, even if he does get to wear a jiffy bag on his head and no one is allowed to laugh.

Still Looking, Not Finding... [17th April 2005]

I haven't written an Epilogue this week, as such. Part of the reason is that I am sitting here with a streaming cold and can barely see the screen through the haze of Ibuprofen, Benylin, Vitamin C, Sudafed, and every other concoction known to pharmaceutical science, that I have been trying to zap it with since it struck me down on Thursday. However, if I am honest, part of the reason also is that I feel the idea may have run its course for the moment, and/or that I might temporarily have lost my way.

Over the last year or so, I have been greatly comforted by the fact that something like faith had come back into my life, albeit simplistic, patchy, and un-coordinated, and I will always be grateful for the support and prayer I got from here on behalf of Russell. You lot probably saved his little catty life.

I am also grateful for learning about the Rule of Benedict, and I am still thinking of ways in which I can use this.

However, I have run up against two big and partially connected problems of late, which I am finding it very difficult to reconcile, and which have increasingly led to me posting Epilogues containing more questions than answers. Since part of what people said they liked about my witterings in the past was that they came to some resolution, however tentative, the fact that I have been unable to reconcile these issues means that resolution has been pretty scarce, and who wants to read yet another diatribe from me with an inconclusive ending?

It's no secret what the issues are, I have been grappling with them for about four or five weeks now. They can be summed up as the conflict between Church and State and my inability to forgive people. Insofar as the State has recently followed a set of actions with which I wildly and profoundly disagree, this has brought the whole issue into very sharp focus for me. Especially with the Election being called in the UK, the start of the Uist Hedgehog Cull for the third year running and the death of the Pope which has led me to think about the place of moral teaching in a Church and to find that there as well I seem to be at odds with the established view. How can I say that the fact that everything will be alright in the next world excuses the injustice, hatred, greed and evil of the actions of our own and other leaders in this one? We are being invited to vote for a bunch of liars and hypocrites, people who are willing to bend any truth, defy any opinion without engaging with it, to ditch any tradition, to deny us any liberty, and start any war, in their ceaseless pursuit of "whatever works". One has been proved to have misled us, but has not resigned. One looks daily more and more like Goebbels, and probably acts like him, one has been put up on every TV and Radio programme going to deny that black is white, or vice versa, but whatever happens to stifle debate and obfuscate the issue, and one has a voice and a manner when interviewed that immediately makes me think of being groomed by a paedophile. *Then* there are the Tories!

Various people at various times have offered by various means to go through this with me, and unfortunately I have been so busy that I haven't been able to spend the time to take up these kind offers. I apologise if I have seemed churlish over not taking up these offers, which I know were sincerely and kindly meant. So I find myself these days preaching to people about things I can't work out for myself, and not having time to join in the debate I myself caused, or listen to the answers!

I don't like finding myself in such a false position, and to carry on down that road would be to become as big a hypocrite as those I accuse of hypocrisy, in government and elsewhere - in fact, to be a *double* hypocrite, because I could not forgive them either. I have gone round and round these loops over the last few days and, for the last couple of weeks, knowing that I was going to come up against this rock face over and over, I have actually faced the task of sitting down to write on a Sunday with a mixture of reluctance and indecision, and I think when you get to that stage, whatever the task is, it's time to take a break. So I am going to hie myself off into the wilderness for a while. Not literally, and probably not for forty days and forty nights, but for long enough to think these knotty coils through so that I become useful once more, to myself and to others. It doesn't mean I won't still drop in, and it doesn't mean that I have gone for good. I can also use the time constructively to work on my book. But for the next few weeks, I think the Holme Valley will have to look after itself, even if I will still be looking after those who rely on me, furry and non-furry, to the best of my ability.

Happy trails everybody

And there the Epilogues stopped, until July 2005 when I finally was presented with a set of circumstances that allowed me to carry out my promise to write an Epilogue to the Epilogues, and bring the story up to date.

We pick up the narrative again with our imminent departure to Scotland on a well earned break in our camper van, which was due to have a special kayak-carrier fitted while it was up there...

§

EPI-EPI-LOGUE

What We Did on our Holidays or: Around Scotland without an Opposable Thumb

Monday 4th July 2005

Set off from Huddersfield at 10am having spent most of Sunday packing the camper. Sunday was a fine day, but of course on Monday morning, as we pulled out of the driveway, dead on cue, a light drizzle started. Slightly dispirited, we drove through the rain to Keswick, and did some shopping in Booths supermarket, also taking the opportunity to break the journey. The original idea had been to get to the Kayak Rack Manufacturers in Coylton, near Ayr, early in the afternoon, but we reckoned without Scotland. Scotland is much bigger than you think it is. That is the first law of Scotland. The second law of Scotland is that for every midge you despatch to the happy hunting grounds, two hundred more take its place.

As the weather improved, our spirits sank, as we had a miserable drive through the central Scottish wasteland, following the motorway up from Moffat towards Glasgow, willing the turning for Ayr to come in sight. Unfortunately, roads in Scotland follow the valleys, which can lead to some spectacular detours, especially further North in the Highlands. Having reached the turnoff and with the Tannahill Weavers on repeat on the CD player in an attempt to get us in the mood, we trailed along the road leading out West towards Ayr, passing through a seemingly endless succession of small towns consisting of two identical rows of bungalows lining a main street, with a shop and occasionally a post office. At the edge of each of these was invariably a school with a speed warning sign: "Twenty's plenty". After three or four of these I took to reciting it aloud in the voice Janet used to use when offering Dr Cameron his tea. Debbie was not amused.

At 4.45pm (so much for "early afternoon" we finally arrived at Coylton (basted in bright, warm, sunshine, unlike England) to fit the kayak bars. The people at Kari-Tech could have been forgiven for having given up and gone home but in fact, once summoned down to the yard by the friendly local farmer with his mobile phone, they mustered around the camper and set to work with a will. And struggled with the job til 8PM at which point we all agreed it had been a long day and it would be much better if we left the kayak with them (until then it had been occupying most of the inside of the camper) found somewhere locally to doss, and came back in the morning.

So it was that we motored on out to the heads of Ayr and stayed the night at Dunmure, watching the sunset over the Isle of Arran. After toasting the fact that the weather had turned with generous slugs of mead, Debbie gazed out over the Firth of Clyde at what she said was a single tree that she could see on top of Goatfell, the tallest mountain on Arran. It turned out that the "single tree" was in fact a dark cloud, and flew off into the sunset to a height of 2000 feet. Obviously confusion between "little" and "far away" is not confined solely to the annals of Father Ted.

Tuesday 5th July 2005

After a slow start, we wended our way back to Coylton, arriving as promised, "first thing" at 12PM! During the three hours struggle that followed, the kayak bar fitting was finally subdued, at the cost of one thumb (mine) which I hurt badly during the shenanigans with hammers, stepladders, spanners, planks and other various assorted items of kit necessary to get what is in effect a large pointy plastic washing up bowl with a seat in it, hoisted 9 feet 1 into the air and sitting atop a VW Transporter. Having spent most of afternoon getting the kayak bars fitted we then paid (I had previously thought this would be the most painful part of the exercise but no, it was definitely my thumb) said our goodbyes to Coylton, and then set off for northbound, over the Erskine bridge, up the side of Loch Lomond, and into the Trossachs, Aberfoyle and Loch Ard. Thumb not v. well, hurting a lot and swelling up. Would be useful for hitchhiking though, if the need arose. No motorist could ignore its angry majesty.

During one of the many breaks while we were struggling with getting the Kari-Tech bars fitted, I was talking to the dairy farmer at Coylton who rents them the space they use to make the bars and other kayak accessories. He's getting out of dairy, and now organises and annual country and western festival instead. It's much, much, more profitable. Last year the local Castle complained about the sound, he said, but it was probably just because they weren't invited.

As we left Ayr on the coast road we were uncomfortably jerked back into the real world by the sight of patrols of armed police, conspicuous around the perimeter of Prestwick airport, coupled with reports of expected rioting and protest at the G8 summit. Coincidentally, I found I was wearing a gillet. Perhaps I could have a summit all of my own.

Deb meanwhile was having a disaster day. We finally got to the shores of Loch Ard and almost the first thing she did was to nearly lose a shoe in a bog having a pee. I know that you *normally* pee in bogs, but *this* bog was *actually* a bog, if you see what I mean. She then came back from her little foray into the woods, changed her shoes, and almost immediately broke one of the curtain holders in the camper, finishing off by dropping a light on my head.

The only adjective I can use to describe the mountains round Loch Ard was that they were very Trossach-y. And there were lots of them, all named improbable things like Ben Lomond, Ben Doon, and Ben Vorlick, which sounds like it ought to be a Scottish bedtime drink. Anyway we soon got fed up and decided it was easier just to call them all "Ben Affleck." A) it saves having to look on the map and B) It suggests the interesting question "who was the first man up Ben Affleck?" [Anyone who answers "Tom Cruise" risks the wrath of m'learned friends, and since there is obviously no truth in such a scurrilous assertion I will pass quickly on.]

Loch Ard had a Crannog in it. Mind you, we decided also that the Ordnance Survey probably just insert them at random all over maps of Scotland (ooh look, a Crannog): see also Castle (or "not ANOTHER bloody castle" to quote Debbie).

Wednesday 6th July 2005

Woke up with thumb angry, swollen and purple - this is generally held to be a bad idea if it's your thumb, but a good idea if it's any other part of your body. Also had a stiff neck. What a crazy mixed up kid I am.

Watched the geese beside Loch Ard. Later, did a painting of Loch Ard, while Debbie paddled it. The Loch, not the painting. A French lass from the hotel came to watch. Apparently lots of French people come to Scotland to work in the catering industry all summer (why?) I suppose she had never seen a guy without an opposable thumb doing a painting before. Maybe she thought I was an impressionist (wanna see me do Marcel Marceau?) Anyway Deb had her paddle, and Tig had a contretemps with some fierce Scottish ducks who tried to waddle out of the water just at the point where she was sleeping. Neither party saw the other until they were about an inch apart, and both were equally astonished and quick to retreat. We now have to add ducks to the long list of things Tig is scared of, which also includes Rabbits (especially Scottish ones) and Sheep. So far I have resisted the temptation to shoot the sheep and then explain to the farmer that they were worrying our dog.

Having packed up at Loch Ard, we tootled back to Aberfoyle to the tourist info, where we also took the opportunity to fill up the water carriers from the tap in the disabled toilets. In fact, a very nice lady seeing me struggling with my thumb, took them off me and did them for me. I thanked her profusely, explaining that while we were self-sufficient, we needed the water "for the dog". And the kettle, and the cooking, and the washing. Aberfoyle boasts, among its many attractions, "The Wee But a Ben Bistro"! Yes, folks, that whirring noise you can hear is Sir Harry Lauder, revolving in his grave at 78RPM.

Now that we were back in (relative) civilization, we found that the mobile phones worked again, (mobiles were a no-no while we were in the shadow of Ben Affleck, which sort of made me wonder what people use to make all these hoax calls that mountain rescue keep complaining about - smoke signals?) When I dialled in to my urgent three now voicemail messages I found that our tender for a major charity had been accepted and there was to be a presentation the day I got back in the office. Argh. Power point by proxy! More work. It makes you wonder why we bother with holidays. Left Aberfoyle for Loch Lomond via Balmaha (gateway to the south?) and Rowardennan (immediately christened by us "Rhododendron") where the road up the Eastern side of Loch Lomond stops. Deb asked "did they run out of money?" I answered "no, they ran out of destination".

We heard there that President Bush had collided on his bike with one of the thousands of policemen sent to protect him. The President, out for a bike ride (in the middle of a summit intended to change the world, he goes off for a bike ride, what is he playing at?) had collided with the policeman (who had probably been drafted in from somewhere like Balamory and never seen anything move faster than a hedgehog trying to escape the deadly syringes of Scottish Natural Heritage before now) sustaining a hand injury and broke the cop's ankle. Thank God for a leader of the free world who is able to see disaster coming and avoid it. Er... oh.

Wednesday night was spent by the shores of Loch Lomond with the midges - I have become convinced that midges are the origin of both all the moves in Scottish Country Dancing (especially the Highland Fling) AND Tourette's syndrome. Also there was no way I could get into the gents at Rowardennan (too many steps, too few rails, not enough thumbs to grip with) and there was no disabled bog so I had to use the (fortunately, at that time of night, deserted) ladies (sorry, Ladies of Rowardennan). That night the camper's bed broke and we had a domestic about it. I can strongly recommend melamine plates to the married couples of England, as they can be thrown over and over again without breaking!

Thursday 7th July 2005
Next morning at Loch Lomond we had an early start, courtesy of the broken bed, and saw the sun rise at about 5AM. Deb was out on the water by 8.15 and I spent an idyllic two hours tidying up and catching up on lost sleep. Then I phoned the mobile phone company and (after negotiating their choices of menus and options, specifically designed to deter people less bloody-minded than I was feeling right then) spent a further hour arguing with someone called Jiten about whether or not the 14 day peace of mind guarantee started when I got my new phone or when they first thought of ringing us up, even though they didn't get round to sending it to us for days afterwards.

I don't want to be unkind to people who work in call centres, but they picked the wrong person to argue with that day. I ended up screaming down the phone to them that they were a useless bunch of oxygen thieves. If you are interested, the company is called Dial-a-Phone, and no barge pole known to man is long enough. I would rather sniff a steelworker's jockstrap than have any more knowing contact with them. They make Russ Abbot look like an MBA.

Because of the conversation with Dial-a-Gooby, lunch was a bit delayed, so I rang home and spoke to Deb's Mum, who had been feeding the cats. She told us of the bombs. I put the BBC on and listened with a mounting sense of anger and hopelessness to the reports. It had to come, sooner or later, our blind support for Bush would come back to bite us on the bum, and now it seemed it had happened. The G8 faded like Shakespeare's "insubstantial pageant". All yesterday's buffoonery (Geldof, concerts, protests - themselves tinged with an edge of frustrated violence at the heavy handed police tactics) all diminished when overtaken by the plain factual truth that someone (and we assumed straight away it was Al-Qaeda) had let off four bombs in London, killing dozens of people. We listened to Blair making his statement, with those odd pauses in. between. the. words. Sadly, the word "sorry" did not feature. In fact it was nothing to do with Iraq. So that's alright then. Must've just been a coincidence.

Sobered, chastened, we headed down from Loch Lomond, back over the Erskine Bridge, heading for Ardrossan and the ferry to Arran. God, what a place. Ardrossan I mean. Still the lady there in the Calmac Terminal did offer to post my postcards for me when I couldn't find a post box, and she was as good as her word, because everyone got them the day after. Strike one for the Royal Mail. It won't happen when it's been privatised.

People have unkindly said that if you want to know what the Isle of Man was like fifty years ago, go to Arran, but I quite like the "timeslip" quality of the place. After landing we went into the Co-op at Brodick, taking care to walk down the aisles the right way so we could read all the signs (they have gaelic on the back) Gaelic was still in conversational use on Skye as recently as 1984, I can report, having sat and listened to two crofters discussing I know not what in Gaelic, to a background of Barry Manilow, in the pub at Carbost.

I bought a bottle of Skye Whisky (established 1933) by Iain MacLeod - purely as thumb anaesthetic you understand - and came to the conclusion as I drank it that all Scottish place names are interchangeable (DunDonald Macdonald Dunmure Dunromininthe gloamin etc)

Leaving Brodick, we stopped off at Lochranza, where the ferry comes in the other side, from Clanaoig on the Mull of Kintrye, for water (from another public bog tap) then drove on down past Pirnmill on the coast road. The weather had dulled and Kilbrannan Sound was a flat calm. Last time we saw seals swimming here, and we were not to be disappointed, as they made a reappearance, swimming around just off shore and hauling out on to the rocks. While we were parked up watching them, a school of porpoises went by, doing perfect synchronised leaping out of the water and then reappearing again a few yards further on. Both of us were pinching ourselves. (Although with my thumb I wasn't being very effective). No, we were not dreaming, we had both seen a school of porpoises just swim by, from left to right in perfect order. The seals were unfazed, they have seen it all before.

That night, having fixed the bed, fortified by Mead and by nips of "The MacLeod" we slept sounder than a sound thing in the layby at Pirnmill. The phones had stopped working again.

Friday 8th July 2005

Began with a slow start and then we spent the afternoon having a prolonged lunch on Pirnmill Beach, discussing (amongst other things) Platonic archetypes, and how it was impossible to disprove Bishop Berkeley's theory that things ceased to exist when you could not see hear or feel them. We had the beach to ourselves, well, actually there was, occasionally, only one other person there, about half a mile away to the North, but for about three hours it was ours and ours alone.

A family with an improbable collection of dogs came along eventually, and stopped to chat. Were we on holiday? Yes, they thought so, because, as they said - "we've been watching you!" Shades of the Wicker Man - perhaps it was a local beach for local people, who knows, anyway they poddled off, taking their pack of various motley mutts with them, while Tig snoozed contentedly on the warm sand by my camping chair, with the superior air of a Geman Shepherd who had been there since early on and claimed her place with a towel.

I was also trying to instil in Debbie some of the rudiments of navigation prior to her embarking on her first sea-kayaking trip. We had trouble with windward and leeward. I managed to get her to recite the compass rose, but Port and Starboard also caused problems. "Why don't they call it something sensible, like Port and Stilton?" Why not, indeed.

Then she went off for a paddle while I did a very indifferent painting, and also, having given up the landscape, painted the points of the compass onto a flat pebble for her. The kayak rack was playing up again and we had to reverse back to the layby with the kayak hanging off the side so we could get it back on top properly. Fortunately you only get one car every 45 minutes along that road, or we would have been toast, wandering about in the gloom.

We drove on to Dougarie Point and found a place to spend Friday night: it was just light enough when we pulled up to see a seal basking on the rocks offshore. The seal did not bat an eyelid (actually, do seals have eyelids to bat?)

Saturday 9th July 2005

Started with the seal of approval, and the approval of a seal. Perhaps they haul out and say "Ooh look, a tin of humans. I wonder if there is any fish in there". After another slow start, we drove round the coast road back towards Brodick and the shops. Once more (at Kilmory) the Ladies was the only bog I could use. The thumb was easing but it's amazing how much you need your thumb to haul yourself up steps. We drove on, past the memorial to the airmen who died when their plane crashed into the Sound of Pladda in 1942, with Ailsa Craig prominent on the horizon (Or "That currant bun", as Debbie referred to it. Clearly her navigational skills still need some honing.)

After shopping in Brodick we parked up and I sat painting a picture of Goatfell and the Arran mountains, while a man busking in the pub garden behind us sang "Amarillo", over and over again. Peter Kaye has a lot to answer for. Deb, however, had a more productive evening and paddled across the bay and saw 5 seals, one on a rock and four swimming round her as she sailed along. Perhaps they thought she was a giant orange seal. It's an easy mistake to make. I told her next time to take a tin of pilchards ("They'll be all over you like a rash")

Back at Dougarie we had a barbecue on the beach. The last of Macleod went down, the thumb was pleasantly numb, the food was vaguely warm, the only thing which unsettled me slightly was Tig's strange behaviour, frequently leaving the fire and always going towards the south west, the direction of home. I speculated at the time that maybe a Barrow-wight from one of the ancient sites had come to the edge of the firelight, drawn from his chambered tomb or cairn by the need for human company. As it turned out, Tig had other reasons to be harking towards home.

Sunday 10th July 2005

We finally got one of the phones working, to find a text message "ring Mum ASAP". When Debbie rang her Mum, we learnt the sad news that Russell, the Baggis Cat, who had defied so much in the way of illness that would have killed off many a lesser mogster, had died on Saturday night.

Deb's mum had been coming round to feed the cats while we were away, and not finding Russ in his usual place, went searching and found him flaked out at the end of our bed. She bundled him up and drove him straight to the vets, they stuck him on a drip, but there was nothing they could do, this time, unlike back in February, he just didn't have the strength this time around to pull off a second miracle. He died about 8 o'clock on Saturday night. Just as Debbie was paddling with the seals.

When Russ was first ill, I happened to be reading the Mass Observation diary of Maggie Joy Blunt, and kept this bit from when she wrote about one of her cats, on 14 March 1947:

> The cat died. Such an insignificant event. A dead cat - target for mockery, small boys, and dust. There are too many cats in the world. Why make all the fuss because now there is one less? Every cat is a miracle of independent, loveable life, if you have the eyes and the feeling to understand it as such. I have loved many cats and I expect I shall love many more. Each one becomes a friend with a distinct individuality, and the loss each time is a deeply personal one. No one else ever replaces that person exactly, but new personalities help you to forget your grief at the loss of others.

I'm not going to re-write Baggis's epitaph now, the one I wrote originally in the Epilogue for him back then still stands, even though, cantankerous little creature that he was, he undermined it, at that time, in typical Russell fashion, by not actually dying!

Deb summed it up by saying he wasn't a good cat, but he was the best bad cat in the world, and always managed make you smile at his antics, even those he shouldn't really have been allowed to get away with, eg swiping food off your plate while you were still eating it... we stopped briefly at the Ruthwell Cross near Dumfries on the journey home, and I couldn't help but be struck by the thought that the last time I was there, I was speaking on the phone to Ian W., also alas, no longer with us. Debbie jerked me out of my reverie by asking me if "this was that place where Jesus visited". No dear, that was Glastonbury. Allegedly.

All Sunday, on that long hot journey back from Ardrossan, down through Scotland, past the lake district and then on via Skipton and finally trundling into the drive about midnight, I was re-living all the times, good and bad, that Russell and I had been through together, me a human, him a cat. I had that old Eagles song going round my head, about "My man's got it made, now he's far beyond the pain, and we who must remain, go on living just the same."

Except it won't be the same, after 13 years, it is the end of an era. And I-church needs a new virtual cat. Russ will be a hard act to follow. In many ways. We buried him the following Wednesday, in the shadow of the honeysuckle hedge in the garden where he liked to go in the shade on hot days, and then in the evening, we lit the chiminea, filled the garden and the deck with tea lights, and finished off the last of the mead.

I am going to stop writing now, for a while, and raise a glass to Russell, now feasting on chicken in aspic up there in cat heaven, along with Ginger, Silvo, Halibut, Reggie and Ossie, all purring to the music of the spheres. Which is, in itself, purring.

And all shall be well and all manner of thing shall be well.

For those who might need it, here is a brief list of "dramatis personae". All of these people assure me that they are real, even the four-legged ones.

Tiggy (Tig): A dog, a female dog...
Freddie: another, smaller, dog, a bit like a wiry Lancashire Heeler
Lucy: a fairly old, ginger dog who looks a bit like a sheep in a bad light
Russell (Russ the Puss, Russbags, The Baggis Cat): a cat (short hair/black & white) the best bad cat in all the world.
Nigel: another cat, ginger this time, with a habit of "giving paw".
Dusty: a cat (large, fat, tortoiseshell, she looks a bit like a Davy Crockett hat)
Kitty: a cat (short hair/black and white, not to be confused with Russell but frequently was bespite being a different sex)
Debbie: a wife (aka Moose-face, Llama Face, etc)
Jonathan: a brother-in-law
Matthew: another of the same
Chris: a brother-in-law
Adrian: and another one
Becky: for variation, a sister-in-law
Granny: a granny, aka Biddy or "The Neighbourhood Witch"
Gez: an author
Chris: another author
Phil: a publisher and van-driver in equal measures
Maisie: an author and sometime typer of letters and envelope-stuffer
Colin: a deceased neighbour who provided half our current house
God: (aka "Big G") a would-be supreme being
Mustardland: the BBC message board devoted to *The Archers*

Others are generally explained as they crop up.